The Syntax of Adjectives

Linguistic Inquiry Monographs
Samuel Jay Keyser, general editor

A complete list of books published in the Linguistic Inquiry Monographs series appears at the back of this book.

The Syntax of Adjectives

A Comparative Study

Guglielmo Cinque

The MIT Press
Cambridge, Massachusetts
London, England

© 2010 Massachusetts Institute of Technology

All rights reserved. No part of this book may be reproduced in any form by any electronic or mechanical means (including photocopying, recording, or information storage and retrieval) without permission in writing from the publisher.

This book was set in Times New Roman and Syntax on 3B2 by Asco Typesetters, Hong Kong.

Library of Congress Cataloging-in-Publication Data

Cinque, Guglielmo.
The syntax of adjectives : a comparative study / Guglielmo Cinque.
   p. cm. — (Linguistic inquiry monographs)
Includes bibliographical references and indexes.
ISBN 978-0-262-01416-8 (hardcover : alk. paper) — ISBN 978-0-262-51426-2 (pbk. : alk. paper) 1. Grammar, Comparative and general—Adjective. 2. Grammar, Comparative and general—Syntax. I. Title.
P273.C56 2010
415'.5—dc22   2009043836

The MIT Press is pleased to keep this title available in print by manufacturing single copies, on demand, via digital printing technology.

A Iliyana

Contents

Acknowledgments xi
Introduction xiii

1 Problems for N Movement in Romance 1
 1.1 An Apparent Restriction on the Number of Postnominal Adjectives in Romance 1
 1.2 Existence of Unexpected Mirror-Image Orders between Germanic and Romance 2
 1.3 Existence of Unexpected Scope Effects in Romance 3

2 A Systematic Contrast between English (Germanic) and Italian (Romance) 5
 2.1 Individual-Level vs. Stage-Level Readings 6
 2.2 Restrictive vs. Nonrestrictive Readings 7
 2.3 Modal vs. Implicit Relative Clause Readings 8
 2.4 Intersective vs. Nonintersective (Adverbial) Readings 9
 2.5 Relative (to a Comparison Class) vs. Absolute Readings 10
 2.6 Comparative vs. Absolute Readings of Superlatives 11
 2.7 Specificity- vs. Non-Specificity-Inducing Readings 12
 2.8 Evaluative vs. Epistemic Readings of 'unknown' 14
 2.9 NP-Dependent vs. Discourse Anaphoric Readings of 'different' 15
 2.10 Summary of the Basic Generalizations 16
 2.11 An Additional Problem for the N-Movement Analysis 22

3 Phrasal Movement and the Two Sources of Adnominal Adjectives 25
 3.1 The Two Sources of Adnominal Adjectives 25
 3.2 A Summary of the Interpretive Properties Associated with Each Source 26
 3.3 A Preview of the Syntactic Properties Associated with Each Source 28
 3.4 Summary of the Semantic and Syntactic Properties of the Two Sources 33

3.5 Some Crosslinguistic and Acquisitional Evidence for the Dual Source of Adnominal Adjectives   34
3.6 Phrasal Movement Over Head Movement or Base Generation   37

4 An Analysis of the Two Sources of Adjectives   43
4.1 A Syntactic Analysis of Direct Modification Adjectives   43
4.2 A Syntactic Analysis of Indirect Modification Adjectives   54

5 An Analysis of English (Germanic)   57
5.1 Prenominal Adjectives in English (Germanic)   57
5.2 Postnominal Adjectives in English (Germanic) and Their Derivation   59
5.3 A Potential Problem   61
5.4 A Reduced Relative Clause Source for Prenominal Participles   64
5.5 *Something Funny*   65

6 An Analysis of Italian (Romance)   69
6.1 Prenominal and Postnominal Adjectives in Italian (Romance)   69
6.2 The Position of PP Complements and Adjuncts vis-à-vis Adjectives in Italian (Romance)   79
6.3 The Position of Demonstrative Reinforcers vis-à-vis Adjectives in Italian (Romance)   82
6.4 Adjectives After *celui* in French   84

7 Further Differences between English (Germanic) and Italian (Romance)   87
7.1 Epithets with Prenominal and Postnominal Adjectives   87
7.2 Idiomatic Readings with Prenominal and Postnominal Adjectives   87
7.3 A Constraint on Romance Prenominal Adjectives   88

Conclusion   91

Appendix: Further Evidence for the Dual Source of Adnominal Adjectives   95
A.1 Chinese   95
A.2 Maltese   98
A.3 Bosnian/Croatian/Serbian   99
A.4 Romanian   102
A.5 Greek   104
A.6 Some Notes on Russian and German   108

Notes   113
References   151
Name Index   187
Subject Index   193

Series Foreword

We are pleased to present the fifty-seventh in the series *Linguistic Inquiry Monographs*. These monographs present new and original research beyond the scope of the article. We hope they will benefit our field by bringing to it perspectives that will stimulate further research and insight.

Originally published in limited edition, the *Linguistic Inquiry Monographs* are now more widely available. This change is due to the great interest engendered by the series and by the needs of a growing readership. The editors thank the readers for their support and welcome suggestions about future directions for the series.

Samuel Jay Keyser
for the Editorial Board

Acknowledgments

This book is a revised and expanded version of a paper circulated in 2005 under the title "The Dual Source of Adjectives and Phrasal Movement in the Romance DP." It grows out of work presented in classes at the University of Venice in 2002, at UCLA in the winter quarter of 2003, at the 2005 Summer Institute of the Linguistic Society of America at Harvard and MIT, at the LISSIM 4 Summer School in Kausani (India, June 2009), at the Ealing 2009 Summer School in Paris (September 2009), and in talks at the Universities of Padua (June 2003), Tromsø (October 2003), New York at Stony Brook (NELS 34, November 2003), Rome (31st Incontro di Grammatica Generativa, February 2005), Lille III (Colloque sur "Les Adjectifs," September 2007), and the Chinese University of Hong Kong (May 2009).

I wish to thank the various audiences, and, in particular, Mark Baker, Adriana Belletti, Paola Benincà, Hagit Borer, Laura Brugè, Anna Cardinaletti, Probal Dasgupta, Alessandra Giorgi, Giuliana Giusti, Alexander Grosu, Liliane Haegeman, Richard Kayne, Ed Keenan, Chris Kennedy, Hilda Koopman, Richard Larson, Anoop Mahajan, David Pesetsky, Cecilia Poletto, Megan Rae, Luigi Rizzi, Walter Schweikert, Elisabeth Selkirk, Petra Sleeman, Dominique Sportiche, Melita Stavrou, and Tim Stowell. For comments on previous drafts of this work I am indebted to Werner Abraham, Nadira Aljović, Stefania Chèvre, Francesca Del Gobbo, Iliyana Krapova, Christopher Laenzlinger, Chi Fung Lam, Nedžad Leko, Thomas Leu, Victor Manfredi, Franc Marušič, Katy McKinney-Bock, Waltraud Paul, Asya Pereltsvaig, Helen Trugman, Tong Wu, Nina Zhang, and four anonymous reviewers. Special thanks go to Richard Larson for his comments, and for his inspiring work on the semantics of adjectives.

Introduction

In Cinque 1990a, 1994, I had proposed that the DP-internal word-order difference between Romance and Germanic (exemplified in (1) with Italian and English) should not be seen as arising from a different base generation of the adjectives (to the left of the N in Germanic, and both to the left and to the right of the N in Romance), but in terms of the Noun raising across some of the adjectives in Romance (though not in Germanic), within one and the same, possibly universal, underlying structure, (2):

(1) a. La **sola possibile** invasione **romana** della Tracia[1]
      the only possible invasion Roman of-the Thrace
   b. The **only possible Roman** invasion of Thrace
   c. *La **sola possibile romana** invasione della Tracia
      the only possible Roman invasion of-the Thrace

(2)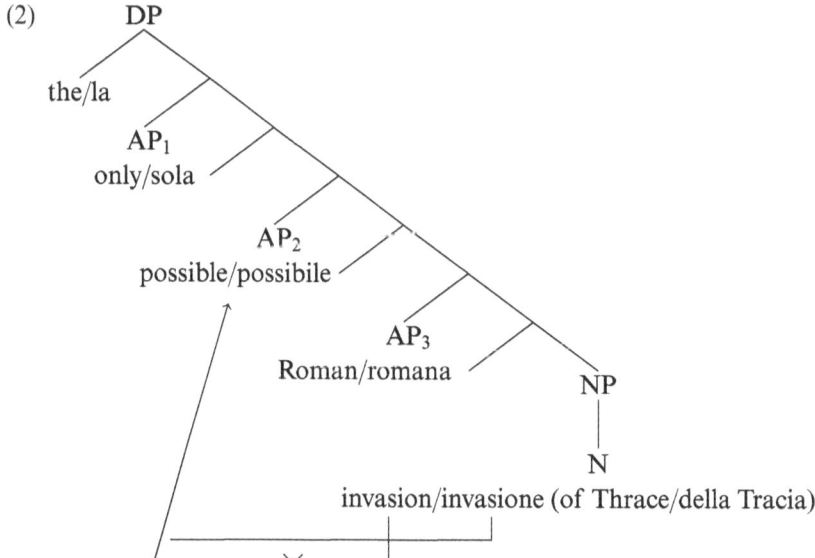

Since then, a number of problems have emerged that demand a reconsideration of that analysis. They will be reviewed in chapter 1. In chapter 2, a more fundamental problem for the head-movement analysis will be addressed, which has to do with its inability to capture the pattern of interpretive differences between pre- and postnominal adjectives in the two language families.

In particular, the head-movement analysis will be seen to be unable to derive the following generalizations:

1. While APs appearing in the prenominal position in Romance are necessarily individual-level, nonrestrictive, modal (for adjectives like *possible*), nonintersective, absolute (i.e., not relative to a comparison class for scalar adjectives; not comparative for superlatives), specificity-inducing (i.e., rendering an indefinite DP in which they are contained specific), evaluative rather than epistemic (for adjectives like *unknown*), and (plural) NP dependent rather than discourse anaphoric (for an adjective like *different*), postnominal APs in Germanic, when possible, generally have the opposite properties: they are stage-level (characteristically), restrictive, intersective, relative to a comparison class (for scalar adjectives) or have a comparative reading (for superlatives), have an implicit relative reading (for adjectives such as *possible*), are non-specificity-inducing, epistemic (rather than evaluative, for adjectives like *unknown*), and discourse anaphoric rather than NP dependent (for an adjective like *different*).
2. Postnominal adjectives in Romance and prenominal adjectives in Germanic are systematically ambiguous between these two sets of readings.
3. The two prenominal readings of Germanic, and the two postnominal readings of Romance, are ordered in a mirror-image fashion: the AP in the outer position (leftmost in Germanic; rightmost in Romance) has the set of interpretations found (when that is possible) postnominally in Germanic, which derive, as has been suggested, from a reduced relative clause source.

To capture these generalizations, an alternative analysis will be developed in chapter 3 in terms of phrasal movement, which seems able to overcome the problems of the head-movement analysis while retaining its basic insight. The phrasal-movement analysis will be argued to compare favorably not only with respect to the head-movement analysis but also with respect to base-generation analyses.

In the course of the discussion, the importance of distinguishing two structural sources for adnominal adjectives will also become evident. Adjectives (more accurately APs) will be seen to enter the DP either as specifiers of dedicated functional projections in the "extended projection" of the NP, or as (reduced) relative clauses.[2] (See chapters 3 and 4.)

Although many adjectives can access both sources, some will turn out to access only one, which will make it possible to isolate and compare the different syntactic and interpretive properties associated with each source. Chapters 5 through 7 will approach the syntax of English and Italian adjectives within the framework developed in the preceding chapters. The appendix contains a brief discussion of some languages that appear to overtly distinguish the two sources of adjectives.

1 Problems for N Movement in Romance

1.1 An Apparent Restriction on the Number of Postnominal Adjectives in Romance

Regarding the idea that postnominal adjectives result from the head N raising past them, an initial problem is provided by the existence of an apparently curious restriction on the number of adjectives found after the N and before a complement (or adjunct) of the N. In Italian, for example, as shown in example (1) of the introduction, repeated here, the N must raise past the thematic adjective *romana*:

(1) a. La **sola possibile** invasione **romana** della Tracia
        the only possible invasion Roman of-the Thrace
   b. The **only possible Roman** invasion of Thrace
   c. *La **sola possibile romana** invasione della Tracia
        the only possible Roman invasion of-the Thrace

As (2) shows, it can also (though it need not) raise past an adjective like *possibile*:

(2) a. La sola **possibile** invasione della Tracia
        the only possible invasion of the Thrace
   b. La sola invasione$_i$ **possibile** t$_i$ della Tracia
        the only invasion possible of-the Thrace
       'the only possible invasion of Thrace'

Yet successive raisings of the N past both *romana* and *possibile* give rise to an unacceptable sentence. Compare (1a) and (2b) with (3):

(3) *?La **sola** invasione **possibile romana** della Tracia
     the only invasion possible Roman of-the Thrace

This problem was noted, but left without a real account, in Cinque 1990a, 1994.[1] The problem, it now seems to me, is connected to the one discussed in the next section, as the other side of the same coin.

1.2 Existence of Unexpected Mirror-Image Orders between Germanic and Romance

As observed in the literature, postnominal adjectives in Romance characteristically enter an order that is the mirror image of the order of prenominal adjectives in Germanic. (See, among others, Lamarche 1991; Bosque and Picallo 1996; Bouchard 1998, 2002, chap. 3; Laenzlinger 2000, 2005a, 2005b; and Dimitrova-Vulchanova 2003.) Although the potentially interfering factor of a DP final position of adjectives derived from relative clauses is not always taken into consideration in these works (with the consequence that some of the arguments lose much of their force),[2] the observation is fundamentally correct, something I failed to recognize in Cinque 1994.

So, for example, if we control for the absence of the interfering factor just mentioned by considering only postnominal adjectives that are nonpredicative (and hence cannot constitute the predicate of a reduced relative clause), we still find the mirror-image effect (cf. Bernstein 1993b, chap. 2, note 38).

In (4), one of the two nonpredicative adjectives in prenominal position, *probable*, precedes and takes scope over the other (*main*). As (5) shows, in Italian, when both adjectives are postnominal, the order, which retains the same interpretive and scope properties of the English order, is necessarily the reverse: *probabile* ('probable') follows *prima* ('main/foremost'):[3]

(4) The most probable main cause of his death (is this)

(5) a. La causa prima più   probabile della sua morte (è questa)
        the cause main most probable of   his death (is this)
        'The most probable main cause of his death (is this)'
    b. *La causa   più   probabile prima della sua morte (è questa)
        the cause   most probable main of   his death (is this)

We now see why (3) is bad—not because of any restriction on the number, or type, of adjectives found between the N and one of its complements or adjuncts, but because the order is the "direct" one found prenominally in English rather than the required mirror image of it, which is actually fine. See (6):[4]

(6) La sola invasione *romana possibile* della Tracia
    the only invasion Roman possible of   Thrace
    'the only possible Roman invasion of Thrace'

Another argument for the conclusion that postnominal adjectives in Romance enter an order that is the mirror image of the one found prenominally in Germanic can be construed on the basis of a case discussed in Bouchard 2002, 124f; 2009, sections 2.1 and 2.2. As he notes, in one of its interpretations, (7) can have *malhonnêtes* taking scope over *chinois*, while itself being under the scope of *présumés* (as indicated by the bracketing):[5]

(7) les [présumés [[[professeurs] chinois] malhonnêtes]]
    the alleged   professors   Chinese dishonest
    'the alleged dishonest Chinese professors'

This is problematic for an analysis that takes postnominal adjectives in Romance to be a consequence of N-movement, with all postnominal mirror-image orders analyzed in terms of a DP final relative clause source for adjectives on the right taking scope over those to their left (as in Cinque 1994). Assuming that *malhonnêtes* is a DP final reduced relative clause (in order to account for its taking scope over *chinois*) would incorrectly lead to the expectation that it also takes scope over the prenominal adjective *présumés*, as does a bona fide relative clause:

(8) les présumés professeurs chinois qui sont malhonnêtes
    the alleged   professors Chinese who are dishonest
    'the alleged Chinese professors who are dishonest'

If some derivation other than one involving a relative clause source for *malhonnêtes* must be at the basis of (7) under the discussed interpretation, then the mirror-image status of the postnominal adjectives in (7) constitutes a real problem for a pure N-raising approach, which gives the wrong result.

1.3 Existence of Unexpected Scope Effects in Romance

Provided that we again control for the absence of a relative clause source for the postnominal adjective (by selecting a nonpredicative one), the head-movement analysis leads one to expect a postnominal adjective not to be able to take scope over a prenominal one. Yet, this seems possible in cases like the following (see Valois 1991a; Svenonius 1994; Bouchard 1998, 2002):

(9) E' una *giovane* promessa *sicura*
    he-is a young promise sure
    'He is a sure young promise'

Here the postnominal adjective *sicura* (which is nonpredicative: *la giovane promessa è sicura* 'the young promise is sure') takes scope over *giovane promessa* (hence over the prenominal adjective *giovane*). This is an unexpected result.

On top of all these problems, there is another, more serious, one for the head-movement approach: its inability to provide a unified analysis for the different pattern we find in the interpretation of prenominal and postnominal adjectives in Germanic and Romance. This will be the subject of the next chapter.

2 A Systematic Contrast between English (Germanic) and Italian (Romance)

In both English and Italian, prenominal and postnominal adjectives differ in interpretation with respect to a number of well-known semantic distinctions. As will become apparent, English (and more generally Germanic) displays a pattern opposite that of Italian (and more generally Romance). While English adjectives are ambiguous between the two values of a number of semantic distinctions in prenominal position, and have only one value in postnominal position (where available), adjectives in Italian are ambiguous in postnominal position and have only one value in prenominal position (which is, in fact, the opposite of the one displayed by English adjectives in postnominal position).

My claim that the prenominal reading of many Italian (Romance) adjectives is also found postnominally is at variance with the often made claim that prenominal and postnominal adjectives in Romance differ systematically in meaning (see, among others, Waugh 1977, 151–152; Bernstein 1993a, note 18; Bernstein 1993b, 56; Alexiadou 2001, 2003; Mallén 2002; Alexiadou, Haegeman, and Stavrou 2007, part III, chapter 1, section 4.2; Pasqui 2007; Katz 2008). In fact, some even go so far as to claim that prenominal and postnominal adjectives in Romance can never have exactly the same interpretations in the two positions. Bouchard (2002, 73ff.), for example, reviews a large number of well-known cases where such differences are obvious (*une femme seule* 'a woman who is alone' versus *une seule femme* 'only one woman'; *une victoire certaine* 'a sure victory' versus *une certaine victoire* 'a certain victory'; pp. 81, 85, etc.), and others where the differences are less obvious, yet real (*un habile chirurgien* 'a skillful surgeon (as a surgeon)' versus *un chirurgien habile* 'a skillful surgeon at something (for a surgeon)'; p. 99). But this is not the point. What needs to be shown is that no cases exist where exactly the same reading is found both prenominally and postnominally (in addition to other, perhaps more salient, readings). Such cases, however, exist.

If one takes nonpredicative adjectives that can occur both pre- and postnominally, the identity of the readings appears more evident, because no other reading is added when one puts the adjective in postnominal position: *questa è una vera e propria falsità, questa è una falsità vera e propria* 'this is a real lie'; *questa è la probabile causa della sua morte, questa è la causa probabile della sua morte* 'this is the probable cause of his death'; *questo è il principale motivo della sua partenza, questo è il motivo principale della sua partenza* 'this is the main reason for his departure' (Cinque 1994, 94).[1]

In general, when one construes the right context, many adjectives in Romance indeed prove to retain in postnominal position the meaning they have prenominally. This conclusion, which has been reached by other authors (for French, by Delomier 1980, 22; Ewert and Hansen 1993, 167, who also cite Brunot 1922, 639; Jones 1996, 321; Abeillé and Godard 1999, 12, 16, and notes 4 and 12; Aljović 2000, 102; Borillo 2001, 42–43; for Spanish, by Contreras 1981, 151; Demonte 1982, 271, 278ff.; Demonte 1999a, 208; Rigau 1999, 351; for Romanian, by Cornilescu 2003, 5; Cornilescu 2006, 60), represents a problem for Bouchard's (2002) analysis. Also see notes 3 and 7 in this chapter.

I now review a number of well-known semantic distinctions, which reveal a very systematic pattern of oppositions between English (Germanic) and Italian (Romance).

2.1 Individual-Level vs. Stage-Level Readings

Building on Bolinger 1967, a number of authors (Ferris 1993, section 3.5; Sadler and Arnold 1994; Svenonius 1994; Larson 1998) note that in prenominal position English adjectives are systematically ambiguous between a reading in which they denote an enduring, or individual-level, property and a reading in which they denote a temporary, or stage-level, one (see (1)), while in postnominal position ((2)) they more typically (though perhaps not always) denote a stage-level property.[2]

English
(1) a. The **visible** stars include Aldebaran and Sirius (*ambiguous*)
    b. 'The stars that are generally visible include Aldebaran and Sirius' (individual-level)
    c. 'The stars that happen to be visible now include Aldebaran and Sirius' (stage-level)

(2) a. The (only) stars **visible** are Aldebaran and Sirius (*unambiguous*)
   b. #'The (only) stars that are generally visible are Aldebaran and Sirius' (individual-level)
   c. 'The (only) stars that happen to be visible now are Aldebaran and Sirius' (stage-level)

In Italian, and more generally in Romance, the situation is the opposite of that more typically found in English. Only one reading is possible prenominally (the individual-level reading; see (3)), while both readings are possible postnominally (see (4)):

Italian
(3) a. Le **invisibili** stelle di Andromeda esercitano un grande
      the invisible stars of Andromeda have   a great
      fascino (*unambiguous*)
      fascination
   b. 'Andromeda's stars, which are generally invisible, have a great fascination' (individual-level)
   c. #'Andromeda's generally visible stars, which happen to be invisible now, have a great fascination' (stage-level)

(4) a. Le stelle **invisibili** di Andromeda sono moltissime (*ambiguous*)
      the stars invisible of Andromeda are   very many
   b. 'Andromeda's stars, which are generally invisible, are very many' (individual-level)
   c. 'Andromeda's generally visible stars, which happen to be invisible now, are very many' (stage-level)

2.2 Restrictive vs. Nonrestrictive Readings

Another well-known distinction affecting the interpretation of adjectives is the restrictive/nonrestrictive distinction (Jespersen 1924, chapter 8; Bolinger 1967; Larson and Marušič 2004; among many others). The two languages again show the same pattern. The adjective is ambiguous in prenominal position in English ((5)), and in postnominal position in Italian ((8)); and it is unambiguously interpreted as restrictive in postnominal position in English ((6)), and nonrestrictively in prenominal position in Italian ((7)).[3]

English
(5) a. All of his **unsuitable** acts were condemned (*ambiguous*)
   b. 'All his acts were condemned; they were unsuitable' (nonrestrictive)

c. 'All (and only) his acts that were unsuitable were condemned' (restrictive)
(6) a. Every word **unsuitable** was deleted (*unambiguous*)
   b. #'Every word was deleted; they were unsuitable' (nonrestrictive)
   c. 'Every word that was unsuitable was deleted' (restrictive)

Italian
(7) a. Le **noiose** lezioni di Ferri se le ricordano tutti (*unambiguous*)
         the boring classes of Ferri remember   all
   b. 'Everybody remembers Ferri's classes, all of which were boring' (nonrestrictive)
   c. #'Everybody remembers just those classes by Ferri that were boring' (restrictive)
(8) a. Le lezioni **noiose** di Ferri se le ricordano tutti (*ambiguous*)[4]
        the classes boring of Ferri remember   all
   b. 'Everybody remembers Ferri's classes, all of which were boring' (nonrestrictive)
   c. 'Everybody remembers just those classes by Ferri that were boring' (restrictive)

2.3 Modal vs. Implicit Relative Clause Readings

Larson (2000a) notes that an adjective like *possible* in English is ambiguous in prenominal position between a modal reading (roughly paraphrasable as 'potential') and an implicit relative clause reading with Antecedent Contained Deletion (see (9)), while postnominally it is unambiguous, just retaining the implicit relative clause reading with Antecedent Contained Deletion (see (10)). Once again, Italian shows the opposite pattern: ambiguity in postnominal position ((12)), and retention of just the modal reading in prenominal position ((11)):[5]

English
(9) a. Mary interviewed every **possible** candidate (*ambiguous*)
   b. 'Mary interviewed every potential candidate' (modal reading)
   c. 'Mary interviewed every candidate that it was possible for her to interview' (implicit relative clause reading)
(10) a. Mary interviewed every candidate **possible** (*unambiguous*)
    b. #'Mary interviewed every potential candidate' (modal reading)
    c. 'Mary interviewed every candidate that it was possible for her to interview' (implicit relative clause reading)

Italian

(11) a.   Maria ha intervistato ogni **possibile** candidato (*unambiguous*)
Maria has interviewed every possible candidate
   b.   'Maria interviewed every potential candidate' (modal reading)
   c.   #'Maria interviewed every candidate that it was possible for her to interview' (implicit relative clause reading)

(12) a.   Maria ha intervistato ogni candidato **possibile** (*ambiguous*)
Maria has interviewed every candidate possible
   b.   'Maria interviewed every potential candidate' (modal reading)
   c.   'Maria interviewed every candidate that it was possible for her to interview' (implicit relative clause reading)

2.4 Intersective vs. Nonintersective (Adverbial) Readings

In prenominal position in English, many adjectives are systematically ambiguous between an intersective and a nonintersective reading. So, for example, as Larson (1995) observed, in *Olga is a beautiful dancer*, *beautiful* can either refer to the set of beautiful entities intersecting with the set of dancers, in which case it is interpreted as applying to the extension, or referent, of *dancer* ("she is beautiful as a person, and is a dancer"), or can modify the intension of *dancer*, in which case its interpretation is "adverbial" rather than intersective ("she dances beautifully"). (See Vendler 1968, chapter 6, and for a more accurate characterization of this ambiguity, Larson 1995, 1998.)

As (13) shows, the ambiguity is preserved even if prenominal *beautiful* is in the comparative form (and the standard of comparison is "extraposed"). Although an adjective like *beautiful* cannot be found by itself in postnominal position (*a dancer beautiful...*), it can if it is followed by the marker and standard of comparison, as in (14a), in which case it only has the intersective interpretation.[6] Once again, Italian contrasts systematically with English. Prenominally, the adjective is unambiguous (it can only be interpreted nonintersectively, or "adverbially"; see (15)), whereas postnominally it is ambiguous between the intersective and the nonintersective interpretations ((16)).[7]

English

(13) a.   Olga is a more **beautiful** dancer than her instructor (*ambiguous*)
   b.   'Olga is a dancer who is also a more beautiful person than her instructor' (intersective)
   c.   'Olga dances more beautifully than her instructor' (nonintersective)

(14) a. Olga is a dancer more **beautiful** than her instructor (*unambiguous*)
   b. 'Olga is a dancer who is also a more beautiful person than her instructor' (intersective)
   c. #'Olga dances more beautifully than her instructor' (nonintersective)

Italian
(15) a. Un **buon** attaccante non farebbe   mai   una cosa del
      a   good forward   not would-do never a   thing of-the
      genere (*unambiguous*)
      kind
   b. 'A forward good at playing forward would never do such a thing' (nonintersective)
   c. #'A good-hearted forward would never do such a thing' (intersective)

(16) a. Un attaccante **buono** non farebbe   mai   una cosa del
      a   forward   good   not would-do never a   thing of-the
      genere (*ambiguous*)
      kind
   b. 'A forward good at playing forward would never do such a thing' (nonintersective)
   c. 'A good-hearted forward would never do such a thing' (intersective)

2.5 Relative (to a Comparison Class) vs. Absolute Readings

As noted by many authors (Bartsch and Vennemann 1972, part II; Bartsch 1972; Kamp 1975; Higginbotham 1985; among others), scalar adjectives (like *big* in *A big tank was coming toward us*) can be understood in an absolute sense ('a big object') or as relative to a comparison class (typically provided by the noun with which they combine, i.e., 'big for a tank').[8]

In prenominal position in Italian such adjectives can only be understood in an absolute way. So, for example, in (19a), *gli altissimi edifici di New York* 'New York's very tall buildings' only means that New York's buildings are extremely tall objects in an absolute sense, not that they are very tall compared to the average height of buildings. In postnominal position, on the other hand, *altissimi* 'very tall' is ambiguous between these two readings (see (20)). In English, it is the prenominal position that is ambiguous ((17a)) (for the postnominal position one cannot tell given that such adjectives cannot occur there):

English

(17) a. New York's very **tall** buildings impress everybody (*ambiguous*)
  b. 'New York's buildings, which are very tall objects, impress everybody' (absolute)
  c. 'New York's buildings, which are very tall compared to the average height of buildings, impress everybody' (relative)

(18) [the postnominal positioning of the adjective cannot be tested]

Italian

(19) a. Gli **altissimi** edifici   di New York colpiscono
      the very-tall buildings of New York strike
      tutti (*unambiguous*)
      all
  b. 'New York's buildings, which are very tall objects, impress everybody' (absolute)
  c. #'New York's buildings, which are very tall compared to the average height of buildings, impress everybody' (relative)

(20) a. Gli edifici   **altissimi** di New York colpiscono tutti (*ambiguous*)
      the buildings very-tall of New York strike   all
  b. 'New York's buildings, which are very tall objects, impress everybody' (absolute)
  c. 'New York's buildings, which are very tall compared to the average height of buildings, impress everybody' (relative)

2.6 Comparative vs. Absolute Readings of Superlatives

A similar pattern is provided by the interpretation of the superlative form of adjectives. In prenominal position a superlative adjective in English is ambiguous between an absolute and a comparative reading. See (21) (for the postnominal position one cannot tell given that such adjectives cannot occur there).[9]

Once again, Italian differs in displaying ambiguity in postnominal position (see (24)), but not prenominally (see (23)), where it only admits an absolute reading:

English

(21) a. Who climbed the **highest** snowy mountain? (*ambiguous*)
  b. 'Who climbed Mt. Everest?' (absolute)

c. 'Who climbed a snowy mountain higher than those that others climbed?' (comparative)

(22) [the postnominal positioning of the adjective cannot be tested]

Italian

(23) a. Chi ha scalato la **più alta** montagna innevata? (*unambiguous*)
        who has climbed the most high mountain snowy
   b. 'Who climbed Mt. Everest?' (absolute)
   c. # 'Who climbed a snowy mountain higher than that which others climbed?' (comparative)

(24) a. Chi ha scalato la montagna innevata **più   alta**? (*ambiguous*)
        who has climbed the mountain snowy   most high
   b. 'Who climbed Mt. Everest?' (absolute)
   c. 'Who climbed a snowy mountain higher than that which others climbed?' (relative)

2.7   Specificity- vs. Non-Specificity-Inducing Readings

Another property distinguishes the prenominal from the postnominal position of the adjective in Romance. This was originally noted by Bosque (1993) for Spanish (also see Bosque 1996, 2001; Ticio 2003, 124ff.; Jacob 2006), and, after him, by Picallo (1994) for Catalan. Similar facts seem to hold in Italian and French, and, we conjecture, throughout Romance. The prenominal position of the adjective renders an indefinite DP specific (in *realis* contexts). See (27), which implies the existence of a specific actor that will come to the party, whether or not the speaker knows his identity. When the adjective is postnominal instead, the indefinite DP need not be specific ((28)). No comparable contrast is detectable in English, for reasons that I come back to (see (25) and (26)):

English

(25) a. John will burn a **nearby** house (*ambiguous*)
   b. 'John will burn some specific house that is near his' (specific)
   c. 'John will burn some house or other among those that are near his' (nonspecific)

(26) a. John will burn a house **nearby** (*ambiguous*)
   b. 'John will burn a specific house that is near his' (specific)
   c. 'John will burn some house or other among those that are near his' (nonspecific)

Italian

(27) a. Domani, alla festa so che interverrà un **famoso** attore (*unambiguous*)
tomorrow, to-the party I-know that will-intervene a famous actor

    b. 'Tomorrow, I know that a certain famous actor will come to the party' (specific)

    c. #'Tomorrow, I know that some famous actor or other will come to the party' (nonspecific)

(28) a. Domani, alla festa so che interverrà un attore **famoso** (*ambiguous*)
tomorrow, to-the party I-know that will-intervene an actor famous

    b. 'Tomorrow, I know that a certain famous actor will come to the party' (specific)

    c. 'Tomorrow, I know that some famous actor or other will come to the party' (nonspecific)

For reasons that remain to be understood, a prenominal adjective no longer forces a specific reading of an indefinite DP in Italian if this is embedded in a modal (*irrealis*) context. Compare (27a) with (29):[10]

(29) a. Se mai incontrerò un famoso attore di Hollywood, gli chiederò un autografo
'If ever I meet a famous Hollywood actor, I'll ask him for an autograph'

    b. Chiunque vorrebbe essere una famosa star del cinema
'Anyone would like to be a famous movie star'

When not in a modal context, exclusively prenominal adjectives like *vecchio* (in the sense of 'long standing'), *povero* (in the sense of 'pitiable'), and so on also induce a specific reading of the DP (*Domani, alla festa ci sarà anche un tuo vecchio amico* 'Tomorrow, at the party there will be an old friend of yours'; *domani forse interverrà anche un tuo povero collega* 'Tomorrow perhaps there will also be a poor colleague of yours').

The specificity-inducing character of the prenominal position of the adjective in Italian emerges more clearly in contexts such as (30a,b), which are incompatible with a specific interpretation of the indefinite DP (because they assert its nonexistence):

(30) a. Purtroppo, su questo argomento, non esiste un ⟨*significativo⟩ articolo ⟨significativo⟩
'Unfortunately, on this topic, no significant article exists'

b. Non credo proprio che ci sia un ⟨*famoso⟩ attore ⟨famoso⟩ per questa parte
'I really don't think that there is a famous actor for this part'

This context contrasts with that in (31), which is instead compatible with a specific interpretation of the indefinite DP:

(31) a. Su questo argomento, Gianni ha già scritto un ⟨significativo⟩ articolo ⟨significativo⟩
'On this topic, Gianni has already written a significant article'
b. Ecco un ⟨famoso⟩ attore ⟨famoso⟩ per questa parte
'Here is a famous actor for this part'

Clear evidence in Spanish that an indefinite DP with a prenominal adjective is interpreted as specific is provided by contrasts like the following, from Bosque (2001, 27) (also see Silva-Villar and Gutiérrez-Rexach 1997, 464):

(32) a. Busco (a) un actor famoso
b. Busco *(a) un famoso actor
'I am looking for a famous actor'

When specific, animate direct objects are necessarily preceded by the preposition *a* ('to') (see Brugè and Brugger 1996 as well as Torrego 1998 for discussion and references); hence the ungrammaticality of (32b) without *a*, given the necessarily specific interpretation induced by the prenominal adjective.[11]

2.8 Evaluative vs. Epistemic Readings of 'unknown'

Abusch and Rooth (1997) note that, when used attributively in an indefinite DP, an adjective like *unknown* is ambiguous between a simple evaluative reading and an epistemic one.[12] See (33) (the interpretation of *unknown* in postnominal position cannot be tested because the adjective cannot occur there).

In Italian, the same ambiguity is found in postnominal but not in prenominal position, where only the evaluative reading is possible (see (35)–(36)):

English
(33) a. Maria lives in some **unknown** village in the South of France (*ambiguous*)
b. Maria lives in some village in the South of France that is not a well-known one (*evaluative*)

c. Maria lives in some village in the South of France, but it is not known which one *(epistemic)*

(34) [the postnominal positioning of the adjective cannot be tested]

Italian
(35) a. Maria vive in uno **sconosciuto** villaggio del sud della
Maria lives in an unknown village of-the South of-the
Francia *(unambiguous)*
France
b. 'Maria lives in some village in the South of France that is not a well-known one' *(evaluative)*
c. #'Maria lives in some village in the South of France, but it is not known which one' *(epistemic)*

(36) a. Maria vive in un villaggio **sconosciuto** del sud della
Maria lives in a village unknown of-the South of-the
Francia *(ambiguous)*
France
b. 'Maria lives in some village in the South of France that is not a well-known one' *(evaluative)*
c. 'Maria lives in some village in the South of France, but it is not known which one' *(epistemic)*

2.9 NP-Dependent vs. Discourse Anaphoric Readings of 'different'

The adjective *different* in English, among its various interpretations (Carlson 1987; Moltmann 1992; Moltmann 1997, section 4.5.2; Beck 1998, 2000), has what Beck (1998, 2000) refers to as the "NP-dependent" ((37b)) and the "discourse anaphoric" ((37c)) readings:[13]

English
(37) a. Detmar and Kordula live in **different** cities *(ambiguous)* (Beck 1998, 19)
b. 'The city that Detmar lives in is different from the city that Kordula lives in' *(NP-dependent reading)*
c. 'Detmar and Kordula live in cities that are different from some salient city' *(discourse anaphoric reading)*

(38) [the postnominal positioning of the adjective cannot be tested]

In Italian, the same ambiguity is again found in postnominal position, but not prenominally, where only the NP-dependent reading is available. See (39) and (40):

Italian

(39) a. Gianni e   Mario vivono in **differenti** città (*unambiguous*)
    Gianni and Mario live   in different cities
  b. 'The city that Gianni lives in is different from the city that Mario lives in' (*NP-dependent reading*)
  c. #'Gianni and Mario live in cities that are different from some salient city' (*discourse anaphoric reading*)[14]

(40) a. Gianni e   Mario vivono in città **differenti** (*ambiguous*)
    Gianni and Mario live   in cities different
  b. 'The city that Gianni lives in is different from the city that Mario lives in' (*NP-dependent reading*)
  c. 'Gianni and Mario live in cities that are different from some salient city' (*discourse anaphoric reading*)

2.10 Summary of the Basic Generalizations

The basic generalizations on the interpretive properties of prenominal and postnominal adjectives emerging from the data of the preceding sections are summarized in tables 2.1 and 2.2.

Table 2.1
English (Germanic)

Prenominal adjectives	N	Postnominal adjectives
stage-level or individual-level reading		stage-level (or individual- level) reading
restrictive or nonrestrictive reading		restrictive reading
implicit relative clause or modal reading		implicit relative clause reading
intersective or nonintersective reading		intersective reading
relative or absolute reading		[cannot be tested]
comparative or absolute reading of superlatives		[cannot be tested]
specificity- or non-specificity-inducing reading		specificity- or non-specificity-inducing reading
evaluative or epistemic reading of 'unknown'		[cannot be tested]
NP-dependent or discourse anaphoric reading of 'different'		[cannot be tested]

Table 2.2
Italian (Romance)

Prenominal adjectives	N	Postnominal adjectives
individual-level reading		individual-level or stage-level reading
nonrestrictive reading		restrictive or nonrestrictive reading
modal reading		modal or implicit relative clause reading
nonintersective reading		intersective or nonintersective reading
absolute reading		relative or absolute reading
absolute reading of superlatives		comparative or absolute reading of superlatives
specificity-inducing reading		specificity- or non-specificity-inducing reading
evaluative reading of 'unknown'		evaluative or epistemic reading of 'unknown'
NP-dependent reading of 'different'		NP-dependent or discourse anaphoric reading of 'different'

2.10.1 An Asymmetric Distribution of Interpretive Possibilities

The asymmetric distribution of interpretive possibilities seen in tables 2.1 and 2.2 can be characterized as follows. In English (Germanic) the prenominal position is systematically ambiguous between the two values of each property, while the postnominal one (when available) has only one value: stage-level (characteristically), restrictive, implicit relative clause, and intersective readings (the fact that it retains an ambiguity for the specificity-/non-specificity-inducing reading, and partly for the stage-/individual-level reading, will later be related to the fact that the adjective is similarly ambiguous in the predicate position of a relative clause).[15]

In Italian (Romance), it is instead the postnominal position that is systematically ambiguous between the two values of each property, while the prenominal one only has the individual-level, nonrestrictive, modal, nonintersective, absolute, absolute with superlatives, specificity-inducing, evaluative, and NP-dependent, readings.[16]

These values necessarily go together. So, for example, the absolute interpretation of the adjective *altissimi* 'very tall', whether in prenominal ((19a)) or postnominal ((20a)) position, is necessarily nonrestrictive, individual-level, and so on.[17] Similarly, the evaluative reading of *sconosciuto* 'unknown' in (35a) (*Maria vive in uno sconosciuto villaggio del sud della Francia* 'Maria lives in some village in the South of France, which happens not to be a well-known one') is also individual-level, nonrestrictive, specific, and so forth.[18]

2.10.2 Postnominal Adjectives in English (Part I)

Postnominal adjectives in English are argued by Sadler and Arnold (1994, 194–196), Larson (1998, 2000a, 2000b), and Larson and Marušič (2004) to be reduced relative clauses (also see James 1979, 692; Ferris 1993, section 3.8; and Jacobsson 1996, 214). Evidence for this conclusion comes from the fact that whenever an adjective can be found both prenominally and postnominally, with different properties, the postnominal one invariably shows a behavior identical to that of the corresponding predicative adjective inside a restrictive relative clause. As noted above, the prenominal position of *possible* in (9a), repeated here as (41a), is ambiguous between a modal reading (roughly equivalent to 'potential') and a reduced relative clause reading with Antecedent Contained Deletion (roughly paraphrasable as 'every candidate that it was possible for her to interview'; see Larson 2000a).

The postnominal position ((41b)) instead only retains the reduced relative clause reading with Antecedent Contained Deletion, equivalent to the corresponding relative clause containing the adjective in predicate position ((41c)):

(41) a. Mary interviewed every possible candidate
   b. Mary interviewed every candidate possible
   c. Mary interviewed every candidate that it was possible for her to interview

(42a,b) is another well-known minimal pair (see Sadler and Arnold 1994, 194, for this and other such pairs, as well as Markus 1997). Prenominal *present* only has a temporal reading, while postnominal *present* only has a locative reading. The corresponding relative clause with *present* in predicate position ((42c)) only has the reading of postnominal *present*: the locative one.

(42) a. the present editors
   b. the editors present
   c. the editors who are/were present

The pair (43a,b) represents an adjectival doublet (see Larson and Marušič 2004, 272–273). One of the two (*live*) can only be found in prenominal position, and the other (*alive*) only in postnominal position (but see Blöhdorn 2009, 80, for a rare example of prenominal *alive*; also see Jacobsson

1961). The only form possible in the predicate position of the corresponding relative clause ((43c)) is the 'postnominal' *alive*.

(43) a. the live/*alive animals
b. the animals *live/alive
c. the animals that are *live/alive

The systematic identity in behavior between adjectives in postnominal position and the same adjectives in the predicate position of a relative clause becomes understandable if the former are actually nothing other than reduced relative clauses.[19]

2.10.3 Order of the Two Readings in Prenominal Position in English (Germanic)

The two readings available prenominally in English can in fact co-occur, and when they do they are strictly ordered (Larson 1998, 2000a, 2000b), the leftmost corresponding systematically to the postnominal (reduced relative clause) reading. See (44)–(52):

(44) *stage-level* > *individual-level* > *N* > *stage-level*[20] (Larson 1998, 155–156)
  a. Every VISIBLE visible star
    (*Every visible VISIBLE star)
  b. Every visible star VISIBLE

(45) *restrictive* > *nonrestrictive* > *N* > *restrictive* (cf. Larson and Marušič 2004, 275)
  a. His MOST UNSUITABLE unsuitable acts
    (*His unsuitable MOST UNSUITABLE acts)
  b. His unsuitable acts MOST UNSUITABLE

(46) *implicit relative clause* > *modal* > *N* > *implicit relative clause* (Larson 2000a)[21]
  a. She tried to interview every POSSIBLE possible candidate
    (*She tried to interview every possible POSSIBLE candidate)
  b. She tried to interview every possible candidate POSSIBLE

(47) *intersective* > *nonintersective* > *N* > *intersective* (Larson and Marušič 2004, 281)[22]
  a. She is a BEAUTIFUL beautiful dancer
    (*She is a beautiful BEAUTIFUL dancer)
  b. She is a beautiful dancer MORE BEAUTIFUL THAN HER INSTRUCTOR

(48) *relative (to a comparison class) > absolute > N > relative (to a comparison class)*
   a. I have never seen QUITE SO TALL tall buildings
      (*I have never seen tall QUITE SO TALL buildings)
   b. I have never seen tall buildings QUITE SO TALL

(49) [comparative superlative > absolute superlative N] (does not apply)

(50) [nonspecificity inducing > specificity inducing N] (does not apply)

(51) *epistemic > evaluative > N*
   a. Maria lives in some UNKNOWN unknown village in the South of France
      (*Maria lives in some unknown UNKNOWN village in the South of France)
   b. [postnominal position cannot be tested]

(52) *discourse anaphoric > NP dependent > N*
   a. John and Mary live in DIFFERENT different cities
      (*John and Mary live in different DIFFERENT cities)
   b. [postnominal position cannot be tested]

Given that they are invariably identical, it is reasonable to consider the leftmost of the two prenominal positions and the postnominal position deriving from a reduced relative clause to be transformationally related. A possibility in line with the tradition would be to consider the leftmost prenominal position as derived through fronting of the postnominal one. For reasons discussed in Cinque 2003, 2008a, and in preparation, I will instead assume (reduced) relative clauses to be merged prenominally. Their ultimate postnominal location is a consequence of their movement to a higher licensing position, followed by merger of a possibly covert complementizer that attracts the entire remnant to its left, along lines recently developed by Kayne (1999, 2000, 2005b). (See sections 3.1 and 4.2 for somewhat more detailed discussion.) Nothing here, however, hinges crucially on that decision.

2.10.4 Order of the Two Readings in Postnominal Position in Italian (Romance)
The two readings available postnominally in Italian (Romance) are strictly ordered in the opposite way (with the leftmost of the two corresponding to the prenominal one):[23]

(53) *individual-level > N > individual-level > stage-level*
   a. una posizione invidiabile (oggi ancor più) INVIDIABILE
      a   position   enviable   (today even more) enviable
      'a (today even more) enviable enviable position'
      (*una posizione (oggi ancor più) INVIDIABILE invidiabile)
   b. una invidiabile posizione (oggi ancor più) INVIDIABILE
      an enviable   position   (today even more) enviable
      'a (today even more) enviable enviable position'

(54) *nonrestrictive > N > nonrestrictive > restrictive*
   a. I   greci   industriosi PIU' INDUSTRIOSI
      the Greeks industrious most industrious
      'the most industrious industrious Greeks'
      (*I greci PIU' INDUSTRIOSI industriosi)
   b. Gli industriosi greci   PIU' INDUSTRIOSI
      the industrious Greeks most industrious
      'the most industrious industrious Greeks'

(55) *modal > N > modal > implicit relative clause*[24]
   a. Cercò   di intervistare ogni   candidato possibile POSSIBILE
      he-tried to interview   every candidate potential possible
      'He tried to interview every possible potential candidate'
      (*Cercò di intervistare ogni candidato POSSIBILE possibile)
   b. Cercò   di intervistare ogni possibile candidato POSSIBILE
      'He-tried to interview   every potential candidate possible'

(56) *nonintersective > N > nonintersective > intersective*
   a. un attaccante buono BUONO
      a   forward   good good
      'a good-hearted good forward'
      (*un attaccante BUONO buono)
   b. un buon attaccante BUONO
      a   good forward   good
      'a good-hearted good forward'

(57) *absolute > N > absolute > relative (to a comparison class)*
   a. edifici   altissimi COSI' ALTI
      buildings very tall so   tall
      'so tall very tall buildings'
      (*edifici COSI' ALTI altissimi)
   b. altissimi edifici   COSI' ALTI
      very tall buildings SO   TALL
      'so tall very tall buildings'

(58) [N absolute superl. > comparative superl.] (does not apply)

(59) [N specificity-inducing > non-specificity-inducing] (does not apply)

(60) *evaluative > N > evaluative > epistemic*
    a. (Vive   in) un villaggio sconosciuto SCONOSCIUTO
       (she-lives in) a village unknown   unknown
       'She lives in an unknown unknown village'
       (*Vive in un villaggio SCONOSCIUTO sconosciuto)
    b. (Vive   in) uno sconosciuto villaggio SCONOSCIUTO
       (she-lives in) an unknown   village   unknown
       'She lives in an unknown unknown village'

(61) *NP dependent > N > NP dependent > discourse anaphoric*
    a. Gianni e   Mario vivono in città differenti DIFFERENTI
       Gianni and Mario live   in cities different different
       'Gianni and Mario live in different different cities'
       (*Gianni e Mario vivono in città DIFFERENTI differenti)
    b. Gianni e   Mario vivono in differenti città DIFFERENTI
       Gianni and Mario live   in different cities different
       'Gianni and Mario live in different different cities'

2.10.5 Summary of the Orders of the Two Readings in English (Germanic) and Italian (Romance)

If we refer to APs with the readings individual-level, nonrestrictive, modal, nonintersective, absolute, specificity-inducing, evaluative, and NP dependent, as "direct modification" APs (to borrow a term from Sproat and Shih 1988, 1991), the surface orderings so far reviewed may be succinctly stated as follows (RC = relative clause):[25]

(62) *English (Germanic)*
    AP from reduced RC > "direct modification" AP > **N** > AP from reduced RC

(63) *Italian (Romance)*
    "direct modification" AP > **N** > "direct modification" AP > AP from reduced RC

2.11 An Additional Problem for the N-Movement Analysis

Assuming that each class of interpretations of an adjective is associated with a particular structural position in the DP, it turns out that N-movement cannot possibly derive the desired generalizations within a unified Merge structure for Germanic and Romance. If we start from a structure like (64), where the readings are associated with the different DP-internal positions indicated there and where "__" signals the possible landing sites of N-movement (in Romance), we can capture the situation of English (Germanic), where no N-movement applies and where the correct readings (in the correct order) are found both prenominally and postnominally. But we cannot capture the situation of Italian (Romance). If N obligatorily moved one notch, past the "direct modification" APs, we would correctly derive the right readings of the postnominal adjectives (in the right order), but would have the wrong readings for the adjectives that remain in prenominal position. The same problem would ensue if the N moved one notch optionally, or the first notch obligatorily and the second optionally. If it instead moved two notches obligatorily we would get the wrong readings both prenominally (no prenominal adjectives would be possible) and postnominally, with the readings in the wrong order as well.[26]

(64) *Putative source 1*

Reduced RC	"Direct modification" AP	N	Reduced RC
__ stage-level	__ individual-level	N	stage-level
__ restrictive	__ nonrestrictive	N	restrictive
__ implicit RC reading	__ modal	N	implicit RC reading
__ intersective	__ nonintersective	N	intersective
__ relative (to a comparison class)	__ absolute	N	relative (to a comparison class)
__ comparative (superlative)	__ absolute (superlative)	N	comparative (superlative)
__ epistemic	__ evaluative	N	epistemic
__ discourse anaphoric	__ NP dependent	N	discourse anaphoric

If we were instead to assume the particular association of readings and structural positions indicated in (65), we could directly capture the Italian (Romance) situation under the assumption that N obligatorily moves one notch, and optionally two notches. In this way, we would correctly derive the fact that in prenominal position only the readings associated with "direct modification" APs are possible, while in postnominal position both are possible (and in an order that is the correct order). However, we would not be able to capture the English (Germanic) situation. The order of the prenominal readings (positions) of (65) is the reverse of the order found in English (Germanic).

(65) *Putative source 2*

"Direct modification" AP	Reduced RC	N	Reduced RC
__ individual-level	__ stage-level	N	stage-level
__ nonrestrictive	__ restrictive	N	restrictive
__ modal	__ implicit RC reading	N	implicit RC reading
__ nonintersective	__ intersective	N	intersective
__ absolute	__ relative (to a comparison class)	N	relative (to a comparison class)
__ absolute (superlative)	__ comparative (superlative)	N	comparative (superlative)
__ evaluative	__ epistemic	N	epistemic
__ NP dependent	__ discourse anaphoric	N	discourse anaphoric

In sum, there appears to be no common structure of Merge for Germanic and Romance that together with N-movement can derive the observed different patterns of interpretation for prenominal and postnominal adjectives in the two language families.

An alternative analysis exists, however, that is compatible with a unique structure of Merge for Germanic and Romance, and that seems to provide a revealing account of the observed generalizations. It does not involve N-movement but movement of (phrases containing) the NP.[27]

3   Phrasal Movement and the Two Sources of Adnominal Adjectives

3.1   The Two Sources of Adnominal Adjectives

As the preceding discussion has implied, the first component of the analysis to be developed here is the idea that adnominal adjectives (APs) have two separate sources.[1] One is a direct adnominal modification source, which I take to involve merger of the different classes of APs in the specifiers of various dedicated functional heads of the extended projection of the NP (evidence for this position over alternatives that have been proposed in the literature will be discussed in section 4.1.1). The other source is a (reduced) relative clause source (to which, I will argue, the former source cannot be reduced; see section 4.1.3). This second source corresponds to Sproat and Shih's (1988, 1990) "indirect modification." As already noted, I will also be assuming that the Merge position of (reduced) relative clauses is prenominal, specifically in the specifier of a projection above the projections hosting direct modification APs, as very roughly sketched in (1):[2]

(1)
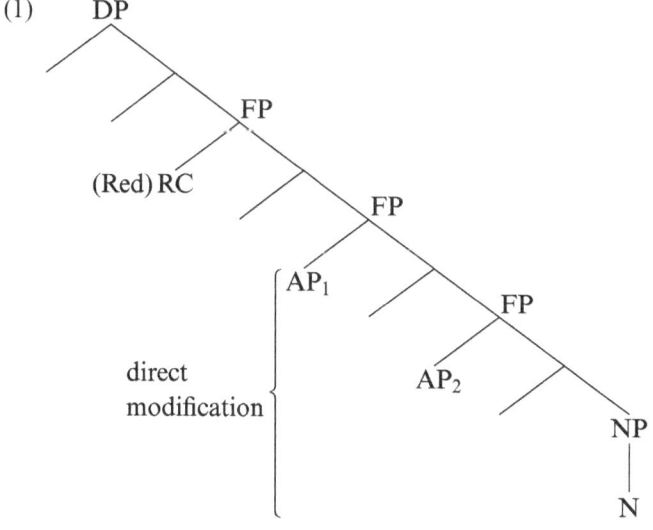

As also mentioned above, the postnominal position of (reduced) relative clauses will be taken to arise as a consequence of the merger of a (possibly covert) complementizer that attracts the NP (plus any direct modification APs, if present) along lines advocated by Kayne (1999, 2000, 2005b):[3]

(2) a. [[IP e recently arrived] nice Greek vases] → (merger of C and attraction of the Head)
 b. [nice Greek vases] C [[IP e recently arrived] t] → (merger of the determiner)
 c. [the [[nice Greek vases] C [[IP e recently arrived] t]]]

3.2 A Summary of the Interpretive Properties Associated with Each Source

As seen, the two sources turn out to have quite different interpretive properties. Each source is associated with a value for the semantic distinctions reviewed above that is in general the opposite of the value associated with the other source. See (6) below, which represents the Merge structure of the two types of modification.

A further distinction between the two sources is suggested by an observation of Larson's (2000b). There he notes that in (3) the first temporal modifier is interpreted deictically ('which took place on Thursday this week'), while the second is interpreted generically ('which ordinarily takes place on Thursday'):

(3) I missed the THURSDAY Thursday lecture

Although the same distinction cannot be reproduced in Italian with adjectives (both the deictic and the generic temporal modifiers take the form of a postnominal PP introduced by *di*, in the generic case typically accompanied by a definite article), it can be reproduced with PPs, which are found in the expected mirror-image order (N > generic > deictic):

(4) la   lezione del   giovedì   di giovedì   (prossimo)
 the class of-the Thursday of Thursday (next)
 '(Next) Thursday Thursday class'

(5) *?la   lezione di giovedì   (prossimo) del   giovedì
 the class of Thursday (next)   of-the Thursday

There is an additional interpretive difference between the two sources. Only direct modification adjectives can give rise to idiomatic readings. Presumably this is a consequence of the nonintersective nature of direct modification versus the necessarily intersective nature of indirect modification (which is incompatible with the semantic noncompositionality of idioms). See the discussion in section 7.2 on the possible idiomatic interpretation of prenominal, but not of postnominal, adjectives in English (as opposed to Italian), the possible idiomatic interpretation of Bosnian/Croatian/Serbian "long-form" adjectives (which can be direct modification adjectives) versus the impossibility of an idiomatic interpretation of "short-form" adjectives (which are only indirect modification adjectives) (appendix, section A.3), and the possible idiomatic reading of Chinese *de*-less adjectives versus the impossibility of an idiomatic reading for the corresponding adjectives with *de* (appendix, section A.1).

The table in (6) summarizes the different properties associated with each source:

(6) *Indirect (reduced RC) modification*   *Direct modification*
   [Det. [stage-level (or individual-   [individual-level   NP]]]
       level)
   [Det. [restrictive   [nonrestrictive   NP]]]
   [Det. [implicit relative clause   [modal   NP]]]
   [Det. [intersective   [nonintersective   NP]]]
   [Det. [relative (to a comparison   [absolute   NP]]]
       class)
   [Det. [comparative (with   [absolute (with   NP]]][4]
       superlatives)   superlatives)
   [Det. [specificity- or non-   [specificity-inducing   NP]]][5]
       specificity-inducing
   [Det. [epistemic 'unknown'   [evaluative 'unknown'   NP]]]
   [Det. [discourse anaphoric   [NP dependent   NP]]]
       'different'   'different'
   [Det. [deictic   [generic   NP]]]
   [Det. [literal interpretation   [possible idiomatic   NP]]]
        interpretation

That is, direct modification has only the "adverbial" individual-level, nonrestrictive, modal, nonintersective, absolute (with both nonsuperlative and superlative scalar adjectives), specificity-inducing, evaluative (for adjectives like 'unknown'), NP-dependent (for an adjective like 'different'), generic, interpretations, and can give rise to idiomatic readings. Indirect modification (the relative clause source) instead has the opposite values, with two apparent exceptions. It has the opposite values: restrictive, implicit relative clause, intersective, relative to a comparison class, comparative (with superlatives), epistemic (for adjectives like 'unknown'), discourse anaphoric (for an adjective like 'different'), deictic, literal; but it appears to be underspecified for the value specificity-/non-specificity-inducing, and, to some extent, for the value stage-level/individual-level, as noted above.

The reason for these two apparent exceptions is very likely the fact that indirect modification has the same readings of predicative adjectives in relative clauses, and predicative adjectives in relative clauses are compatible with both values of such distinctions. See (7a), where reference may be to a specific house that is nearby, or to some house or other that must satisfy the property of being nearby, and (7b), where *navigable* may be interpreted as 'currently navigable' (stage-level) or 'generally navigable, though maybe not at the present moment' (individual-level):

(7) a. He wants to burn a house that is nearby
 b. This is the only river that is navigable

3.3 A Preview of the Syntactic Properties Associated with Each Source

There are also syntactic properties that go together with these clusters of semantic properties.

3.3.1 Relative Distance from N

As seen with English prenominal adjectives and Italian postnominal ones, direct modification adjectives (with the interpretive properties associated with them) are closer to the N than adjectives deriving from relative clauses (with the opposite interpretive properties). This is especially visible in languages in which the two series are morphologically distinct, as in some of the languages that I briefly discuss in the appendix.[6] So, for example, articulated adjectives in Maltese Arabic, which appear to derive from a relative clause source, are invariably further away from the noun than articleless ones, which are direct modification only. (See the appendix, section A.2; also see the cases of Chinese, Bosnian/Croatian/Serbian, and Greek, in sections A.1, A.3, and A.5 of the appendix.) This property will be made to follow from the different height at which (reduced) relative clauses and direct modification adjectives are merged (see chapter 4).

3.3.2 Rigid and Nonrigid Ordering

A second syntactic difference between the two sources involves their word-order properties. As already suggested in Sproat and Shih 1988, 1990, direct modification adjectives, like *de*-less adjectives in Chinese (see the appendix, section A.1), are rigidly ordered, while adjectives deriving from relative clauses are not. The same is true of articleless adjectives in colloquial Slovenian, whose order is rigid (Marušič and Žaucer 2006, 190), as opposed to the free order of adjectives preceded by the "article" TA, which Marušič and Žaucer argue derive from reduced relative clauses. The rigidity of the order of direct modification adjectives is especially clear in languages like Yoruba that only have direct modification adjectives (i.e., that lack predicative adjectives that can enter the relative clause source), or Iká, whose direct modification adjectives are morphologically distinct from predicative adjectives. (For discussion, see section 3.5.1.2.) Other languages reported to have a rigid order of adjectives are Muna (Austronesian—Berg 1989, section 5.9.1), Nabak (Papuan—Fabian, Fabian, and Waters 1998, 72–73), and Nawdm (Niger-Congo—Albro 1998, 3).

As to languages like English or Italian, which appear not to have an absolutely rigid order but only a "preferred" or unmarked one, it is interesting to note that their unmarked order corresponds to the rigid order of languages that do have one.[7] I interpret this as suggesting that English and Italian also have a rigid order with their direct modification adjectives, even though this is obscured by the existence of adjectives that can be used either as direct modifiers or as indirect modifiers (i.e., also as predicative adjectives that enter a relative clause source, thus giving rise to an apparent reversal of the rigid order). (See sections 5.1 and 6.1.)

The hypothesis that even in English and Italian direct modification adjectives are rigidly ordered is confirmed by the rigidity of the order in cases in which the adjectives have no independent predicative usage, and thus can only be direct modifiers of the NP, like "classificatory" and "adverbial" adjectives ((8)), or in cases in Italian where they appear in prenominal position, which is only open to direct modification adjectives ((9)):

(8) a. He is an old electrical engineer vs. *He is an eléctrical old engineer
   b. He is an occasional hard worker vs. *He is a hárd occasional worker

(9) a. I   cari vecchi tempi andati vs. *I   vecchi cari tempi andati
       the dear old   times past   vs. the old   dear times past
   b. la sua povera ex   moglie vs. *la sua ex   povera
       the his poor former wife   vs. the his former poor
       moglie (in the sense of 'pitiable')
       wife
       'his poor former wife'   vs. 'his former poor wife'

Surrendering to the appearance that (direct modification) adjectives in English or Italian have no ordering restrictions would leave such cases as (8) and (9) as exceptions, and the very existence of an unmarked order that corresponds to the rigid order shown by other languages as something of a coincidence.[8]

The apparent nonrigid ordering of adjectives (where found) may have a number of explanations. One has already been mentioned: when the lower of two adjectives that are rigidly ordered when in direct modification can also be used predicatively and can thus access the higher reduced relative clause source. In some such cases there is a discernible change of meaning. See (10)–(11). In others, this may be present, but harder to pin down, as in (12):[9]

(10) a. He is an alleged heavy drinker
 b. He is a heavy alleged drinker

(11) a. He is a former heavy smoker
 b. He is a heavy former smoker

(12) a. a beautiful old house
 b. an old beautiful house

The failure to take the two sources of adjectives into consideration has in fact led many authors to the conclusion that (certain) languages have no strict ordering of adjectives, or just a partial one, possibly determined by semantic or informational conditions. (See Malouf 2000; Bouchard 2002, 2009; Kremers 2003, 74–75; Knittel 2005; Truswell 2004a, 2004b, 2009; Teodorescu 2006; Szendrői 2008, section 3; among others.)

For a discussion of Teoderescu's (2006) pair *a famous alleged actor* and *an alleged famous actor*, see section 5.1. More interesting are cases like her pair *an **alleged** former thief* and *a **former** alleged thief*, where both adjectives are direct modification adjectives only.

Perhaps *former* is merged in two different positions of the extended projection of the NP, which is possibly at the root of its systematic ambiguity with a possessive adjective.[10] For example, *former* can be under the scope of *my*, thus modifying the NP 'intension' ([my [former [mansion]]] = a current possession of mine that used to be a mansion), or may be merged higher, taking scope over *my*, which has plausibly moved past it ([my$_i$ [former [t$_i$ [mansion]]]] = the mansion that was formerly mine). Possible evidence for the different height of merger is the fact that the two readings can co-occur. In a scenario in which each of us strives for possessing a house that was a former mansion, it seems possible to say

"Now I have a new one. My former former mansion was in too poor a state to be inhabited."[11]

Another source of apparent freedom of order is when all of the adjectives involved can have a reduced relative clause source, as in (13), namely when all of them also have a predicative usage, maybe in addition to a direct modification one (see Sproat and Shih 1988, 1990; Baker 2003b, 3):

(13) a. Loro accettavano   solo studenti stranieri ricchi
       they used-to-accept only students foreign   rich
       'They used to accept only rich foreign students'
    b. Loro accettavano   solo studenti ricchi stranieri
       they used-to-accept only students rich   foreign
       'They used to accept only foreign rich students'

Given that the corresponding nonreduced relative clauses are not rigidly ordered with respect to each other (see (14)), we do not expect the reduced ones to show any rigid ordering either.

(14) a. Loro accettavano solo studenti che fossero stranieri che fossero (anche) ricchi
       'They used to accept only students that were from abroad that were (also) rich'
    b. Loro accettavano solo studenti che fossero ricchi che fossero (anche) stranieri
       'They used to accept only students that were rich that were (also) from abroad'

Yet another source of apparent freedom is given by asyndetic coordination. This is what Sproat and Shih (1988, 477–478; 1990, section 2.3) call "parallel modification," whereby each adjective belongs to a separate intonational phrase and modifies the NP independently of the others ("in parallel" rather than "hierarchically," as when the adjectives are stacked). See (15), from Sproat and Shih 1988, 478:

(15) a. She loves all those Oriental, orange, wonderful ivories
    b. She loves all those wonderful, orange, Oriental ivories
    c. She loves all those orange, Oriental, wonderful ivories
    d. She loves all those wonderful, Oriental, orange ivories

Apparent violations of the order of direct modification adjectives are also found whenever the lower of the two adjectives is in the (definite) superlative form (Abney 1987, 340; Matushansky 2002, 160–161).[12] So, for example, while the unmarked order of shape and color adjectives is shape > color (see (16)), and that of evaluative and size adjectives is evaluative > size (see (17)), if the color adjective or the size adjective is in the definite superlative form, the order is reversed (see (18) and (19)):

(16) a. a long white plane
b. %a white long plane

(17) a. a nice small apartment
b. %a small nice apartment

(18) a. *?the long whitest plane (that I saw)
b. the whitest long plane (that I saw)

(19) a. *?the nice smallest apartment (that I know of)
b. the smallest nice apartment (that I know of)

This is even more striking when the adjectives involved are both nonintersective, their order thus being quite rigid. See (8b), repeated here as (20a,b). If the lower of the two is in the definite superlative form, their order can, in fact must, be reversed. See (21a,b).

(20) a. an occasional hard worker
b. *a hard occasional worker (in the intended meaning)

(21) a. *?the occasional hardest worker (that I know)
b. the hardest occasional worker (that I know)

I interpret this as suggesting that the superlative morpheme is merged high up in the functional structure of the DP, from where it attracts the lower of the two adjectives. (See Heim 1999 as well as Stateva 1999, 2000. Also see Sharvit and Stateva 2002, Matushansky 2008, and Kayne 2008, note 18.)

Apparently, this position can even be higher than the position of (finite) restrictive relative clauses, as shown by cases like (22), where it is the superlative adjective that licenses negative polarity *any* inside the relative clause:[13]

(22) the highest mountain that anyone climbed...

All in all, it would seem hasty, if not downright wrong, to conclude from the cases of apparent free ordering and order reversals just reviewed that no ordering exists among (direct modification) adjectives in English and Italian, or, for that matter, universally.

3.4 Summary of the Semantic and Syntactic Properties of the Two Sources

We can summarize the clusters of properties associated with each source as follows:

(23) *Indirect (reduced RC) modification*   *Direct modification*

[Det.	[stage-level (or individual-level)	[individual-level	NP]]]
[Det.	[restrictive	[nonrestrictive	NP]]]
[Det.	[implicit relative clause	[modal	NP]]]
[Det.	[intersective	[nonintersective	NP]]]
[Det.	[relative (to a comparison class)	[absolute	NP]]]
[Det.	[comparative (with superlatives)	[absolute (with superlatives)	NP]]]
[Det.	[specificity- or non-specificity-inducing	[specificity-inducing	NP]]]
[Det.	[epistemic 'unknown'	[evaluative 'unknown'	NP]]]
[Det.	[discourse anaphoric 'different'	[NP dependent 'different'	NP]]]
[Det.	[deictic	[generic	NP]]]
[Det.	[literal interpretation	[possible idiomatic interpretation	NP]]]
	further away from the N	closer to the N	
	not rigidly ordered	rigidly ordered	
	possible in predicate position	not possible in predicate position	

The question of why direct and indirect modification adjectives have the cluster of interpretive properties that they have, rather than the opposite, is a deeper question, and one to which I cannot offer a definite answer. Bolinger's (1967) idea seems to me to have some merit. He suggests that attributive adjectives (what I referred to here, following Sproat and Shih 1988, 1990, as "direct modification" adjectives) are nonintersective, nonrestrictive, individual-level, and so on as a consequence of their modifying the *reference* of the nominal phrase (but see Umbach 2006, 154 for complications), while predicative adjectives have the properties they have (intersective, restrictive, etc.) as a consequence of their modifying the *referent*. (For possible refinements of this idea, see Waugh 1976, 1977; Pustejovsky 1995, chapter 6; Jackendoff 1997, 62–66; Bouchard 1998, section 3; Bouchard 2002, chapter 2; Larson 1998; McNally 2005.)

I suggested above that direct modification adjectives are merged below (reduced) relative clauses (and numerals). In Cinque 2003, 2008a, I tentatively suggested that they are also merged below a "small" indefinite dP (itself merged below relative clauses) that qualifies as the Head of the relative clause itself (and is matched by an identical constituent inside the relative clause; see Cinque in preparation for more detailed discussion):

(24)

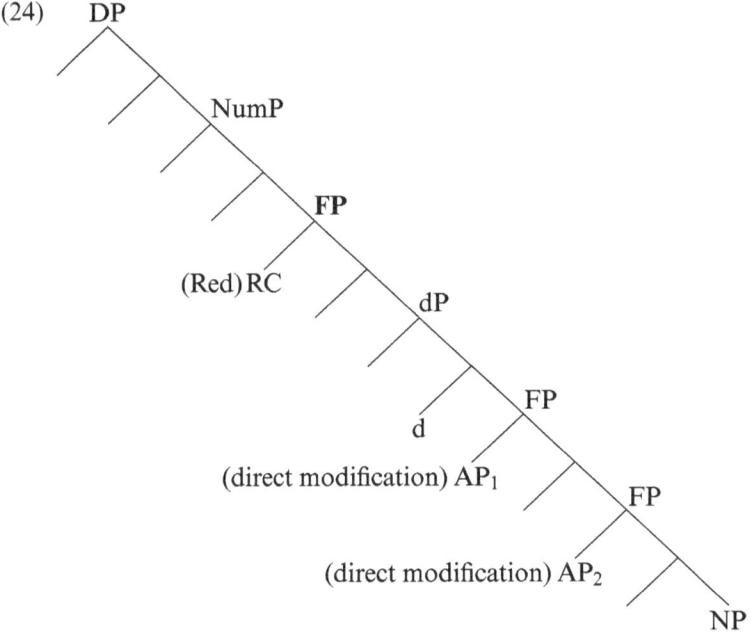

If we think of d as assigning some referential import (though not the uniquely individuating referential import of the higher D, which marks the (maximal) intersection of the set contributed by dP and the set contributed by the relative clause), it is evident that direct modification adjectives, which are below d, modify something that is still predicative in nature, while (full and) reduced relative clauses, which are higher than d, modify something that already has some referential status.

3.5 Some Crosslinguistic and Acquisitional Evidence for the Dual Source of Adnominal Adjectives

3.5.1 Languages Lacking One of the Two Sources

Additional evidence for the two sources for adnominal adjectives comes from the existence of languages that lack one, or the other, of the two sources (see Baker 2003a, section 4.2.4; Cinque 2006, introduction).

3.5.1.1 Languages Lacking Direct Modification Adjectives
As noted in Baker 2003a, 207, Slave (Athapaskan) appears to be one language where adjectives can be used as predicates (also within relative clauses) but not as adnominal (direct modification) attributes:[14]

(25) a. yenene (be-gho) sho hi̧li̧ (Rice 1989, 389–390)
    woman (3-of) proud/happy 3-is
    'The woman is happy/proud (of him/her)'
   b. *yenene sho (Rice, p.c. to Mark Baker)
    woman proud/happy
    'a proud/happy woman'

Other languages lacking adnominal adjectives are apparently Lango (Noonan 1992, 103), and Hixkaryana and Tiriyó (Dixon 2004, 28–29). Also see the discussion in Rijkhoff 2002, 133ff.

3.5.1.2 Languages Lacking Predicative (Hence Indirect Modification) Adjectives
Adjectives in Yoruba form a closed class, and can appear only in adnominal (attributive) position ((26a)),[15] not in predicate position ((26b)) (hence not in the predicate position of a relative clause). See Ajíbóyè 2001, 6, and the references cited there.[16]

(26) a. Mo rí [ajá ńlá] (= (30b) of Ajíbóyè 2001)
    I see dog big
    'I saw a big dog'
   b. *Ajá ńlá (= (29b) of Ajíbóyè 2001)
    dog big
    'The dog is big'

In predicate position, what one finds instead of the impossible (26b) is (27a), with an intransitive stative verb, *tóbi* 'to (be) big' (cf. 'to tower'), which, conversely, cannot be used adnominally ((27b)). As Ajíbóyè (2001, 7) observes, "In order to use *tóbi* as a modifier, one must nominalize it, or form a relative clause, [(28a,b)]."

(27) a. Ajá tóbi (= (29a) of Ajíbóyè 2001)
    dog be-big
    'The dog is big'
   b. *Mo rí [ajá tóbi] (= (30a) of Ajíbóyè 2001)
    I see dog be-big
    'I saw a big dog'

(28) a. Mo rí [ajá tí-tóbi] (= (31a) of Ajíbóyè 2001)
    I   see dog NOM-be-big
    'I saw a big dog'
  b. Mo rí [ajá [tí ó tóbi]] (= (31b) of Ajíbóyè 2001)
    I   see dog REL 3SG be-big
    'I saw a dog that is big'

In the introduction to Cinque 2006, the closed-class character of the exclusively adnominal adjectives of Yoruba is taken to be an indication that adnominal-only adjectives are functional (also see section 4.1.1 below).

Another African language apparently lacking predicative adjectives is Gbaya Mbodómó (an Adamawa-Ubangi (Niger-Congo) language of Cameroon; see Boyd 1997, section 3.1.3). Differently from Yoruba, however, Mbodómó in predicate position utilizes a nominalization of the adnominal-only adjective (which is only a secondary strategy in Yoruba). Compare (29) with (30):[17]

(29) a. so   ada
        sharp machete
    b. we   lï
        hot water

(30) a. ada   ná so-a
        machete has sharp-ness
        'The machete is sharp'
    b. lï   ná we-a
        water has hot-ness
        'The water is hot'

3.5.2 Possible Evidence from Acquisition

As noted by Cardinaletti and Giusti (2007), the acquisition of adjectives in both English and Italian shows characteristics that can be taken to support the existence of direct and indirect modification adjectives, with their respective properties. The fact that in both English (Blackwell 2001, 2005) and Italian (Cardinaletti and Giusti 2007), stage-level adjectives (like 'dirty', 'clean', 'wet', 'dry', 'hot', 'cold', 'happy', 'sad', 'sick', etc.) systematically appear later than individual-level adjectives (like 'round', 'straight', 'pretty', 'ugly', 'long', 'green') seems to show that the acquisition of indirect modification is delayed with respect to that of direct modification. No child produces stage-level adjectives before individual-level ones. Furthermore, when they produce stage-level adjectives, children appear to have "learned" reduced relatives. See Cardinaletti and Giusti 2007 for illustration and more detailed discussion.

3.6 Phrasal Movement over Head Movement or Base Generation

A feature of the analysis developed so far is that only phrasal movement (more precisely, movement of phrases containing the NP) plays a role in the grammar of Romance and Germanic, as in other language families.[18] As seen in chapter 1 and chapter 2, section 2.11, N-movement alone would be unable to derive the desired generalizations.[19]

In addition to the raising of the reduced relative clause Head (i.e., the NP plus the projections dominating it that contain direct modification adjectives) around the reduced relative clause APs, further phrasal movements of the NP around some of the direct modification adjectives will be needed to account for the pre- and postnominal positioning of these adjectives, as schematically shown inside the box in (31) (see chapter 6 for illustration):

(31)

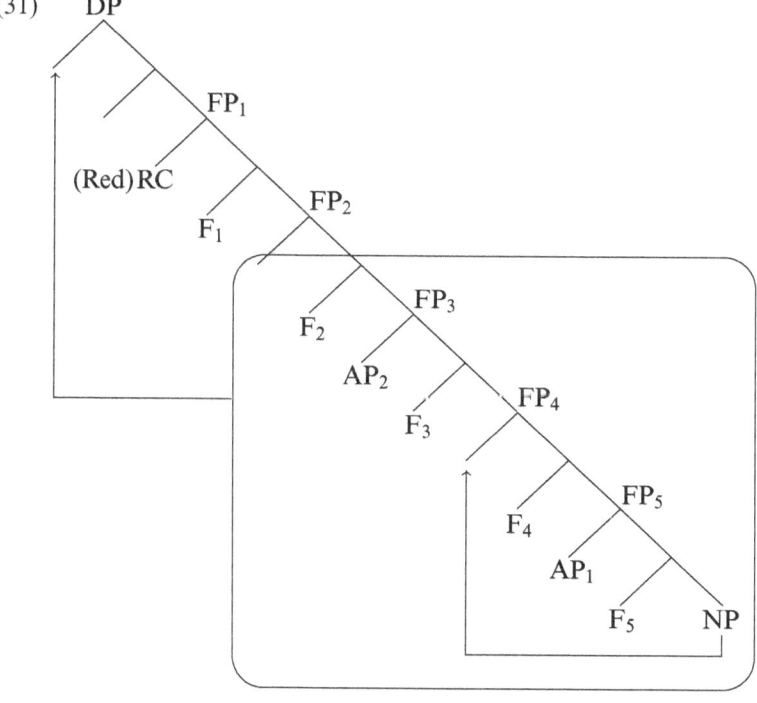

Even if one were to concede that phrasal movement is superior to head movement for the reasons just noted, it might still be objected that one could, perhaps should, do away completely with movement in favor of a base-generation analysis.

I think that in addition to considerations pertaining to antisymmetry, there are conceptual and empirical reasons to prefer a movement to a base-generation analysis.[20] The main reason lies in the fact, first noted in Greenberg 1963 (see Cinque 1996, 2005, for discussion), that crosslinguistically one finds prenominally only one order, while postnominally there are (at least) two—either the same one as the prenominal order, or its exact opposite:

(32) a. Dem > Num > A > N
    b. *A > Num > Dem > N
    c. N > Dem > Num > A
    d. N > A > Num > Dem

The same is true, at a finer-grained level, of the order of (direct modification) adjectives (for example, size, color, and nationality adjectives; see Cinque 2009 and the references cited there):

(33) a. *English, Chinese...*
        $A_{size} > A_{color} > A_{nationality} > N$
    b. 0
        $*A_{nationality} > A_{color} > A_{size} > N$
    c. *Welsh, Irish...*
        $N > A_{size} > A_{color} > A_{nationality}$
    d. *Indonesian, Yoruba,...*
        $N > A_{nationality} > A_{color} > A_{size}$

Under a base-generation analysis, each of these orders would have to be generated independently of the others even if one feels that they are the same order at a more abstract level (they are either literally the same, or mirror images of each other).

In a base-generation analysis it would also be impossible to state the principle (whatever that turns out to be) that governs the ordering of the different classes of adjectives with respect to the N. It has for example been proposed that the more abstract identity of the various orders of adjectives across languages is expressed by a principle that determines the relative distance of each class of adjectives from the head N, thus accounting for what are the two most common orders, (33a,d), and for the impossibility of (33b). But, if one takes this line, (unless some movement is admitted) one can only state the principle as a tendency given that the fourth order, (33c) (which is documented, even if rarer) plainly violates it.

The principle, whatever it ultimately follows from, can instead be stated as an absolute principle rather than just a tendency, if we are willing to abandon the symmetrical view underlying the base-generation account (as in fact Kayne's 1994 Linear Correspondence Axiom would force us to), and to adopt a more abstract, asymmetrical view, whereby there is only one order/structure available for all languages ((34)), and whatever word-order difference there is among them is a function of independently motivated types of movement.

(34)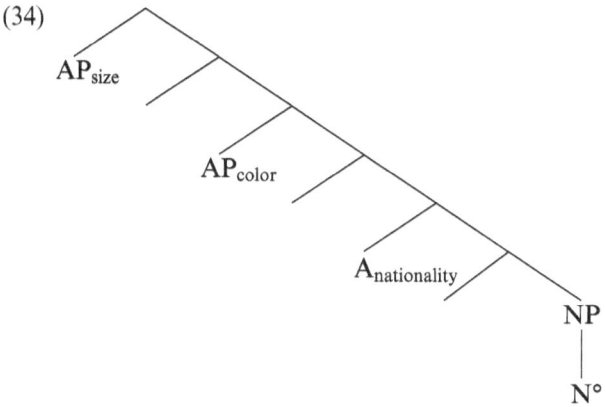

We know that languages vary with respect to whether they displace interrogative *wh*-phrases or not. In English, (single) *wh*-phrases must be displaced to sentence initial position (as in (35)), while in Indonesian (see (36)) they remain in situ. We also know that depending on certain conditions movement can affect just the phrase bearing the feature triggering the movement—here the *wh*-feature—(as in (35)). Alternatively, it can affect a larger phrase containing the phrase bearing the relevant feature (as in (37)); this is what Ross (1967) called pied piping:

(35) [*Who*] did you see ⎵ ?

(36) Siti mau *apa*? (Cole, Hermon, and Tjung 2005, 553)
Siti want what
'What does Siti want?'

(37) [[*Whose*] pictures] did you see ⎵ ?

In Cinque 1996, 2005, I suggested that precisely these two independent parameters (whether the relevant phrase remains in situ or moves; and, if it moves, whether it moves by itself, or by pied piping each time the immediately dominating phrase as in (37)) can account for the three attested orders of (33) and for the principled absence of the fourth, (33b). The phrase bearing the relevant feature triggering the movement (a nominal feature) is in this case NP.

If NP does not move, we get (33a). If NP moves by itself (all the way up), as shown in (38), we get (33c). If it moves (all the way up) each time pied piping the immediately dominating phrase, as in (39), we get (33d). (33b) cannot be derived because the NP has not moved and the base structure has the modifiers in the wrong order. Crucially $A_{nationality}$, A_{color}, or A_{size} cannot move by themselves, just as phrases not bearing the *wh*-feature cannot move by themselves to the sentence initial +*wh*-position.[21]

(38) Agr_wP

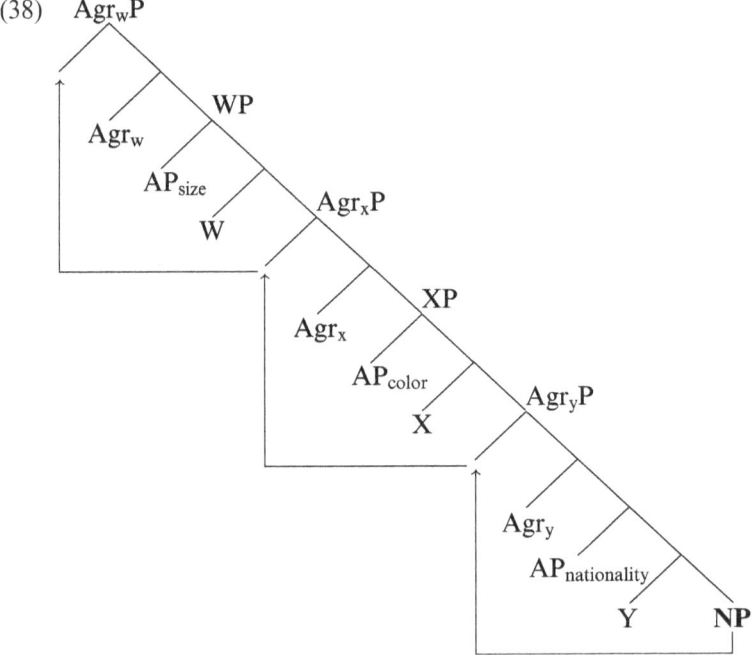

(39)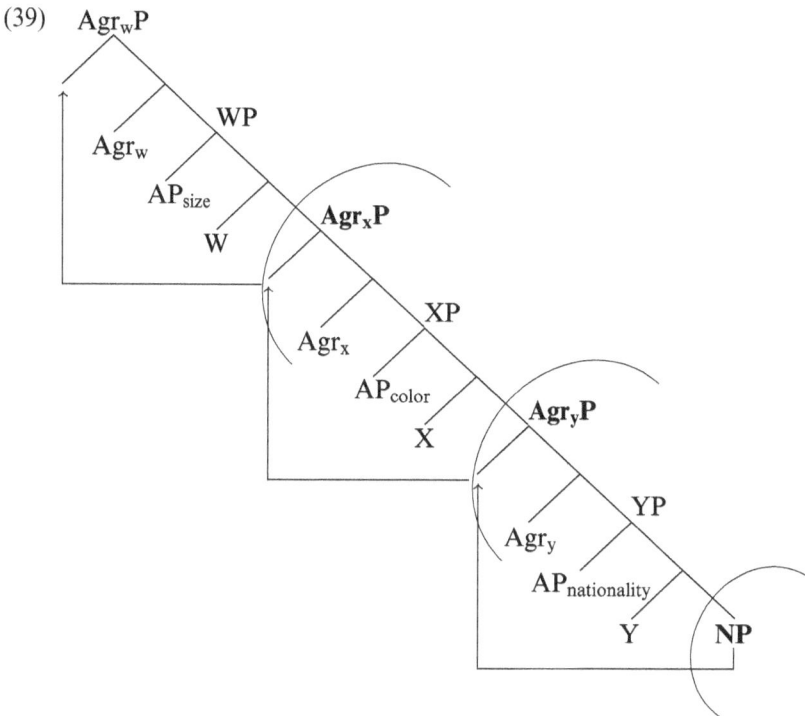

Note that if the principle governing the degree of proximity of each modifier to the head is stated on the "base level" (34), before movement takes place that disrupts the original order of elements, it can be stated as an absolute principle forcing $AP_{nationality}$ to be merged closer to the head than AP_{color}, and AP_{color} closer to the head than AP_{size}.

Furthermore, a (phrasal) movement analysis appears more equipped than a pure base-generation analysis to derive the comparative observation that the adjectives that are obligatorily postnominal in Romance (nationality, classificatory, etc.) correspond to the adjectives that are the lowest (closest to the N) prenominally in Germanic. While this is an accident for a purely base-generation analysis, the leftward, bottom-to-top, character of (NP) movement makes it natural that partial movement of the NP will typically affect the lowest elements of the structure, rendering the reversal of higher adjectives without the previous reversal of the lower ones more marked. For a discussion of marked and unmarked DP-internal movements, see Cinque 2005.

4 An Analysis of the Two Sources of Adjectives

4.1 A Syntactic Analysis of Direct Modification Adjectives

As hinted at above, direct modification adjectives will be argued here to be functional elements (section 4.1.1), with phrasal status, merged as specifiers of distinct heads of the extended projection of the NP (section 4.1.2), not derivable from (reduced) relative clauses (section 4.1.3).

4.1.1 The Functional Nature of Direct Modification Adjectives

Evidence that adnominal direct modification adjectives are functional[1] appears to come from the fact that in many languages, like in the Yoruba and Gbaya Mbodómó cases discussed in the previous chapter, they constitute a closed, often quite small, class of elements (see Dixon 1982, 1994, 2004).[2] The fact that adjectives seem to constitute an open class in certain languages (English, and Germanic more generally, Romance, Slavic, Fijian and Dyrbal,[3] Japanese,[4] Cherokee,[5] etc.), and a closed class in others (many Niger-Congo, Papuan, and sundry languages of India, America, and the Pacific; see Hagège 1974, Dixon 1982, 3ff., Dixon 1994, 34, and the references in note 17 in chapter 3), may appear particularly puzzling. In the introduction to Cinque 2006, I conjectured that this apparent inconsistency is due to the two different functions adjectives typically serve: as predicates and as adnominal modifiers. If in a language adjectives qualify as predicates, they will usually appear to be an open or very large class (as predicates typically are).[6] If on the other hand they only qualify as (direct) adnominal modifiers (with verbs or nouns taking over the task of expressing "adjectival predication"), they will appear to be a closed class. Suggestive evidence for this conclusion comes, as noted above, from the case of Yoruba and Gbaya Mbodómó, and from the other languages mentioned in note 17 in chapter 3.

In different Uto-Aztecan languages adjectives appear either reduced, as prefixes on the noun (which I take to be a sign of their functional character) or as independent words, with special suffixes (see Langacker 1977, 74, and Grune 1997, 6, on Hopi; Dayley 1989, 263–264; Gould and Loether 2002, 82; and McLaughlin 2006, 27ff., on different dialects of Shoshoni; Tuggy 1979, 75, on Tetelcingo Nahuatl; and Givón 1980, 290–291, on Ute). In view of the fact that the former "are usually more idiomatic" (Dayley 1989, 264) and are individual-level and nonrestrictive, in opposition to the stage-level and restrictive readings of the latter (McLaughlin 2006, 27; Givón 1980, 290–291), it is tempting to take the former as (functional) direct modification adjectives and the latter as indirect modification adjectives deriving from a relative clause source (as Givón himself suggests).

Further evidence for the functional nature of direct modification adjectives may come from language impairment. If functional elements are characteristically impaired in agrammatic speech, then the fact that adnominal adjectives in such sentences as *Old sailors tell sad stories* "fail to be integrated in Broca's aphasia" (Rizzi 1985, 157, and the references cited there) may be taken as an additional indication that at least certain types of adjectives (those in direct modification, I conjecture) are functional.

Concerning the putative functional nature of adjectives, it is sometimes claimed, in analogy with adverbs, that if their order followed from independent semantic scope principles no motivation would exist for their generation in the Spec of dedicated functional projections (see note 8 in the previous chapter). Despite the appealing simplicity of this idea, that remains to be seen. Minimally, one has to distinguish those semantic aspects that are grammatically relevant from those that are not, and even then the question remains whether these are directly encoded in the syntax or not.[7]

4.1.2 The Phrasal Nature of Direct Modification Adjectives

Prenominal adjectives have often been claimed not to be phrasal (see, among others, Berman 1974, Abney 1987, Sadler and Arnold 1994, Truswell 2005, for English; Sproat and Shih 1988, 1990, for Chinese; Lamarche 1991, Valois 1991a, 1991b, 1996, Bouchard 1998, 2002, and in part Bernstein 1991, 1993b, for French; Delsing 1993a, 1993b, and others mentioned in Julien 2005, 6, for Scandinavian; and Baker 2003a, section 4.2, for adnominal adjectives in general).

The main grounds for this conclusion are that prenominal adjectives (in contrast to postnominal ones, and to adjectives in predicate position) often manifest properties and restrictions that are unexpected of a phrasal category. For example, in many languages prenominal adjectives cannot take complements or adjuncts:

(1) a. *Spanish* (Luján 1973, 399)
   *Los [fáciles de resolver] problemas
   the easy to solve problems
   b. *Italian* (Giorgi 1988, 303)
   *Il [simile ad un vocabolario] libro di Gianni
   the similar to a dictionary book of Gianni
   'Gianni's book similar to a dictionary'
   c. *English* (Abney 1987, 326)
   *the [proud of his son] man

Indeed this would follow if prenominal adjectives were heads, rather than phrases, either taking a portion of the nominal extended projection as their complement (Abney 1987, 327), or incorporating (left-adjoining) to the N (Valois 1991a, 1991b, 1996; Sigurðsson 1993, 178—but see Sigurðsson 2005, note 10). The same result would also follow if they made up a compound with the following N (Sproat and Shih 1988, 1990; Lamarche 1991).[8]

Notice that the fact that prenominal adjectives do take complements in other languages, either to the left of the adjective (Germanic other than English, literary Italian, etc.—see (2)), or to the right of the adjective (Russian, Bulgarian,[9] Greek, etc.—see (3)), does not necessarily weaken that hypothesis, at least if one can show that the languages in question also have prenominal reduced relative clauses with the same properties, which seems to be true (see (4)–(5)):[10]

(2) a. *German* (Fanselow 1986, 343)
   die [dem Mann treue] Frau
   the the-DAT man faithful woman
   'the woman faithful to her husband'
   b. *Swedish* (Platzack 1982, 275; also see Platzack 1982–1983, 55 n. 7)[11]
   en [mig motbjudande] tanke
   a me repulsive thought
   'a thought repulsive to me'
   c. *Literary Italian* (cf. Cinque 1994, 93 n. 12)
   l'a noi più invisa sete di potere
   the to-us more displeasing thirst of power
   'the thirst for power more hated by us'

(3) a. *Russian* (Bailyn 1994, 25)
   [dovol'nyi vyborami]   prezident
   satisfied   elections-INSTR president
   'the president satisfied with the elections'
   b. *Bulgarian* (Tasseva-Kurktchieva 2005, 285)
   [mnogo gordiyat săs svoeto   dete] bašta
   very   proud-the with SELF-the child father
   'the father very proud of his child'
   c. *Greek* (Androutsopoulou 1995, 24)
   i   [perifani ja to jo   tis] mitera
   the proud   of the son her mother
   'the mother proud of her son'

(4) a. *German* (Holmberg and Rijkhoff 1998, 97)
   der gestern   geschriebene Brief
   the yesterday   written   letter
   'the letter that was written yesterday'
   b. *Swedish* (Delsing 1993a, 123)
   en mördad   man
   a murdered man
   c. *Literary Italian* (see note 1 in chapter 6)
   il da poco restaurato museo   atestino
   the recently renovated museum of-Este

(5) a. *Russian* (Babby 1973, 358)
   Sidjaščaja okolo pal'my devuška (očen' krasiva)
   sitting   near palm   girl   (very pretty)
   'The girl sitting near the palm (is very pretty)'
   b. *Bulgarian* (Iliyana Krapova, p.c.)
   naskoro pristignaliyat Prezident
   recently arrived-the   president
   'the recently arrived president'
   c. *Greek* (Melita Stavrou, p.c.)
   ta prósfata sideroména me   prosohi pukámisa
   the recently ironed   with care   shirts
   'the shirts recently ironed with care'

Quite generally, then, the impossibility for an adjective (or a verbal participle) to take complements in prenominal position does not tell us much about whether the adjective is a head or a phrase (in specifier position). Languages simply differ as to whether they allow a complement or adjunct to follow the adjective,[12] or whether they allow a complement at all. Given this, if adjectives have two sources, it could be claimed that when they take a complement (if any) they are reduced relative clauses (indirect modification adjectives), and that direct modification adjectives, being heads, never take complements.

However, some evidence exists that even direct modification adjectives are (or, at least, can be) phrasal. Excluding adjectives that may have access, like the ones in (2) and (3), to the relative clause source, we still have reasons to posit more structure for those that do not have a relative clause source. In Bulgarian and Greek, for example, nonpredicative adjectives like "main" can be followed, in prenominal position, by an adjunct. See (6a,b):[13]

(6) a. *Bulgarian* (Iliyana Krapova, p.c.)
glavnata po značenie pričina
main-the in significance reason
'the main reason for importance'
b. *Greek* (Melita Stavrou, p.c.)
o kírios kata protereótita lógos
the main by priority reason
'the main reason in terms of priority'

In other languages, nonpredicative adjectives can take modifiers, if not complements:[14]

(7) *Italian*
a. la **più** verosimile causa del suo rifiuto
the most likely cause of his refusal
b. il mio **più** vecchio collaboratore
the my most old collaborator
'my oldest collaborator'
c. i **più** alti dignitari
the highest dignitaries

(8) *English*
a. the **most** probable winner
b. (I felt) the **most** utter fool (Tallerman 1998, 44)
c. a **very** poor soul (Richard Kayne, cited in Bernstein 1993b, chap. 2, note 68; also see her note 57)
d. (They are) hard **enough** workers to earn that kind of money[15]

It could be claimed that (7) and (8) do not show conclusively that the adjective heads a phrase in a specifier position of the extended projection of the NP, because the adjective could still be a head of the extended projection of the NP with the modifier in its Spec. This however leads to some incorrect expectations. As noted in Svenonius 1994, if adjectives were heads, one would expect that a modifier modifying the first of several adjectives should take scope not just over the adjective to its immediate right but over all adjectives following it. Yet, this expectation is not fulfilled. In the Norwegian example *alt-for heit sterk kafee* 'much too hot strong coffee', as Julien (2005, 8) notes, the modifier *alt-for* 'all too' only modifies the adjective *heit* 'hot'; it does not also modify the adjective *sterk* 'strong', suggesting that it and the first adjective form a phrase that excludes the second adjective and the N. Also see Leu 2008, 75, 94–95.

Furthermore, nonpredicative adjectives can, in some languages, undergo *A-bar* movement to a DP initial position (see Corbett 1979; Giusti 1996; Rijkhoff 1998, 352–353; Rijkhoff 2002, 267, 272; Campos 2009): a clear sign of their phrasal status. In English, for example, in so-called Degree and Negative Degree Inversion, they can target the specifier of a functional projection above the (indefinite) DP. (See Hendrick 1990; Valois 1991a, 34; Bernstein 1993b, chapter 2, note 21; Kennedy and Merchant 2000, section 4.2; Matushansky 2002; Troseth 2004, 2009; Felber and Roehrs 2004; Borroff 2006):[16]

(9) *English*
  a. [[how old] a friend] is he?
  b. [[how big] an eater is he?
  c. [[how natural] a successor] will he be?

Also, as Rowlett (2007, 88 n. 33) observes, "The existence of a single SpecFP position for each class of adjectives explains why where two adjectives of the same class appear together, coordination is required."

The fact that adjectives such as 'mere', 'utter', 'pure' and 'simple' can be coordinated may be construed as evidence, at least within Antisymmetry theory (Kayne 1994), that nonpredicative adjectives have phrasal structure, because heads in that theory cannot be coordinated:[17]

(10) *Italian*
  a. Questo è un imbroglio puro e   semplice
     this   is a swindle pure and simple
  b. Questa è una scusa bella   e   buona
     this   is an excuse beautiful and good
     'This is a clear excuse'

Another piece of evidence that adnominal adjectives are phrases rather than heads appears to come from their behavior in code switching. If in contexts of intrasentential code switching "the language of a head determines the position of its complements" (Santorini and Mahootian 1995,

15), then the fact that "the language of an adnominal adjective does not determine the position of the noun it modifies, and all possible codeswitching combinations are attested" (p. 15) suggests that adnominal adjectives are phrases rather than heads taking (an extended projection of) the NP as their complement.[18]

French DP internal sandhi facts (*liaison*) have sometimes also been taken to show that prenominal adjectives are heads rather than XPs (Lamarche 1991; Valois 1991b) (and that prenominal adjectives are related to the noun in a way tighter than postnominal ones are; Bouchard 1998, 2002). I fail to see how a not yet completely understood phenomenon like liaison (especially with respect to the exact syntactic conditions of its operation) can provide a clear argument one way or the other. The different degree of application of liaison to prenominal and to postnominal adjectives may perhaps indicate that a prenominal adjective and the adjective or noun that follows it are in a structural configuration different from that in which the noun and a postnominal adjective are found, but (at present) it can hardly indicate anything more precise than that. And some structural difference between AN and NA sequences is in any event what many analyses of adjectival syntax assume, the present one included.[19]

Further arguments against the head, or the incorporated, status of (prenominal) adjectives are discussed in Svenonius 1994, sections 3.1–3.2; Matushansky 2002, appendix 2; Julien 2005, section 1.2.2; Knittel 2005, 203ff.; and Laenzlinger 2005a. Also see Roehrs 2006, 19ff.

It thus seems plausible to conclude that even direct modification adjectives are phrasal.[20]

4.1.3 Some Reasons for Not Deriving Direct Modification Adjectives from Relative Clauses

A long tradition in generative grammar (beginning with Chomsky [1955] 1975, 539–540; Chomsky 1957; Smith 1961) has treated prenominal attributive adjectives as deriving from predicate adjectives in a (postnominal) relative clause through some preposing operation. In a sense, this derivation comes for free given that it must be available for reduced relative clauses in general (*the letters* [*recently arrived*] and *the* [*recently arrived*] *letters*). Unless expressly blocked, the same derivation applying to a reduced relative clause containing just an adjective in predicate position directly relates such cases as *a star* [*visible*] to *a* [*visible*] *star*. This derivation would also appear to allow one to state the conditions on both predicative and attributive adjectives only once (Chomsky [1955] 1975, 539–540; Berman 1974, 144; Sussex 1975, 6; Hamann 1991, 663).

Though attractive in its simplicity as it may be, this analysis encounters a number of problems. For one thing, as Winter (1965), Motsch (1967), Bolinger (1967), Levi (1973, 1975), Berman (1974, chapter 3), Emonds (1976, section V.3), among others, have observed, not all prenominal adjectives can apparently undergo such a derivation, the reason being that several of them cannot be used predicatively (*the former minister* < **the minister former* < **the minister who is/was former*; cf. **the minister is/was former*).

Second, the preposing operation that optionally turns a postnominal adjective into a prenominal one would have to be made obligatory in some cases (*the house [*red*] → *the* [*red*] *house*), and to be blocked in others (*the people* [*ready*] → *the [*ready*] *people*).[21]

Third, as seen in chapter 2 with English and Italian, prenominal adjectives appear to have readings not found with the corresponding postnominal adjectives (their putative source).

Fourth, as often noted, no rigid order would be expected of adjectives (contrary to what we saw in section 3.3.2) if these were derived from relative clauses, which can stack in no particular order among each other. See for example Alexiadou, Haegeman, and Stavrou 2007, 356, as well as McKinney-Bok 2009, section III.5.3.

A fifth problem for analyses deriving all adjectives from relative clauses may be represented by those constructions where (full and reduced) relative clauses, as well as adjectives more clearly derived from relative clauses, like those that can be postnominal in English, are ruled out, and yet some adjectives (direct modification adjectives, I claim) are possible. Two such constructions, singling out exactly the same classes of admitted and nonadmitted forms, are the following (from Italian and French, respectively):[22]

Elliptical DPs Introduced by the Definite Article in Italian[23]
(11) a. *Le che sono state pubblicate
   the that have been published (understood: riviste 'journals')
  b. *Le recentemente arrivate
   the recently arrived (understood: riviste 'journals')
  c. *Le di Gianni
   the of Gianni (understood: scarpe 'shoes')
  d. *Le orgogliose dei propri figli[24]
   the proud of their children (understood: madri 'mothers')
  e. *Le presenti (understood: persone 'people')[25]
   the present

(12) Le altre/precedenti/principali/(più) probabili/etc.²⁶
the other/former/main/(most) probable/etc. (understood:
conseguenze 'consequences')

DPs Introduced by Possessive Adjectives in French (Bernstein 1993b, 17–
18; Bouchard 2002, 143; both based on Ronat 1974, 62–71, 1977, 163)²⁷
(13) a. *Je te   donnerai mes livres qui sont rouges
        I you will-give my books that are red
    b. *Je te   donnerai mes livres récemment arrivés
        I you will-give my books recently   arrived
    c. *Je te   donnerai mes livres sur la table
        I you will-give my books on the table
    d. *Je te   donnerai mes livres susceptibles de te   plaire
        I you will-give my books likely   to you please
    e. *Je te   donnerai mes livres disponibles/présents
        I you will-give my books available/present

(14) Je te   donnerai mes livres rouges/principaux/...
     I you will-give my books red/main/...
    'I'll give you my red/main/... books'

Both contexts need to be better investigated, however.

Concerning the putative derivation of all adjectives from relative clauses, one possibility to consider, which could perhaps provide an answer to the first and fourth problems above, is that nonpredicative adjectives derive from adverbs (contained in relative clauses) rather than from adjectives in predicate position (see for example Bach 1968, 101ff.; Givón 1970, 828; Giry-Schneider 1997). Thus *the former president* could be thought of as deriving from something like 'the x (who was) formerly a president', *an alleged murderer* from something like 'an x (who is/was) allegedly a murderer', and so on. Though appealing and apparently manageable if we limit our attention to these few cases, a derivation along these lines soon proves difficult to control if we extend its application. Givón's (1970) attempt at deriving all adjectives from relative clauses is a good illustration of this. As soon as we try to derive further types of nonpredicative adjectives from a relative clause, we are forced to posit more and more complex derivations from sources that differ more and more from one another. So, for example, a case like *a poor typist* cannot have the same (relatively simple) derivation as *the former president* or *an alleged murderer* (cf. '*an x (who is/was) poorly a typist'), but should rather derive from something like 'the x who types poorly' (Givón 1970,

828). While the same derivation might extend to *an early riser*, it could not extend to *an early arrival*. The latter can neither derive from 'an x that arrives early' (as with *a poor typist*), nor, for that matter, from 'an x (that is/was) early an arrival' (as with *the former president* or *an alleged murderer*). A more plausible source would seem to be 'an x (that is/was) an event of arriving early' (cf. Givón (1970, 829). *The chief/main reason* can neither derive from 'the x (that is/was) chiefly/mainly a reason' (as with *the former president* or *an alleged murderer*), nor from 'the x that reasons chiefly/mainly' (as with *a poor typist*), nor from 'an x (that is/was) an event of reasoning chiefly/mainly' (as with *an early arrival*). For Givón (1970, note 12), a more sensible source would seem to be: 'the reason that is chiefly emphasized here'. *This particular spot* cannot have any of the above derivations. Again, Givón (1970, note 12) suggests the following as a possible source: 'The spot was chosen for the particular reason (with the particular purpose in mind)'. Examples like these could easily be multiplied: *the only man there* ('He was present there alone'; Givón 1970, note 12), *the very day* ('the x such that it was exactly the day'), *a shocked silence* ('an x such that they were silent out of shock').[28] Whether or not some such sources are plausible, it is clear that such a line of analysis eventually gets out of control.[29] Also, if some such sources are admitted, one would have to somehow block possible derivations such as *their bad need* or *our lucky chairman* from sources like 'the x that they badly needed' and 'the x who is/was luckily our chairman' (also see Fedorowicz-Bacz 1977, 40). The derivation of all adnominal adjectives from a reduced relative clause source would also, it seems, have little to say about the different interpretive properties of prenominal and postnominal adjectives reviewed above for Romance and Germanic, nor would it shed light on the overt distinction between two classes of adjectives in the languages examined in the appendix, nor for the rigid order of direct modification adjectives seen in section 3.3.2, given that relative clauses can in principle stack in any order.[30]

An analysis recognizing two sources for adnominal adjectives seems instead able to capture the basic insight of the traditional analysis while providing an account for the observations that could not easily be subsumed under it. The same conclusions appear to hold for nonrestrictive adjectives, which are sometimes taken to derive from nonrestrictive relative clauses (cf., e.g., Chomsky 1965, 217 n. 26; Blinkenberg 1969, 108 n. 1; Luján 1973; Kayne 1994, 111). Many of them do not even have a parallel predicative usage, which makes such derivation difficult (see (15a,b)):

(15) *Italian*
  a. La sua povera
     the his poor (= pitiable)
     mamma (≠ la sua mamma, che era povera)
     mother (≠ his mother, who was poor)
     'his poor (pitiable) mother'
  b. quel dannato imbroglione (*quell'imbroglione, che è dannato)
     that damn swindler (that swindler, who is damn)

Another difficulty for the idea that nonrestrictive adjectives have their source in nonrestrictive relative clauses comes from one observation of Aoun's (reported in Authier 1988, 175 n. 3). While nonrestrictive adjectives cannot modify the inalienably possessed DP in the Romance external possessor construction (Kayne 1975, 169; Cinque and Krapova, 2009; see (16a)), nonrestrictive relative clauses can (see (16b)).

(16) *French*
  a. *Oscar s'est lavé les mains propres
     'Oscar washed his clean hands'
  b. Oscar s'est lavé les mains, qui pourtant étaient propres
     'Oscar washed his hands, which however were clean'

Also, the derivation of a nonrestrictive adjective modifying a proper name ((17)) from a nonrestrictive relative clause ((18)) does not immediately account for the fact that the article is possible in front of the proper name modified by the adjective, but not in front of the proper name modified by the relative clause:

(17) *Italian*
  a. *(L') amata Londra cominciava a deluderlo
     the beloved London was-starting to disappoint-him
     'Dear London was starting to disappoint him'
  b. *(the) incomparable Callas (cf. Matushanky 2005b, 430)

(18) *Italian*
  a. (*La) Londra, che era (da lui) amata, cominciava a
     the London, which was (by him) loved, was-starting to
     deluderlo
     disappoint-him
     'London, which was dear (to him), was starting to disappoint him'
  b. (*the) Callas, who was incomparable,...

Finally, taking restrictive and nonrestrictive adjectives to derive from restrictive and nonrestrictive relative clauses, respectively, would lead one to expect restrictive adjectives to occur closer to the N than nonrestrictive ones, like their putative sources. But, as we have seen with postnominal adjectives in Italian (Romance) in section 2.10.4, just the opposite is true (see (54)).[31]

4.2 A Syntactic Analysis of Indirect Modification Adjectives

As mentioned in section 3.1, I take indirect modification adjectives to originate in the predicate position of a reduced relative clause (Sproat and Shih 1988, 1990), merged prenominally (Cinque 2003, 2008a, in preparation).

Some facts seem to suggest that the prenominal Merge position of indirect modification adjectives is higher than the projections hosting direct modification adjectives, and lower than the Merge position of numerals. For example, in German, participial reduced relative clauses, which are obligatorily prenominal (see (19a,b)), have to precede direct modification adjectives (see (20)), and have to follow numerals (see (21)).[32]

(19) *German*
    a. Er ist ein [sein Studium seit langem   hassender] Student
        he is a   his   study   for a long time hating   student
        'He is a student who has been hating his studies for a long time'
    b. *Er ist ein Student [sein Studium seit langem   hassend(er)]
        he is a   student his   study   for a long time hating

(20) *German* (Walter Schweikert, p.c.)
    a. der [kürzlich angekommene] ehemalige Botschafter von Chile
        the recently arrived   former   ambassador of Chile
    b. *?der ehemalige [kürzlich angekommene] Botschafter von Chile
        the former   recently arrived   ambassador of Chile

(21) *German* (Walter Schweikert, p.c.)
    a. diese drei [in ihren Büros arbeitenden] Männer
        these three in their office working   men
        'these three men working in their office'
    b. ??diese [in ihren Büros arbeitenden] drei   Männer
        these in their office working   three men
        'these three men working in their office'

Analysis of the Two Sources of Adjectives

This suggests a (partial) structure as in (22)

(22)
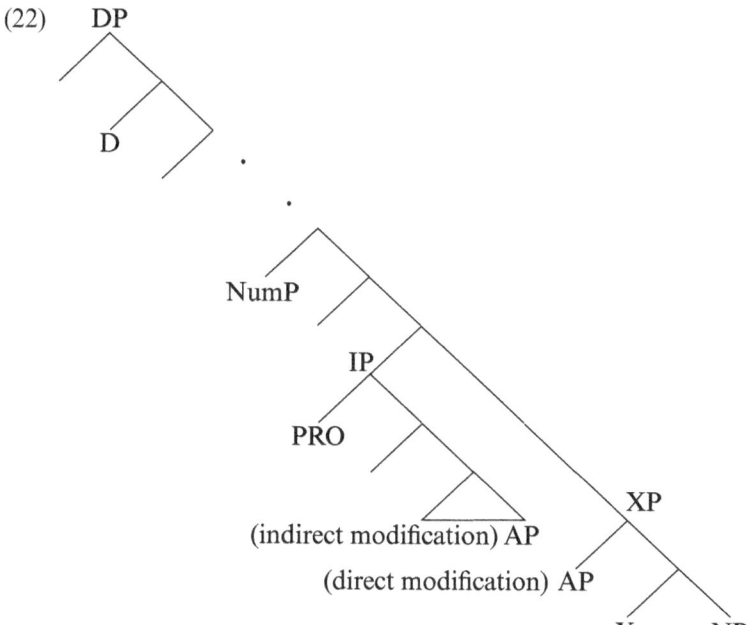

In the nonfinite reduced relative clause IP of (22) I have assumed the presence of a subject PRO, distinct from and matched with the Head of the reduced relative clause—that is, [$_{XP}$ (direct mod.) AP + NP].

German appears to provide direct evidence for the presence of such a PRO.[33] In participial reduced relative constructions in German, the determiner, the head N, and the participle agree in Case. See (23):

(23) *German*
(Wir sahen) die$_{AccPl}$ angekommenen$_{AccPl}$ Studenten$_{AccPl}$
(we saw) the arrived students
'(We saw) the students who had arrived'

As noted in Fanselow 1986, such "floating" distributive phrases as *einer nach dem anderen* 'one after the other' agree in Case with the DP with which they are construed. See (24a,b):

(24) *German*
   a. Wir$_{Nom}$ haben Maria$_{Acc}$ einer$_{Nom}$/*einen$_{Acc}$ nach dem anderen
      we have Maria one after the other
      geküßt
      kissed
      'We have kissed Maria one after the other'

b. Maria$_{Nom}$ hat die Männer$_{Acc}$ einen$_{Acc}$/*einer$_{Nom}$ nach dem
   Maria   has the men   one   after the
   anderen geküßt
   other   kissed
   'Maria kissed the men one after the other'

As Fanselow further observes, if such floating phrases are construed with the PRO subject of an infinitive, they invariably bear nominative Case. This is particularly evident in such cases as (25), where the controller of PRO bears a different Case:

(25) *German*
    Weil ich die Männer$_{Acc}$ überzeugte, PRO Renate
    as   I   the men   convinced   Renate
    einer$_{Nom}$/*einen$_{Acc}$ nach dem anderen zu küssen, ...
    one   after the other   to kiss, ...
    'As I convinced the men to kiss Renate one after the other, ...'

Now, what we observe in the reduced relative clause case is that the floating distributive phrase also appears in nominative Case, irrespective of the Case borne by the Head with which it is construed:

(26) *German*
    (Wir sahen) die$_{Acc}$ [einer/*einen$_{Acc}$ nach dem anderen
    (we saw)   the   one   after the other
    angekommenen$_{Acc}$] Studenten$_{Acc}$
    arrived   students
    '(We saw) the students arrive one after the other'

This clearly points to the presence of a PRO with which the floating distributive phrase is construed.

This does not exclude the possibility that, in addition to the "matching" analysis sketched in (22),[34] there may also be a "raising" analysis of reduced relative clauses, especially considering that idiom chunks may be modified by them (*The headway made so far is not negligible*). See Cinque (in preparation).

5 An Analysis of English (Germanic)

5.1 Prenominal Adjectives in English (Germanic)

If we ignore for a moment the limited cases of postnominal adjectives seen above (to which we return in the next section), it is possible to say that English (Germanic) directly manifests the structure of Merge, with no movements involved. The adjectives displaying the interpretive properties of indirect modification precede (as noted in section 2.10.3) those displaying the properties of direct modification.[1]

		Indirect modification	Direct modification	
(1)	a. Mary interviewed every	póssible	possible	candidate
	b. They described every	(in)vísible	visible	star
	c. She is a	beaútiful	beautiful	dancer

If modification by (speech act, epistemic, etc.) clausal adverbs is diagnostic of the presence of a clausal constituent, one should expect only indirect modification adjectives, which enter a reduced relative clause, to allow them. Direct modification adjectives (like *heavy*, in one of its readings, *former, main*, etc.) should instead be incompatible with them, even if they allow degree modification (*he is an extremely heavy drinker*). This is apparently what we find. While (2a–c) are fine, (3a–c) are definitely worse:

(2) a. These are frankly unacceptable conditions
   b. This is a probably favourable situation
   c. This is a certainly important contribution

(3) a. *These are frankly heavy drinkers
   b. *This is his probably main contribution
   c. *This is a certainly former player

English (and this seems true of the other Germanic languages) is generally taken to have an unmarked order of adjectives, with (to name just a few classes) value adjectives preceding size adjectives, which in turn precede shape adjectives, which precede color adjectives, themselves preceding provenance/nationality adjectives.[2] Violations of these orders are also possible, though, and are generally taken to be marked, or special. So, for example, in comparing (4a) and (4b), Vendler (1968, 130) says that "the first adheres to the natural order" of the two adjectives, meaning "that he drove out in his car which is yellow and which is new," while the second "means that he drove out in the yellow one of his new cars," and adds that "such inverted phrases usually are uttered with a strong emphasis on the first adjective."[3]

(4) a. He drove out in his new yellow car
    b. He drove out in his yellow new car

As noted in section 3.3.2, such more marked orders, which reverse the "natural" order of two adjectives, should not be taken to show that no rigid order exists among direct modification adjectives. In this way, we would lose the possibility of accounting for what is felt as the unmarked order, which, interestingly, corresponds to the absolute rigid order found among direct modification adjectives in those languages, like Yoruba (see chapter 3, note 15, and relative text), which overtly distinguish them from adjectives derived from relative clauses. Such order variations should rather be understood, I submit, in terms of the two sources of adjectives. The adjective of color in the examples in (4) is once merged as a direct modification adjective, in which case it necessarily follows the adjective *new*; and once as the predicate of a reduced relative clause. The order "reversal" we see here is thus due to the fact that adjectives derived from relative clauses precede (and take scope over) direct modification adjectives:

	Indirect modification	Direct modification	
(5) a. He drove out in his	⟨yéllow⟩	new ⟨yellow⟩	car
b. He is certainly a	⟨fámous⟩	alleged ⟨famous⟩	actor
(cf. section 3.3.2)			

This proposal immediately leads to the expectation that such reversals of the "natural" order should not be available when the lower adjective is of the nonpredicative type (and thus cannot be merged as the predicate of a reduced relative clause in the space above direct modification adjectives). This is what we find:

(6) a. *He is a núclear young physicist (cf. a young nuclear physicist)
    b. *He is a heávy former drinker (cf. a former heavy drinker)
    c. *He is a hárd alleged worker (cf. an alleged hard worker)

These facts also show that reversals of the "unmarked" order cannot be due to the fronting of the lower of the two adjectives to a focus position, as has sometimes been proposed (Scott 2002, 92; Truswell 2004a, 2004b, 40ff.; Alexiadou, Haegeman, and Stavrou 2007, 320; Svenonius 2008, 35). If that were the case the examples in (6) should all be grammatical, and the fronted adjective should be able to reconstruct under the scope of the other adjective, as happens with fronted superlative adjectives (see (20) and (21) in chapter 3).[4] The ungrammaticality of cases like (6), involving direct modification adjectives, are also not easy to understand in scope induced reorderings of the kind discussed in Szendrői 2008, or in accounts like that suggested in McKinney-Bock 2009, section III.

5.2 Postnominal Adjectives in English (Germanic) and Their Derivation

5.2.1 Adjectives with Complements or Adjuncts

In addition to the particular classes of adjectives seen above in section 2.10.2, which can (or must) be postnominal in English, adjectives with complements (or adjuncts) are also found postnominally (*the man proud of his son, a proposal different in spirit*), as their prenominal position is barred by the presence of the postposed complement (or adjunct):

(7) a. *The proud of his son man
    b. *A different in spirit proposal

For this particular case, it might be thought that, due to the recursion restriction mentioned in note 12 of chapter 4, their postnominal position is in essence identical to their prenominal one without the complement or adjunct: namely one of a direct modification.[5] Their properties, however, turn out to be quite different from those displayed by their prenominal counterparts without complements or adjuncts, and they seem, in this case too, to point to the adjectives' status as reduced relative clauses. A first piece of evidence to this effect comes from an observation of Sadler and Arnold's (1994, 196, 221–222). As they note, a prenominal adjective which is under the scope of another prenominal adjective to its left, like *rotten* is in (8a), ceases to be under its scope when found in postnominal position (with a complement or adjunct). Consider the following pair of noun phrases:

(8) a. a fake rotten antique
 b. a fake antique rotten with age

In (8a) what may be fake is the rotten status of the antique. Not so in (8b), where being rotten is an asserted property of the fake antique. This follows if *rotten with age* is a reduced relative clause taking scope over the N and the direct modification adjective *fake*.

A second piece of evidence may come from Williams's (1994, 92) observation that a nonintersective adjective like *alleged*, when in prenominal position (as in (9a)), suspends the speaker's commitment to the appropriateness of the attribution of the term *murderer* to a certain individual. However, when it is in postnominal position with a sentential complement (as in (9b)), it loses this capacity and becomes intersective (the referent of the noun phrase is now given by the intersection of the set of murderers, not alleged murderers, and the set of individuals who are alleged to have killed their own parents):[6]

(9) a. The alleged murderer was deported
 b. The murderer alleged to have killed his own parents was deported

A third piece of evidence that postnominal adjectives with complements (or adjuncts) are reduced relative clauses comes from the fact that nonpredicative adjectives cannot appear postnominally even if followed by a complement (or an adjunct). This follows if postnominal adjectives are reduced relative clauses with the adjective occupying a predicate position. See

(10) a. *What is their reason main in importance? (cf. What is their main reason?)
 b. *He is a drinker heavier than his father (cf. He is a heavy drinker)[7]
 c. *The winner sure from every possible viewpoint is John (cf. The sure winner is John)

It thus seems that, in line with Larson and Marušič's (2004) conclusion, *all* postnominal adjectives in English are (reduced) relative clauses, which in English *can or must* occur in postnominal position depending on the presence of complements (or adjuncts) (full finite relative clauses instead *must* occur there).[8]

The reason postnominal adjectives in English (Germanic) never display the interpretations available to direct modification adjectives suggests that

Analysis of English (Germanic)

direct modification adjectives do not "extrapose" (in antisymmetrical terms, raise leftward to be later overtaken by the remnant). See section 5.3 for further discussion.

5.2.2 Other Classes of Postnominal Adjectives in English

As seen above, *-ble* adjectives, in addition to the prenominal position have also access to the postnominal one, in which case they typically (though not necessarily) receive a stage-level interpretation. Other adjectives, like *nearby, adjacent, handy, guilty*, etc. (see Ferris 1993, chapter 3), can be found both pre- and postnominally.[9] Adjectives that are necessarily postnominal include the stage-level ("locative") *present*, and *ready* ((11)), as well as the adjectives formed with the prefix *a-* (*asleep, afraid, alive, alone*, etc.; see (12)):[10]

(11) a. the people present (≠ the present people)
    b. the papers ready (*the ready papers)

(12) a. the cat asleep (*the asleep cat; Bouldin 1990, 70)
    b. the child afraid (*the afraid child; Bouldin 1990, 70)

A possible reason for the optional or obligatory postnominal position of such adjectives is suggested at the end of the next section.

5.3 A Potential Problem

If predicative adjectives found in postnominal position are analyzed as (reduced) relative clauses, the problem arises why we do not find all potentially predicative adjectives in postnominal position in English (Germanic) as we find them, I argued above, in Romance. This problem is especially acute given that participial reduced relative clauses *can* be postnominal in English, as noted.

Yet, except for the few classes of adjectives reviewed in the previous section, this is not the case. Quite generally, reduced relative clauses containing only "bare" APs cannot be found postnominally:

(13) a. *A child intelligent (could do that in five minutes) (Ferris 1993, 45)
    b. *The documents confidential (were kept in the safe)
    c. *the shirt new (went lost)
    d. *a colleague angry (just stepped in)
    e. *the children thirsty (are crying)

I interpret this at face value as indicating that the conditions on the "extraposition" of full finite relative clauses, participial or complex AP reduced relative clauses, and "bare" AP reduced RCs are different.[11]

In the case of full finite relative clauses, leftward attraction and subsequent remnant movement is obligatory (*The [(that) we saw] boy versus The boy [(that) we saw]). In the case of participial reduced relative clauses, leftward attraction and subsequent remnant movement is apparently optional (The [recently sent] letters and The letters [recently sent]), unless "extraposition" is rendered the only option by the right recursion restriction mentioned in note 12 in chapter 4 (see *The [sent recently] letters versus The letters [sent recently]) (the same restriction is also at play with APs followed by a complement or an adjunct: *The [rotten with age] fake antique versus The fake antique [rotten with age]). Finally, 'bare' AP reduced relative clauses appear not to be able to "extrapose."

The fact, noted in section 2.4, that *a dancer more beautiful than her instructor* actually behaves as a reduced relative clause (as shown by its necessary intersective interpretation) vs. *a more beautiful dancer than her instructor*, which can have a nonintersective interpretation (also see (10b) versus the example of note 7 in this chapter), suggests that *a dancer more beautiful than her instructor* is not simply derived from either one of the two prenominal sources (**a more beautiful than her instructor dancer*) by "extraposition," rendered obligatory by the restriction banning rightward recursion of prenominal adjectives. If that were so, one would expect the "extraposed" variant to be able to retain all interpretations available prenominally (i.e., both the intersective and the nonintersective one). The facts seem instead to indicate that direct modification adjectives cannot "extrapose," because the interpretations associated with them are unavailable postnominally. Given this impossibility, and the cited recursion restriction, there is simply no output for direct modification APs containing complements or adjuncts (except for those cases where the complement or the adjunct itself can "extrapose" as in *a more beautiful dancer than her instructor*—on which see Escribano 2005 and references cited there, as well as Zwart 1996 and Van Canegem-Ardijns 2006 for corresponding Dutch cases). Since, on the other hand, participial or complex AP reduced relative clauses *can* extrapose the interpretive properties associated with them will be found postnominally. In line with the evidence that reduced relative clauses may be merged lower than full finite relative clauses,[12] it could be that "bare" AP relative clauses are merged even lower, with each position subject in English to partially different conditions on "extraposition":[13]

Analysis of English (Germanic)

(14)

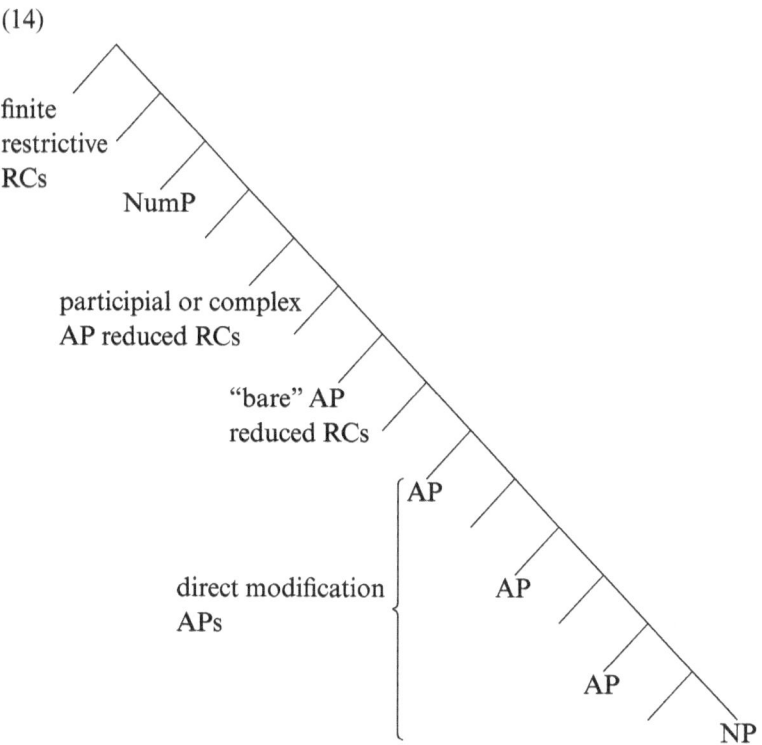

This structure may have to be rendered a little more complex if Larson (1998, 1999, 2000a, 2000b) (also see Larson and Cho 1999, Larson and Marušič 2004, and Larson and Takahashi 2007) is right in arguing that adnominal modification involves two domains, a lower one bound by a generic operator (responsible for the individual-level interpretation of the modifiers closer to the head N) and a higher one bound by an existential operator (responsible for the stage-level interpretation of higher modifiers).[14]

As noted, "bare" AP reduced relative clauses cannot in general appear postnominally even when they have a stage-level interpretation (see (13d,e) above), although when they do they are generally stage-level and restrictive, as argued by James (1979). The very few which occur postnominally (*present, nearby, ready*, and so on, the adjectives in *-ble*, and those prefixed by *a-*) may be postnominal for the same orthogonal reason that forces APs with following complements and adjuncts to "extrapose." See Larson and Marušič's (2004) conjecture mentioned in note 10 above that *a-* is a head taking the morpheme following it as its complement. For the *-ble* adjectives there is perhaps a comparable optional right branching structure, or an unpronounced complement/adjunct ([*available* [TO...]], [*possible* [FOR...]], etc., as, we conjecture, with *ready* (*ready* [TO VP]), and *present* (*present* [AT HERE/ THERE PLACE]). See König 1971, 51–52, Stowell 1991, and Escribano 2004, 28, for a similar conjecture.[15]

5.4 A Reduced Relative Clause Source for Prenominal Participles

The analysis of English (and UG) adnominal/attributive adjectives suggested here crucially assumes two prenominal sources for them: one of direct modification (where the APs are in specifiers of dedicated functional projections above NP), and one of indirect modification (where the APs are in the predicate position of a reduced relative clause merged above the specifiers hosting direct modification adjectives). I take the latter source to be indirectly supported by the independent existence in English of prenominal participial reduced relatives.

It has sometimes been suggested that prenominally all modifiers in English (whether underived or morphologically derived from active or passive participles) are categorially adjectives. Some have even proposed that the mere occurrence in prenominal position in English is a diagnostic of adjectivehood (Freidin 1975; Wasow 1977, 338; Bresnan 1978, 1982; Levin and Rappaport 1986; Haspelmath 1994; among others). But such a conclusion does not seem to be justified. Adjectives differ from verbs in being compatible with *very*, but not with (*very*) *much* (while the latter are compatible with *very much* but not with *very*) (see, for example, McCawley 1970, note 3):

(15) a. Marxism was very (*?much) influential in the sixties
    b. a very (*?much) influential philosophy

(16) John likes Susan very *(much)

Now, the fact that some prenominal participles can be modified by (*very*) *much* suggests that those participles are verbal, presumably within a reduced relative clause:[16]

(17) a. a very much respected scholar
    b. a very much debated issue
    c. a very much appreciated service
    d. the much talked about new show (Sadler and Arnold 1994, 190)

Some (New Zealand) English speakers appear to (marginally) accept both (15a) and (15b) (Megan Rae, personal communication). Rather than taking *very much* to be able (for them) to directly modify the AP as part of its extended projection, it is tempting to think that for them *very much* can modify the predicate of a (reduced) clause even when this contains a simple AP (just as it modifies the predicate of a verbal clause: *I very much like it*/*I like it very much*). This conjecture receives some support from the fact that they make a clear distinction between (15) and the examples in (18), which contain gradable adjectives that are nonpredicative (hence cannot enter the predicate of a reduced relative clause). In such cases only *very* is possible for them too (examples due to Megan Rae):

(18) a. a very (*much) heavy drinker
 b. a very (*much) beautiful dancer
 c. a very (*much) poor typist

Thus it seems that the active and passive participles in (17) are not simple adjectives, but are embedded within a reduced relative clause, and more generally that the prenominal position in English is no diagnostic of adjectivehood.[17]

5.5 *Something Funny*

Both bare and nonbare adjectives have to follow indefinite pronouns such as *something, nothing, someone, no one*, and so on. Larson and Marušič (2004) (also see Cardinaletti and Giusti 2006, section 2.3.1) provide (in my view) convincing evidence that the construction is not derived in English by movement of the N across a prenominal adjective, as proposed in Abney 1987, 287, and Kishimoto 2000, 560 (*some funny thing* → *something funny* t). See also Emonds 1985, 207, and Hulk and Verheugd 1992. Leu (2004) further shows, on the basis of the corresponding French and Swiss German constructions, that the indefinite pronouns in question consist of two functional categories, a quantifier and a functional nominal head (ranging over a limited set of functional nouns: thing, one, body, time, place, etc.), which takes a complement containing the adjective and an empty nominal head. See (19), adapted from his (24):

(19)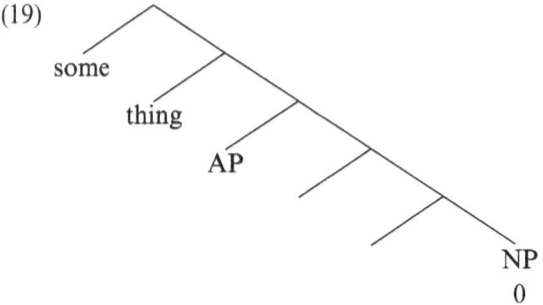

For English, Larson and Marušič (2004) show that the adjective following the indefinite pronoun has all the properties of English postnominal (not prenominal) adjectives, which they argue derive from relative clauses. I take this last conclusion to indicate that indefinite pronouns cannot co-occur in English with direct modification adjectives because the empty nominal category following the adjective is not simply N, or NP, but a bigger portion of the extended projection of the NP that comprises the NP plus all direct modification adjectives, and is just below the prenominal Merge position of reduced relative clauses:[18]

(20)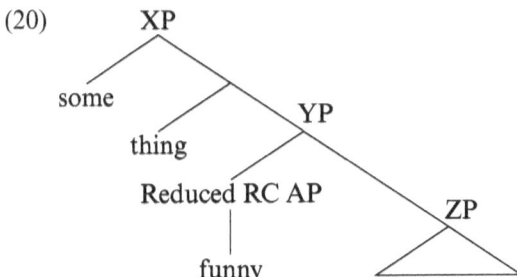

Roehrs (2006, 2008), however, shows that other Germanic languages (German and Dutch) provide evidence that the AP from a reduced relative clause source may remain prenominal. For example, in German it has adjectival inflection like all prenominal adjectives and reduced relative clause participles (see the appendix, section A.6), and displays all the restrictions of prenominal adjectives (cannot be followed by *genug* 'enough', by complements, etc.).[19]

In Slovenian instead, as shown by Marušič and Žaucer (2008), some indefinite pronouns (e.g., *nekaj* 'something') combine with an AP that is *prenominal* to a null N, like German indefinite pronouns, while others (e.g., *nekdo* 'someone') combine only with *postnominal* APs like English indefinite pronouns.

In French, as in other Q/N N contexts (e.g., *beaucoup de livres* 'many books', *une vingtaine d'articles* 'about twenty articles'), the genitive preposition *de* has to be inserted (*quelque chose de lourd* 'something heavy'; Kayne 2005b, 19). Following Kayne (2002, 2005b), I take the derivation to involve raising of the [AP NP] to the specifier of a functional head merged above the XP of (20), followed by insertion of *de* (0 in English) and subsequent attraction of the remnant:[20]

(21) a. [some [thing [funny NP]]] → (merge of X° and attraction of [funny NP])
 b. [[funny NP] X° [some [thing t]]] → (merge of 0 and attraction of the remnant)
 c. [[some [thing t]]] 0 [[funny NP] X° t]]

6 An Analysis of Italian (Romance)

6.1 Prenominal and Postnominal Adjectives in Italian (Romance)

For Italian (Romance) the order of Merge is not immediately visible due to the intervention of (various) movements, which in some cases are obligatory and in others optional.

It was noted above that indirect modification APs (with their interpretations) necessarily follow the N (plus any direct modification APs, if present). See, for example:

		Indirect modification		Direct modification
(1) a.	Maria intervistò ogni	potenziale	candidato	possíbile
b.	Maria intervistò ogni candidato	potenziale		possíbile

c. *Maria intervistò ogni possíble ⟨potenziale⟩ candidato/candidato ⟨potenziale⟩.
'Maria interviewed every possible (that it was possible for her to interview) potential candidate'

This implies that the entire constituent made up of the NP and its direct modification adjectives (the [$_{FP2}$] of (2)) (obligatorily) raises above the indirect modification AP found in the reduced relative clause (like, I would claim, it obligatorily raises above a full relative clause, merged prenominally).

(2)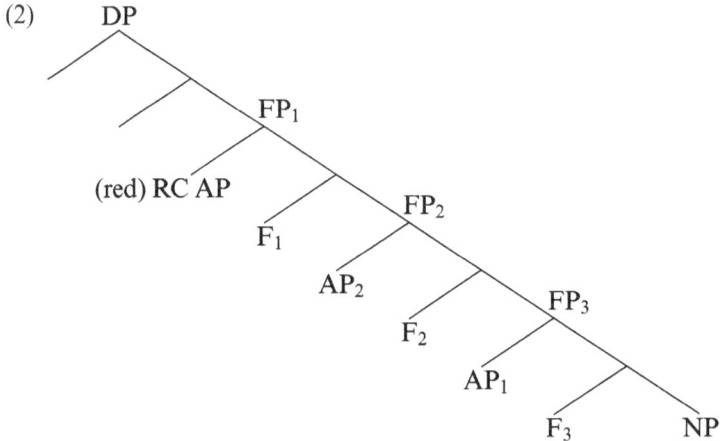

This is rendered plausible by the fact that Romance (as opposed to Germanic) similarly allows no reduced relative clauses to precede the N. Compare (3) with (4):

(3) a. *Italian*
     *le   recentemente arrivate lettere
      the recently   arrived letters
   b. *French*
     *les récemment arrivées lettres
      the recently   arrived letters
   c. *Spanish* (Luján 1980, 49; Demonte 1999b, 54)
     *la escrita carta/*el roto   libro
      the written paper/the broken book
   d. *Romanian* (Carmen Dobrovie-Sorin, p.c.; Dumitrescu and Saltarelli 1998, 187)
     *deja   sositele   cărţi/*nişte căzute frunze
      already arrived-the letters/some fallen leaves
      'the already arrived letters/some fallen leaves'

(4) a. *English* (Barkaï 1972)
      the inadvertently killed passangers
   b. *German* (Walter Schweikert, p.c.)
      die kürzlich angekommenen Briefe
      the recently arrived   letters
   c. *Swedish* (Delsing 1993a, 110)
      en mördad   man
      a murdered man

Analysis of Italian (Romance)

In other words, in Romance, all kinds of relative clauses, whether full or reduced, seem to have to end up after the NP and its direct modifiers.[1] The fact that most direct modification APs (with their interpretations) also follow the noun implies that the NP also raises above (most) direct modification APs inside the constituent that raises above reduced relative clauses (as shown by the arrow inside the box in (5)):

(5)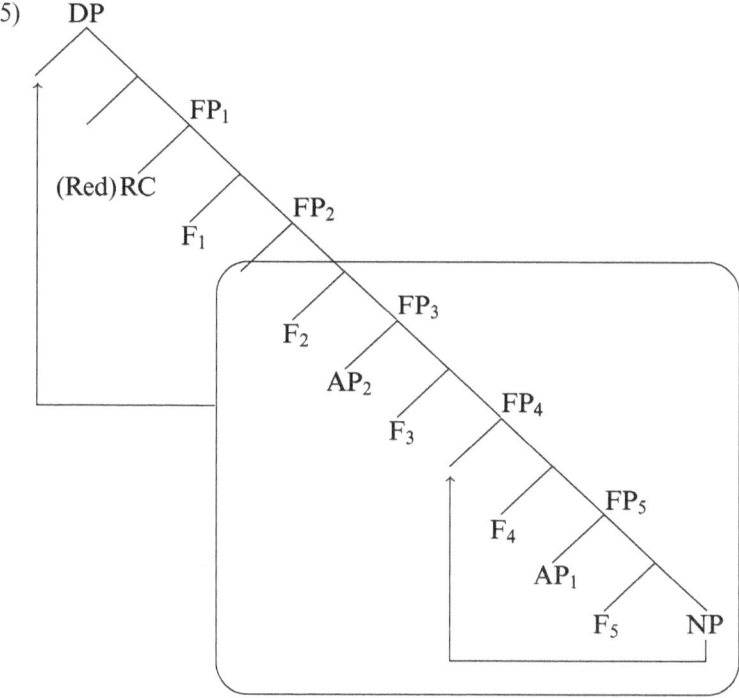

For the latter type of raising one has to distinguish the case where the raising of the NP (or of a bigger phrase containing the NP) around direct modification adjectives is obligatory from the cases in which it is optional or impossible. In Italian, for example, the NP obligatorily raises above classificatory adjectives (see (6)–(7)), and adjectives of provenance/nationality ((8)–(9)),[2] but appears to raise above higher adjectives (of color, shape, size, value, etc.) only optionally (see (10)–(11)).[3]

Italian
(6) a. *Gianni è un **elettronico** ingegnere
    b. Gianni è un ingegnere **elettronico**
        'Gianni is an electrical engineer'

(7) a. *il **centrale** comitato
    b. il comitato **centrale**
       'the central committee'

(8) a. *un **cinese** vaso
    b. un vaso **cinese**
       'a Chinese vase'

(9) a. *la **romana** invasione della Tracia
    b. l'invasione **romana** della Tracia
       'the Roman invasion of Thrace'

(10) a. le **verdi** colline della Toscana
     b. le colline **verdi** della Toscana
        'the green hills of Tuscany'

(11) a. il **tondo** ovale del suo viso
     b. l'ovale **tondo** del suo viso
        'the round oval of her face'

(12) a. l'**enorme** sagoma della cupola
     b. la sagoma **enorme** della cupola
        'the enormous outline of the cupola'

(13) a. il **prezioso** contributo di Gianni
     b. il contributo **prezioso** di Gianni
        'Gianni's precious contribution'

The question why NP raising across classificatory and provenance/nationality APs is obligatory, while it is optional with higher classes of adjectives (except some, across which it is impossible: *mero* 'mere', *povero* 'pitiful', *vecchio* 'longtime, of long-standing', *futuro* 'future', etc.) remains to be understood. The national Romance languages (Italian, French, Catalan, Spanish, Portuguese, Romanian), despite certain differences,[4] are remarkably similar in this respect. Greater variation is found when one takes dialects, or older stages, of these languages into consideration. For example, in Walloon (Bernstein 1991, 105 and note 5; 1993b), the NP does not cross any AP except for nationality ones,[5] while in Old Italian the NP could fail to cross nationality adjectives (Giorgi, forthcoming, sections 4.1.6–4.1.7; Giusti, forthcoming, sections 2.3–2.4; Thiella 2008, chapter 4), as well as the lower classificatory ones (cf. *le sette liberali arti* 'the seven liberal arts', from Dante's *Novellino*, cited in Benincà and Cinque (2008, section 3.2.1)). In Sardinian (Jones 1993, section 2.1.4),

Analysis of Italian (Romance)

and in some Central Italian dialects (Saltarelli 1999), on the other hand, the NP raises obligatorily across all APs except a handful.

Since the order of postnominal direct modification APs in Italian (Romance) is the mirror image of the English (Germanic) prenominal order (compare (14a–c), and especially (17)–(18) below, with their English translations), the raising must be (pace Dehé and Samek-Lodovici 2007, sections 4.2–4.3) of the "roll-up" kind—that is, it must involve at each step pied piping of the *whose-picture* type (Cinque 2005), as sketched in (15) below:

(14) *Italian*
    a. un cane nero enorme
       a dog black enormous
       'an enormous black dog'
    b. un tavolo cinese rotondo
       a table Chinese round
       'a round Chinese table'
    c. una piazza grande bellissima
       a square big beautiful
       'a beautiful big square'

(15)

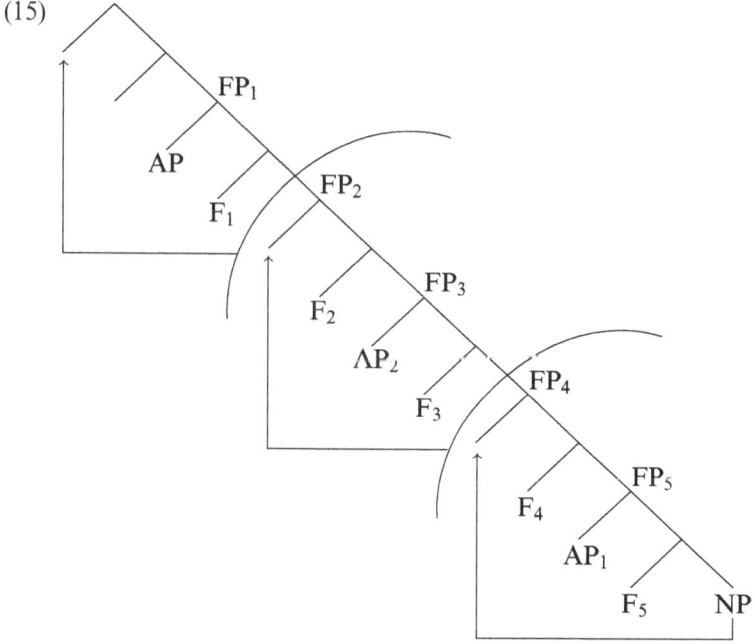

Of course, as in the English case of (*I want*) *a brówn big dog* seen above, in Italian too the opposite order is possible (though more special) alongside the unmarked order seen in (14):

(16) *Italian*
   a. un cane enorme néro
   b. un tavolo rotondo cinése
   c. una piazza bellissima gránde

As in the English case, I take the unmarked order of (14) to reveal the (derived) rigid order of direct modification adjectives in Italian (which is the mirror image of the English one), and I interpret the more special order of (16) as the result of merging the rightmost adjective higher up as a reduced relative clause (which eventually ends up postnominally after the direct modification adjective).[6]

The reversal of the order seen in (16) should be impossible whenever the adjective closer to the N is one of direct modification only, because this cannot access the relative clause source. As with the English cases seen above, this expectation is confirmed:[7]

Italian
(17) a. la ripresa   economica americana
        the recovery economic   American
    b. *la ripresa   americana economica
        the recovery American economic
        'the American economic recovery'

(18) a. l'unico   cliente   abituale possibile
        the-only customer regular possible
    b. *l'unico   cliente   possibile abituale
        the-only customer possible regular
        'the only possible regular customer'

A traditional observation is that certain adjectives can never be postnominal. In the present system, this can be taken to mean that such adjectives cannot be crossed over by the NP (or a larger phrase containing it). In some cases this may depend on the fact that the adjectives are merged in positions which are higher than the positions to which the NP (or the phrase containing it) may raise.[8] It is thus interesting that adjectives which, judging from the position in the clause of the corresponding adverbs (Cinque 1999), are possibly among the highest (*presunto*, *sedicente* 'alleged', *ex* 'former', *futuro* 'future, next in turn'), are exclusively prenominal:[9]

Italian

(19) a. (Si è fatto vivo) un sedicente erede
    (has appeared) an alleged heir
    An alleged heir appeared
  b. (Si è fatto vivo) *un erede sedicente
    (has appeared) a heir alleged
    An alleged heir appeared

(20) a. l' ex primo ministro (è stato arrestato)
    the former prime minister (has been arrested)
  b. *il primo ministro ex (è stato arrestato)
    the prime minister former (has been arrested)

The exclusively prenominal occurrence of an adjective (under a certain interpretation) may also be at the basis of certain meaning contrasts. Cases like (21) and (22), where the adjective appears to change meaning according to whether it occurs prenominally or postnominally, can be seen to depend on the fact that the adjective occupies two distinct positions, one of which (the prenominal one) is high in the direct modification space and is not crossed over by the NP (see (23)), while the other (the postnominal one) is either low in the direct modification space and is crossed over by the NP, or is an indirect modification adjective, merged higher and crossed over by the constituent comprising the NP plus any direct modification adjectives. This can be seen more clearly when both positions are filled (as in *le numerose famiglie numerose che si erano presentate* 'the many numerous families that had come'). See (24):

Italian

(21) le numerose famiglie che si erano presentate
    the numerous (= many) families that had come

(22) le famiglie numerose che si erano presentate
    the numerous (= with many members) families that had come

(23) a. le [numerose (= many) [...[...[famiglie]]]]... → raising of NP
  b. le [numerose (= many) [famiglie [...[t]]]

(24) a. le [numerose (= many) [...[numerose (= with many members) [famiglie]]]]... → raising of NP
  b. le [numerose (= many) [famiglie [numerose (= with many members) [t]]]

There are also more subtle minimal pairs, like (25), which involve the subject-oriented and manner readings of adjectives such as *brutale* 'brutal', discussed in Cinque 1994, section 2:

(25) *Italian*
 a. la loro brutale aggressione all'Albania
    the their brutal aggression to Albania
 b. la loro aggressione brutale all'Albania
    the their aggression brutal to Albania
    'their brutal aggression against Albania'

The adjective in prenominal position has a subject-oriented interpretation while the adjective in postnominal position has a manner interpretation. This suggests that subject-oriented adjectives are higher than manner adjectives (Cinque 1994, section 2), much like the corresponding adverbs in the clause (Jackendoff 1972, chapter 3; Cinque 1999, 19–20), and fail to be crossed over by the NP, which instead necessarily crosses over the lower manner adjective position.

A high location of the adjective cannot however explain all cases of exclusively prenominal adjectives. There are exclusively prenominal adjectives that apparently follow in linear order (are lower than) direct modification adjectives that can be postnominal as well as prenominal. See the combination of the exclusively prenominal *perfetto* (under the relevant reading of 'applying perfectly')[10] with the pre- and postnominal adjective *possibile* 'possible':

(26) *Italian*
 a. un possibile perfetto sconosciuto
    a possible perfect stranger
 b. *un perfetto possibile sconosciuto
    a perfect possible stranger
 c. *un possibile sconosciuto perfetto
    a possible stranger perfect
 d. un perfetto sconosciuto possibile
    a perfect stranger possible
    'a possible perfect stranger'

Also compare the case of *il primo ministro giapponese* with its English translation *the Japanese prime minister*.

This suggests that reasons other than height of merger may be at the basis of the exclusively prenominal character of certain classes of adjectives. These reasons may be in part different in different Romance languages. Although, as noted, Romance languages are in essence identical in the class of adjectives that are necessarily postnominal, necessarily prenominal, and either pre- or postnominal (see Bernstein 1993b on French and Spanish, Cornilescu 2003, Cinque 2004b on Romanian, Gonzaga

2004 on Portuguese, and the present chapter on Italian), there are nonetheless (limited) differences. So, for example, *bon/buono* 'good' in its "approximate" use is only prenominal in French (*il faudra une bonne heure/*heure bonne*; Bouchard 2002, 91), but can be postnominal in Italian (*per arrivare ci vorrà un'ora buona/(?)una buona ora* 'to arrive a good hour will be necessary'). For certain (limited) differences between Italian and Romanian regarding adjective positions, see Giusti 2005, section 2.1.

There are also differences with respect to temporal adverbs used as nominal modifiers in Italian and Spanish. While in the former *allora* 'then' is possible, but neither *ora* 'now' nor *oggi* 'today', etc. (*l'allora/ *l'ora/*l'oggi primo ministro giapponese* 'the then/now/today Japanese prime minister'), in the latter all three are acceptable (see Silva-Villar and Gutiérrez-Rexach 1997, 460).

As noted by Abeillé and Godard (2000, 340), some exclusively prenominal adjectives in French can also appear postnominally if coordinated with another adjective. So, for example, *vrai* 'real' and *faux* 'fake' cannot by themselves be postnominal (*Des vrais coupables/*Des coupables vrais* 'real culprits'; *Des faux coupables/*Des coupables faux* 'fake culprits'). But they can, if coordinated together (*Des vrais ou faux coupables/Des coupables vrais ou faux* 'real or fake culprits'). Similar facts hold in Italian (Compare *una vera menzogna/*una menzogna vera* 'a true lie' with *una menzogna vera e propria* 'a lie true and real', *una pura coincidenza/*una coincidenza pura, una semplice coincidenza/*una coincidenza semplice* with *una coincidenza pura e semplice* 'a coincidence pure and simple'.[11]

I tentatively interpret this fact as suggesting that when coordinated they count more easily as emphasized ("heavy"), and can thus access the Spec of a lower FocusP, ending up in postnominal position as a consequence of the subsequent movement of the remnant (with their pre- or postcomplement position depending on the relative height of the P with respect to FocusP—for which see the discussion in the next section).[12]

Italian (Romance) prenominal adjectives (whether obligatorily prenominal or not) are, as noted, only direct modifiers, with certain associated interpretive properties (individual-level, nonrestrictive, nonintersective, etc. readings). As such, they are, qua direct modifiers, also nonpredicative. This means that, should one of these adjectives also appear in predicate position, it ought to be ambiguous between a direct modification usage and a usage as a predicative, indirect modification, adjective (with the other set of associated interpretive properties: restrictive, intersective, etc. readings). A case in point appears to be the adjective *falso* 'false, fake'. This adjective can appear prenominally, thus qualifying as a direct modifier, with the associated nonrestrictive, nonintersective, etc. readings ((27)); yet it can also be found in predicate position ((28a)), and postnominally ((28b)), with all the properties (restrictive, intersective, etc.) of indirect modification adjectives:

Italian
(27) Questo è un falso problema
　　　This　 is a false problem

(28) a. Questa notizia　　è falsa
　　　　This　 piece of news is false
　　 b. Questa è una notizia falsa
　　　　This　 is a　false piece of news

As one should expect, the meaning of *falso* in (27) is not the same as the meaning of *falso* in (28). In (27), it is a "privative" adjective (Partee 2003a, 2003b), one that denies that the N is an appropriate description for a certain situation (the interpretation being that 'it is not a (real) problem'). In (28), instead, the adjective does not deny the appropriateness of the noun as a description of the facts. The piece of news may well be real news, though not one corresponding to the truth. This is particularly clear in the following minimal pair:

(29) *Italian*
　　 a. Le false banconote con cui　giocano...
　　　　the fake bills　　with which play-they...
　　　　'The fake bills with which they play...'
　　 b. Le banconote false con cui　giocano...
　　　　the bills　　fake with which play-they...
　　　　'The fake bills with which they play...'

In the first case one refers to something that is not a real bill (e.g., Monopoly money); in the second case to something, possibly indistinguishable from real money, that has been counterfeited.[13]

The fact that certain languages only have the direct modification, "privative," reading of 'false, fake' (as is apparently the case of Mandarin Chinese; see note 7 of the appendix) indirectly confirms the conclusion, drawn here on word order and interpretive grounds, that two separate uses of *falso* (a direct modification and an indirect modification one) should be posited. In this respect, English seems to pattern with Italian, even if the distinction between the two usages of 'false/fake' is less evident than in Italian (due to the fact that in English both are prenominal), and is generally not recognized in the semantic literature (Kamp 1975; Kamp and Partee 1995; Partee 2003a, 2003b).

6.2 The Position of PP Complements and Adjuncts vis-à-vis Adjectives in Italian (Romance)

An apparent problem for an analysis that postulates movement of the NP (or of a larger phrase containing it) rather than of just the head N is the fact that PP complements of the noun, rather than being dragged along by the NP in its raising, appear to be stranded at the end of the DP. Under the traditional analysis that first merges Ps with their complement, and then the resultant PP with the "head" N, this is indeed problematic. However, the apparent stranding of complement (and adjunct) PPs at the end of the DP is exactly what is to be expected under Kayne's (2000, 2002, 2004) analysis of prepositions. According to that analysis, prepositions are heads merged high in the extended projection of the NP (or outside of the DP altogether). They attract their "complements," and force (in VO languages) the entire remnant to raise to their left, which makes them final in the DP. More accurately, their DP-final position is achieved as sketched in (30):[14]

(30) a. [those [two [nice [books [syntax]]]]] → (merge of K(ase) and attraction of the DP to its Spec)
   b. [[syntax] K [those [two [nice [books t]]]]] → (merge of P (*on*) and attraction of the remnant)
   c. [[those [two [nice [books t]]]] on [[syntax] K t]]

In Romance, while postnominal adjectives found between the head N and its (PP) complement(s) can either be direct modification adjectives or indirect modification adjectives, adjectives following a (PP) complement of the N are necessarily indirect modification adjectives.

This is clearly exemplified in Italian by the different interpretations associated with the different positions occupied by the adjective *industriosi* in (31a–c):[15]

(31) *Italian*
   a. Gli **industriosi** greci di Megara di sicuro saranno premiati
   b. I greci **industriosi** di Megara di sicuro saranno premiati
   c. I greci di Megara **industriósi** di sicuro saranno premiati
      'The industrious Greeks of Megara will certainly receive a prize'

(31a) has a nonrestrictive interpretation only ('all the Greeks of Megara, who are industrious, will receive a prize'). This is expected, as we saw, from the prenominal status of the adjective. (31b) is ambiguous. It can either have the nonrestrictive interpretation of (31a), or a restrictive interpretation ('among the Greeks of Megara, only those who are industrious will receive a prize'). This follows from the two possible sources of the adjective. It can either be merged as a direct modifier, and be crossed over by the NP (in which case it will retain all and only the readings of direct modification adjectives; in the case at hand, the nonrestrictive one), or it can be merged higher up, as the predicate of a reduced relative clause, and be crossed over by the NP plus its direct modifiers, if any (in which case it will have only the restrictive reading). (31c) is unambiguous. It only has the restrictive reading of indirect modification adjectives.

Under the analysis sketched above, after Kayne's, the necessary indirect modification character of adjectives following a PP complement may be seen to follow from the fact that both complements and relative clauses (but, I would add, no direct modification adjectives), may undergo movement to a higher position followed by merger of a P or of an (overt or covert) complementizer that subsequently forces movement of the entire remnant to their left, making them DP-final.

Depending on whether C or P is merged higher than the other, the (reduced) relative clause or the PP complement/adjunct will be absolutely final and the other next to final (see the two alternative derivations in (32) and (33)):[16]

Italian
(32) a. [gli [industriosi [greci [Megara]]]] → (merge of K(ase) and attraction of the DP to its Spec)
   b. [[Megara] K [gli [industriosi [greci t]]]] → (merge of P (*di*) and attraction of the remnant)
   c. [[gli [industriosi [greci t]]] di [[Megara] K t]] → (merge of C_1 and attraction of *industriosi*)
   d. [industriosi C_1 [[i [t [greci t]]]] di [[Megara] K t] (merge of C_2 and attraction of the remnant)
   e. [[[[i [t [greci t]]]] di [[Megara] K t] C_2 [industriosi C_1 t]] → **i greci di Megara industriosi**

(33) a. [gli [industriosi [greci [Megara]]]] → (merge of C_1 and attraction of *industriosi*)
   b. [industriosi C_1 [[i [t [greci Megara]]]]] → (merge of C_2 and attraction of the remnant)
   c. [[i [t [greci [Megara]]]] C_2 [industriosi C_1 t]] (merge of K and attraction of the DP to its Spec)
   d. [[Megara] K [[i [t [greci]]] C_2 [industriosi C_1 t]] → (merge of P and attraction of the remnant)
   e. [[[i [t [greci]]] C_2 [industriosi C_1 t]] di [[Megara] K t]] → **i greci industriosi di Megara**

In other words, the ordinary derivation is that shown in (33), where merger of a (covert) C precedes merger of P. In (32) the C which is merged later than P is presumably a Focus head.

If direct modification adjectives (unlike adjectives merged as predicates of a reduced relative clause) cannot be attracted to a (covert) C higher than the position where Ps are merged (in fact, cannot be attracted *tout court*), they will necessarily be to the left of the PP. Only indirect modification APs will thus be able to follow a PP complement or adjunct of the head. Given that when they follow the PP, as noted, they must be heavily stressed, modified, coordinated, or followed by a complement or adjunct, it is reasonable to assume that they actually move to the Spec of a FocusP.[17]

Interestingly, the only classes of modifiers that can appear after a PP without being specially stressed are those that are allowed postnominally in English (and after *celui* in French, for which see section 6.4).

This suggests that they count as "heavy," perhaps for the reasons discussed in section 5.3, in connection with English. That is, because they involve nonpronounced structure (as (37) shows, they can follow the noun's complement even without being heavily stressed, modified, coordinated, or followed by a complement or adjunct):

Italian

(34) *Full relative clause*
I sostenitori di Gianni che conosciamo
'the supporters of Gianni that we know'

(35) *Reduced relative clause*
I sostenitori di Gianni convocati recentemente
'the supporters of Gianni summoned recently'

(36) *PP modifiers*
I sostenitori di Gianni di convinzioni liberali
'the supporters of Gianni of liberal convictions'

(37) *Special classes of adjectives*
i sostenitori di Gianni presenti/disponibili/pronti/...
'the supporters of G. present/available/ready/...'

In other words, bare indirect modification adjectives under normal conditions can undergo a derivation like (38), but not one like (39):

Italian

(38) a. [$_{YP}$ fedeli [$_{NP}$ sostenitori Gianni]] merge of X and attraction of NP to its Spec, followed by merger of D →

b. [i [[sostenitori Gianni] X [$_{YP}$ fedeli [$_{NP}$]]]] merge of K and attraction of *Gianni* to its Spec →
c. [Gianni K [i [[sostenitori t] X [$_{YP}$ fedeli [$_{NP}$]]]]] merge of *di* and attraction of the remnant →
d. [i [[sostenitori t] X [$_{YP}$ fedeli [$_{NP}$]]]] di [Gianni K [t]]]
'(lit.) the supporters faithful of G.'

(39) [unavailable]
a. [$_{YP}$ fedeli [$_{NP}$ sostenitori Gianni]] merge of K and attraction of *Gianni* to its Spec →
b. [Gianni K [$_{YP}$ fedeli [$_{NP}$ sostenitori t]]] merge of *di* and attraction of the remnant →
c. [$_{YP}$ fedeli [$_{NP}$ sostenitori t]] di [Gianni K t] merge of C$_1$ and attraction of *fedeli* →
d. [fedeli C$_1$ [$_{YP}$ t [$_{NP}$ sostenitori t]] di [Gianni K t]] merge of C$_2$ and attraction of the remnant →
e. [(i) [$_{YP}$ t [$_{NP}$ sostenitori t]] di [Gianni K t] C$_2$ [fedeli C$_1$ t]]
'(lit.) the supporters of G. faithful'

With 'heavy' indirect modification adjectives both derivations are instead possible (cf. *i sostenitori fedeli al loro leader di Gianni* '(lit.) the supporters faithful to their leader of G.', and *i sostenitori di Gianni fedeli al loro leader* '(lit.) the supporters of G. faithful to their leader').

The fact that subject PPs generally precede oblique PPs (the direct order) in Romance, despite the adjectives showing an inverse order, is taken by Giurgea 2009 to be a problem for a DP-internal phrasal movement analysis, and for a cartographic approach more generally. But under Kayne's analysis of prepositional phrases adopted here this conclusion is not necessary. In particular the order subject PP > oblique PPs is reminiscent of superiority, and can be treated along similar lines (see Krapova and Cinque 2008, section 7).

6.3 The Position of Demonstrative Reinforcers vis-à-vis Adjectives in Italian (Romance)

Just as complement (and adjunct) PPs in Italian constitute a divide between direct modification adjectives (only possible to their left) and indirect modification adjectives (possible both to their left, and to their right if focused), so do demonstrative reinforcers (like the *qui* of (40)), studied for Romance in Brugè 1996, 2002, Brugè and Giusti 1996, Bernstein 1997, and Ihsane 2003 (also see Leu 2007, 2008):

(40) questi (tre) (bei) libri **qui**
these three nice books here (dem. reinf.)
'these here three nice books'

As shown by the examples in (41), which contain direct modification adjectives, these can only occur to the left of the reinforcer:[18]

(41) *Italian*
   a. Questo figlio ⟨unico⟩ qui ⟨*unico⟩ se l'è cavata benissimo
      this child ⟨only⟩ here ⟨only⟩ managed very-well
      'This only child managed very well'
   b. Quel salario ⟨medio⟩ lì ⟨*medio⟩ non farebbe gola
      that salary ⟨average⟩ there ⟨average⟩ would tempt
      a nessuno
      no one
      'That average salary would tempt no one'
   c. Quel sistema ⟨immunitario⟩ lì ⟨*immunitario⟩ è simile al
      that system ⟨immune⟩ there ⟨immune⟩ is similar to
      nostro
      ours
      'That immune system is similar to ours'
   d. Quel fisico ⟨atomico⟩ lì ⟨*atomico⟩ era un genio
      that physicist ⟨atomic⟩ there ⟨atomic⟩ was a genius
      'That atomic physicist was a genius'

Adjectives that are not necessarily direct modifiers, like those in (42), can instead appear either before or after the demonstrative reinforcer:

(42) *Italian*
   a. Questi cuori ⟨infranti⟩ qui ⟨infranti⟩ mi fanno pena
      these hearts ⟨broken⟩ here ⟨broken⟩ make me feel sorry
      'These broken hearts make me feel sorry'
   b. Quella penna ⟨rossa⟩ lì ⟨rossa⟩ non è nostra
      that pen ⟨red⟩ there ⟨red⟩ not is ours
      'That red pen is not ours'
   c. Questi piatti ⟨pronti⟩ qui ⟨pronti⟩ vanno serviti
      these dishes ⟨ready⟩ here ⟨ready⟩ have to-be-served
      subito
      immediately
      'The dishes ready have to be served immediately'

Modifying in part Brugè's (2002) and Bernstein's (1997) analyses, I will assume that the demonstrative and the demonstrative reinforcer is a constituent merged immediately below the determiner; the XP of (43) (but see Leu 2007, 2008, for a more articulated analysis).[19]

(43) [Det [[$_{XP}$ questi qui] [tre [bei [libri]]]]]
     Det these-here   three nice books

To derive the order in (40), one may assume that the demonstrative first raises to Spec,Det (cf. Leu 2007, 2008),[20] after which there is attraction of *qui* to the Spec of a higher head, followed by merger of a head that attracts the entire remnant (the latter head actually appears to be spelled out in Spanish, as *de*; see (45)).

Italian
(44) a. [*questi* [Det [[t *qui*] [*tre* [*bei* [*libri*]]]]]] → merger of a head and attraction of *qui*
   b. [t *qui* X [*questi* [Det [[t t] [*tre* [*bei* [*libri*]]]]]] → merger of a head and attraction of the remnant
   c. [*questi* [Det [[t t] [*tre* [*bei* [*libri*]]]]]] Y [t *qui* X t]

(45) este (...) libro de aquí[21]
     this   book of here
     'this book'

As with the adjectives following a complement or adjunct PP, I will assume that the adjectives following a demonstrative reinforcer have accessed the Spec of a focus head higher than the position targeted by the demonstrative reinforcer (which excludes, as noted, direct modification adjectives).

6.4 Adjectives After *celui* in French

The account proposed for those adjectives that follow a PP and the demonstrative reinforcer in Romance may prompt an account of the parallel fact that no indirect modification adjective (nor direct modification adjective, for that matter) can be found after *celui* in French (see (46)), except for those classes that can appear postnominally in English and after a complement or a demonstrative reinforcer in Italian. See (47)–(51) (cf. Kayne 1994; Sleeman and Verheugd 1998a, 1998b; Bouchard 2002, 172ff.; and references cited there).

French
(46) *celui jaune (Kayne 1994, 100)

(47) *Full relative clause*
Le livre que Ida m'a donné ne m'a pas plu, mais celui
the book that Ida to-me gave didn't to-me appeal, but the-one
que Paul m'a donné m'a beaucoup plu
that Paul to-me gave a lot to-me appealed

(48) *Reduced relative clause*
   a. celui envoyé à Jean
      the-one sent to Jean
   b. celui à faire
      the-one to do

(49) *PP modifiers*
celui de Marie n'est pas beau, mais celui de Pierre est beau
the-one by Marie is-not nice, but the-one by Pierre is nice

(50) *Adjectives followed by a complement (or adjunct)*
celui fier de son fils regardait Paul
the-one proud of his son looked-at Paul

(51) *Special classes of adjectives* (Bouchard 2002, 174)
   a. ceux présents auront droit à un rabais
      those present will-have right to a rebate
   b. ceux coupables/responsables seront punis
      those guilty/responsible will-be punished
   c. ceux prêts doivent être envoyés immédiatement
      those ready must be sent immediately

If *celui* is high in DP (perhaps in Spec, DP; Kayne 1994, 101), and there is an unpronounced C/P merged higher, then only those indirect modifiers that can be attracted to a focus head higher than C/P (crucially, neither direct modification adjectives nor bare indirect modification adjectives) will be found to co-occur with *celui*. Only focused indirect modification APs or APs with a larger (overt or covert) structure will be able to.

7 Further Differences between English (Germanic) and Italian (Romance)

Here three more differences between English (Germanic) and Italian (Romance) are discussed, which seem to follow from the analysis sketched so far.

7.1 Epithets with Prenominal and Postnominal Adjectives

As observed in Stowell 1981, 287, in English epithets resuming a previously introduced referent can only have prenominal, not postnominal adjectives (see (1)). This is presumably due to the fact that such epithets can only contain nonrestrictive modifiers and that only prenominal adjectives can be interpreted nonrestrictively in English:[1]

(1) I tried to visit the mayor last week, but [the angry old man]/*[the man angry at his constituents] refused to see me

This is not true for Italian (Romance), where postnominal APs can also be interpreted nonrestrictively:

(2) Ho   cercato di parlare con Gianni, ma [quel **maledetto**
    I-have tried to talk   with Gianni, but that damn
    imbroglione]/[quell'imbroglione **maledetto**] non si   è   fatto
    swindler   /that swindler   damn   not himself has made
    trovare
    find
    'I tried to talk to Gianni, but that damn swindler was not to be found anywhere'

7.2 Idiomatic Readings with Prenominal and Postnominal Adjectives

As noted by Sadler and Arnold (1994, 194–195), in English "prenominal adjective noun combinations allow idiomatic interpretations whereas postnominal and predicative adjectives do not." See (3) and (4):

(3) a. A red herring
    b. *A herring red in character
    c. *A herring which is red (on the intended meaning)
(4) a. A white lie
    b. *A lie white in spirit
    c. *A lie which was white (on the intended meaning)

In Italian, instead, both pre- and postnominal adjectives allow for idiomatic interpretations:

(5) a. Di bassa lega (lit. 'of low alloy' = vulgar/of bad taste)
    b. Di buon senso (lit. 'of good sense' = of common sense)
(6) a. Ad armi pari (lit. 'at weapons even' = with equal chances)
    b. Ai ferri corti (lit. 'at the irons short' = in bad terms (with someone))

This follows if idiomatic readings are only possible with direct modification APs, because only these are nonintersective, and if in Italian postnominal adjectives can also involve direct modification.[2]

7.3 A Constraint on Romance Prenominal Adjectives

Demonte (1999b, 68ff.) mentions the observation found in traditional grammars of Spanish "that adjectives preceding a series of singular coordinated nouns which they modify "agree [in gender and number] with the immediately following noun," as in [(7a)], while "the adjective specifying various preceding singular (nouns), all of the same gender, should show plural agreement," as in [(7c)]" (p. 68). Also see Camacho 2003, 127ff.

(7) *Spanish* (Real Academia Española, 391)
    a. con **ferviente** devoción y cariño
       with fervent (sing.) devotion (sing.) and affection (sing.)
    b. ??con **fervientes** devoción y cariño
       with fervent (pl.) devotion (sing.) and affection (sing.)
    c. con devoción y cariño **fervientes**
       with devotion (sing.) and affection (sing.) fervent (pl.)

A similar restriction is noted for French in Noailly 1999, 90:

(8) *French* (Noailly 1999, 90)
    a. avec une **étonnante** grâce et sincérité
       with an astonishing (sing.) grace (sing.) and sincerity (sing.)

b. ??avec d'**étonnantes**   grâce   et   sincérité
   with astonishing (pl.) grace (sing.) and sincerity (sing.)

As Noailly (1999, 90) notes, "La seule solution qui reste, c'est donc de postposer l'adjectif en le mettant au pluriel":

(9) *French*
   avec une grâce   et   une sincérité   **étonnantes**
   with a   grace (sing.) and a   sincerity (sing.) astonishing (pl.)

Italian behaves similarly:

(10) *Italian*
   a. (Ci trattò)   con grande   amore   e
      ((s)he treated us) with great (sing.) love (sing.) and
      affetto
      affection (sing.)
   b. *?(Ci trattò)   con grandi   amore   e
      ((s)he treated us) with great (pl.) love (sing.) and
      affetto
      affection (sing.)
   c. (Ci trattò)   con amore   e   affetto
      ((s)he treated us) with love (sing.) and affection (sing.)
      grandi
      great (pl.)
      '(S)he treated us with great love and affection'

This can perhaps be made sense of if, as noted, prenominal adjectives in Romance are only direct modification adjectives modifying a constituent smaller than dP, the first nominal constituent with referential import (see the brief discussion in section 3.4). As a consequence of that, the coordination that follows them cannot count as the coordination of two singular referential dPs, making up a plural referential dP.[3]

Because postnominal adjectives can (also) be derived from a relative clause source, merged higher than dP (see structure (24) of chapter 3), they will be able to modify a coordination of two singular referential dPs making up a plural referential dP, with which they agree in the plural. This is, I claim, the case in (7c), (9), and (10c).

Note that this leads one to expect that adjectives that are direct modifiers only will not be able to enter the postnominal plural option, because this is only open to the higher indirect modification adjectives. The expectation appears fulfilled. See the examples in (11), with adjectives that have no predicative usage:

(11) *Italian*
    a. ??in   sicurezza   e   padronanza   complete
       with confidence (sing.) and command (sing.) complete (pl.)
       (cf. in completa/??complete sicurezza e padronanza 'with complete (sing./??pl.) confidence and command)
    b. ??con protervia   e   arroganza   probabili
       with insolence (sing.) and arrogance (sing.) probable (pl.)
       (cf. con probabile/??probabili protervia e arroganza 'with probable (sing./??pl.) insolence (sing.) and arrogance (sing.))
    c. ??per calcolo   e   interesse puri e semplici
       for calculation (sing.) and interest (sing.) simple (pl.)
       'for simple calculation and interest'
       (cf. per puro e semplice/??puri e semplici calcolo e interesse 'for simple (sing./??pl.) calculation (sing.) and interest (sing.)')

The constraint observed for Romance is not detectable in English given that prenominally both direct and indirect modification adjectives are available and the adjective does not overtly agree in number with the noun. In German, where the adjective does show number agreement with the noun, instead of the expected possibility of both singular agreement (with direct modification adjectives) and plural agreement (with indirect modification adjectives), only singular agreement is apparently possible, for reasons that remain to be understood:

(12) *German*
    a.   mit offenbarer/großer   Sympathie und Liebe
         with apparent/big (sing.) sympathy and love
    b. *mit offenbaren/großen Sympathie und Liebe
         with apparent/big (pl.) sympathy and love

Conclusion

The major point of this book is that adjectives enter the structure of DPs in two different ways: either as direct phrasal specifiers of dedicated functional heads of the extended projection of the Noun or as predicates of reduced relative clauses, merged above the functional projections hosting the former type of adjectives. The two types of adjectives were seen to be associated with different interpretive and syntactic properties. A second, related, goal was to see if a better understanding could be achieved of the syntax of Romance and Germanic adjectives on the basis of the dual source of adjectives.

The account of the main properties and generalizations concerning Germanic and Romance adjectives can be briefly summarized as follows. First, the APs that have a reduced relative clause source, and that precede the direct modification APs in prenominal position in Germanic, are found in postnominal position in Romance following the direct modification APs (if any are present). This was attributed to the obligatory "extraposition" of reduced relative clauses in Romance as opposed to the impossibility of extraposing bare adjective reduced relative clauses in Germanic.

Second, the APs that are merged as direct modifiers in dedicated functional projections above N remain prenominal in Germanic, while (except for few classes) they optionally or obligatorily end up after the N in Romance, depending on the specific class they belong to.

Third, the postnominal orders of Romance, which are the mirror image of the orders of Germanic follow from two types of roll-up phrasal movement, that involving indirect modification APs and that involving direct modification APs:

	Indirect modification	Direct modification	Direct modification	
(1) a. the		American	musical	comedy of the 1950s
b. the only		possible	Roman	invasion of Thrace
c. She interviewed every	possible	potential		candidate

	Direct modification	Direct modification	Indirect modification	
(2) a. la commedia	musicale	americana		degli Anni '50
b. la sola invasione	romana	possibile		della Tracia
c. Intervistò ogni candidato	potenziale		possibile	alla presidenza

Fourth, the existence of the unexpected scope effects of the type in (3), noted in section 1.3, derives from the possibility of pied piping the lower adjective with the N around the higher one, as shown in (3):

(3) a. E'   una *sicura*   [*giovane*   promessa] →
    (he)-is a   sure   young   promise
  b. E'   una [*giovane* promessa] *sicura* t
    (he)-is a   young promise   sure
  'He is a sure young promise'

(with "Direct modification" / "Direct modification" labels above *sicura* and *giovane* respectively)

Fifth, prenominal APs in Romance are unambiguous because they can only have a direct modification source given that all types of (reduced) relative clauses obligatorily end up postnominally in Romance.

Sixth, as noted, certain direct modification adjectives can only be prenominal (*vecchio* 'longtime, of long standing'; *povero* 'pitiable'; etc.). In the present analysis, this follows from the impossibility for the NP to cross over them (for reasons that remain to be clarified).

Seventh, postnominal APs in Romance are instead ambiguous because they can either arise from a direct modification source, or from an indirect modification source.

Eighth, the difference in meaning of certain adjectives between the prenominal and the postnominal position was analyzed here as due to the possibility for those adjectives to be used either as direct modifiers or as predicates of a reduced relative clause, and from the necessarily prenominal location of the direct modification usage of those adjectives (which leaves the reduced relative clause source as the only possible source for the postnominal adjective).

Conclusion

Ninth, in addition to the ambiguity deriving from the possibility of having both a direct and an indirect modification source, certain adjectives display further ambiguities if they belong to more than one class of direct modification adjectives, and come to occupy different positions in the extended projection of the NP.

Color adjectives are a particularly clear case. *Giallo* 'yellow' can be a low, obligatorily postnominal, direct modification classificatory adjective in *un libro giallo* 'a thriller (lit. a novel yellow)',[1] as well as a nonrestrictive, nonintersective, etc., prenominal direct modification adjective in *le gialle colline dell'Andalusia* 'the yellow hills of A.', in addition to being able to occur as a (relative clause–derived) restrictive, intersective, etc., obligatorily postnominal, adjective in *(Passami) la cravatta gialla* '(Pass me) the yellow tie'.[2] As seen, depending on where it is inserted, the same adjective will thus display different syntactic/semantic and word-order properties. For discussion of several cases of this sort, see Adamson 2000 and Scott 2002.

Appendix: Further Evidence for the Dual Source of Adnominal Adjectives

In this appendix a number of languages are briefly discussed that appear to overtly distinguish the two sources.[1]

A.1 Chinese

Mandarin Chinese is one language that has been claimed to overtly distinguish direct modification from indirect modification adjectives (derived from reduced relative clauses).[2] Sproat and Shih (1988, 1990) point out that while adjectives followed by the marker *de* display no rigid order among each other, those that appear without *de* do display rigid ordering. Compare (1) (their 1990 (2a)) with (2) (their 1990 (4a)):

(1) a. xiăo-de lü-de huāpíng
      small DE green DE vase
      'a small green vase'
   b. lü-de xiăo-de huāpíng
      green DE small DE vase
      'a small green vase'

(2) a. xiăo lü huāpíng
      small green vase
      'a small green vase'
   b. *lü xiăo huāpíng
      green small vase
      'a small green vase'

They suggest that the first type of modification, which displays the same marker *de* found in relative clauses, is in fact nothing other than a (reduced) relative clause (hence the nonrigid order of the adjectives typical of relative clauses; cf. also Aoun and Li 2003, 150), while the second is a nominal compound (hence the rigid order, typical of compounds; cf. also Aoun and Li 2003, 149, Cheung 2005, and Yang 2005, chapter 6).[3]

Subsequent research, however, has shown the picture to be more complex. Paul (2005) provides evidence against Sproat and Shih's (1988, 1990) (and Cheng 1986, and Duanmu's 1998, and Simpson's 2001) idea that adjectives with *de* in Mandarin Chinese are necessarily to be analyzed as relative clauses and that Ns preceded by *de*-less adjectives necessarily form compounds. Concerning the first point, she shows that in contrast to what is sometimes claimed in the literature (see Sproat and Shih 1988, 1990) even nonpredicative adjectives, like *yiqian* 'former', can (and must) be followed by *de* in adnominal position (see (3), (4), as well as (ia,b) in note 4).[4]

(3) Beijing daxue   yiqian de xiaozhang (Paul 2005, note 7)
    Beijing University former DE president
    'the former president of Beijing University'

(4) benlai de yisi (Paul 2005, section 2)
    original DE meaning
    'the original meaning'

Concerning the second point, Paul (2005, 2009) (and Sio 2006, 112–113, for Cantonese) show that some [A N] sequences behave as compounds (i.e., single words, whose components are invisible to syntactic processes), while other [A N] sequences behave like fully transparent syntactic phrases.[5]

Once the phrasal status of (certain) [A N] sequences is established, it becomes interesting to consider what syntactic and semantic differences there are between *de*-less adjectives and the same adjectives with *de*. The properties of *de*-less adjectives appear to be consistently those isolated above for direct modification adjectives. I have already noted after Sproat and Shih 1988, 1990, that they enter a particularly rigid order (also see Paul 2005, section 3.3).[6] Also, as noted in Huang 1982 and Cheung 2005, section 2.1, they only enter hierarchical (stacked) readings, while adjectives with *de* can enter either hierarchical or conjoined readings. From an interpretive viewpoint, they seem to differ from adjectives with *de* in being 'defining', or individual-level, nonrestrictive (they do not contrast one object with another, which may also explain why *de*-less adjectives are not possible with just any N—cf. Fu 1987, 290ff.; Wang 1995, section 4.2.2; Paul 2005, section 3.2, 2009; Cheung 2005; Sio 2006, 117ff.), and nonintersective.[7] Wei (2004), as reported in Sio 2006, 129 n. 5, observes that bare adjectives in Mandarin, along with their literal meaning, can also have nonintersective idiomatic readings, which are lost when the adjective is followed by *de*. See, for example, (5):

(5) tā dà zuǐbà
he big mouth
'He has a big mouth' or 'He is gossipy'

Moreover, as noted by Fu (1987, 288) and Sproat and Shih (1990, 571) (also see Yang 2005, chapter 6, section 4.6; Cheung 2005, section 2.2; Sio 2006, chapter 5, section 2.1.2), adjectives with *de* can only occur outside of *de*-less ones (see (6) and (7)):[8]

(6) a. hēi-de xiǎo shū (Sproat and Shih 1990, 571)
    black-de small book
  b. *xiǎo hēi-de shū
    small black-de book
    'small black book'

(7) a. na san-ge hong de da
    that three-classifier red DE big
    qiu (Cheung 2005, examples (19a,b))
    ball
    'those three red big balls'
  b. *na san-ge da hong de qiu
    that three-classifier big red DE ball
    'those three big red balls'

Also see Cheung 2005 and Yang 2005, 211, where it is pointed out that while adjectives with *de* can occur, within the sequence Demonstrative Numeral+Classifier N, either before the Demonstrative, or in between the Demonstrative and the Numeral+Classifier (typical relative clause positions), as well as between Numeral+Classifier and N, *de*-less adjectives can only occur in the latter position.[9]

Given the possibility seen above for *de* to occur with (some) nonpredicative adjectives, one should perhaps posit the existence of two *de*'s, one of which (the one also following full or reduced relative clauses) is necessarily pronounced; the other (the one following direct modification adjectives) sometimes is not pronounced (see, in particular, the discussion in note 7).[10]

In conclusion, it seems reasonable to say that while not all direct modification adjectives are *de*-less, those *de*-less adjectives that do not form compounds are only direct modification adjectives.

A.2 Maltese

Maltese also appears to distinguish direct modification adjectives from indirect modification adjectives in terms of the absence versus presence of an adjectival determiner. In definite noun phrases, "The definite article occurs on the noun and may be repeated, in the appropriate allomorphic form, on the adjective" (Plank and Moravcsik 1996, 187). See (8), their (12a):[11]

(8) il-mara (t-)twila
    the-woman (the-)tall
    'the tall woman'

As Plank and Moravcsik (1996, 187) further note, "Re-articulated and bare adjectives are not in free variation." The former have a restrictive reading, and the latter a nonrestrictive one (pp. 187–188), an observation that goes back to Sutcliffe 1936, as Fabri (2001, 158) notes. In fact Fabri (1993, 38ff., 2001) provides extensive evidence for the restrictive nature of articulated adjectives. To give one example, he observes that when an adjective like *hot* modifies a noun like *sun* it cannot be articulated. Rearticulation of the adjective would only be "acceptable in the context of a science fiction story in which a fictitious world or planet had more than one sun" (2001, 164; see also 1993, 48–49). Similar considerations are at the basis of contrasts like the following, also given in Fabri 1993, 2001:

(9) Xagħar Simon twil/*t-twil jogħġob-ni (Fabri 1993, 53)
    hair   Simon long/the.long pleases-me
    'I like Simon's long hair'

In the present analysis, the restrictive nature of articulated adjectives is an unambiguous diagnostic of their derivation from a reduced relative clause. That in turn implies that it should not be possible to rearticulate adjectives that cannot be predicates (hence predicates of a relative clause). This appears confirmed by various observations found in the literature on Maltese. So, for example, nonintersective adjectives cannot be rearticulated ((10a,b), and the same is true of classificatory adjectives (10c–e)):

(10) a. ir-rumanz (*l-)ewlieni (Fabri 1993, 51)
        the-novel (the-)single
        'the only novel'
     b. l-ispirtu (*l-)awtentiku (Plank and Moravcsik 1996, 188)
        the-spirit (the-)authentic
        'the authentic spirit'

c. il-qagħada (*l-)internazzjonali (Plank and Moravcsik
   the-situation (the-)international   1996, 188)
   'the international situation'
d. l-istudju (*l-)grammatikali (Borg 1996, 16; Borg and
   the-studies (the-)grammatical   Azzopardi-Alexander 1997, 71)
   'grammatical studies'
e. l-ilsien (*il-)Għarbi (Plank and Moravcsik 1996, 188)
   the-language (the-)Arabic
   'the Arabic language'

Also, as reported in Duffield 1995, 337 n. 34, and 1999, section 2.3, based on Fabri 1993, 55, when both an articleless (in my interpretation, direct modification) adjective and a rearticulated (i.e., indirect modification) adjective co-occur, the articulated adjective must be outside of the articleless adjective, much the way in English and Italian (modulo their pre- and postnominal position) indirect modification adjectives are outside direct modification ones. See (11):[12]

(11) a. ?il-bozza hamra l-ġdida
        the-bulb red   the-new
     b. *il-bozza l-hamra ġdida
        the-bulb the-red new
        'the new red bulb'

A.3 Bosnian/Croatian/Serbian

Bosnian/Croatian/Serbian adjectives display two distinct morphological forms: a "short" (traditionally "indefinite") form, and a "long" (traditionally "definite") form (Leko 1988, 1992, 1996, 1999; Aljović 2000, 2002, 2010).[13] Syntactically, both forms can appear before the N:

(12) a. nov   kaput
        new (short form) coat
        'a new coat'
     b. novi   kaput
        new (long form) coat
        'the/a new coat'

In predicate position, however, only the short form is possible (Leko 1999, 234):[14]

(13) Njegov kaput je nov/*novi
     his   coat is new (short form)/*new (long form)

I take it to mean that the short form can only be used as a predicate—either an overt one (as in (13)), or a covert one (as in (12a), where it is the predicate of a reduced relative clause). Evidence for this conclusion comes from the fact that adnominal short-form adjectives display properties that were seen above to characterize indirect modification adjectives (those derived from relative clauses).[15]

So, for example, unlike long-form adjectives, short-form adjectives cannot give rise to nonintersective (idiomatic) collocations; they can only give rise to literal (nonidiomatic) readings. See, for instance, (14)–(15), from Leko 1992, 623–624:

(14) a. slijepi   miš
        blind (long form) mouse
        'bat'
     b. slijep   miš
        blind (short form) mouse
        'blind mouse'

(15) a. strani   jezik
        strange (long form) language
        'foreign language'
     b. stran   jezik
        strange (short form) language
        'some unfamiliar language'

Short-form adjectives show no strict order whatsoever. See (16), from Aljović 2002, 34, as well as note 17 below, and the relative text, for the distinct behavior of long-form adjectives:

(16) a. pouzdano$_{short}$ màlo$_{short}$ crno$_{short}$ auto
        reliable   small   black   car
        'a reliable small black car'
     b. crno$_{short}$ pouzdano$_{short}$ màlo$_{short}$ auto
        black   reliable   small   car
        'a black reliable small car'

Interestingly, adjectives that cannot be used predicatively do not even possess a short form; they only have the long form. See, for example, the "adverbial" adjectives *navodni* 'alleged (long form)' and *budući* 'future (long form)' (Aljović 2000, 103ff.):

(17) a. navodni/*navodan   komunista
        An/the-alleged (long form)/(*short form) communist

b. budući/*buduć   predsjednik
a/the-future (long form)/(*short form) president

and the classificatory adjectives of (18) (Rutkowski and Progovac 2005):

(18) a. centralni/*centralan   komitet
a/the-central (long form)/(*short form) committee
b. polarni/*polaran   medved
a/the-polar (long form)/(*short form) bear
c. generalni/*generalan   director
a/the-general (long form)/(*short form) director

For many speakers (though not for all; cf. Zlatić 1997, 61; Aljović 2002, note 14), short- and long-form adjectives can occur together prenominally. If they do, short-form adjectives necessarily precede long-form adjectives (Leko 1988, 140–141; Leko 1992, 623; Olga Tomić, personal communication):[16]

(19) a. siromašan   bolesni   dječak
a/the-poor (short form) sick (long form) boy
'the poor sick boy'
b. *bolesni   siromašan   dječak
a/the-sick (long form) poor (short form) boy

(20) a. bolestan   siromašni   dječak
a/the-sick (short form) poor (long form) boy
'a/the sick poor boy'
b. *siromašni   bolestan   dječak
a/the-poor (long form) sick (short form) boy

As to long-form adjectives, it seems that they can either have a direct modification source, or an indirect modification one, since they are systematically ambiguous between the two sets of properties associated with the two sources seen above (Nadira Aljović, personal communication), and do not have an absolutely rigid order among each other, only a preferred one (Nedžad Leko, personal communication).[17] They thus appear to be like prenominal adjectives in English, which are ambiguous between the two sources, and have a preferred, but not an absolutely rigid, order (see for discussion sections 3.3.2 and 5.1).

In any event, by virtue of their possible direct modification source, only long-form adjectives give rise to nonintersective (idiomatic) collocations, as noted in relation to (14)–(15), and only they give rise to a specific interpretation of the DP (Aljović 2000, 189ff.; Aljović 2002; cf. also Trenkić

2004).[18] Also, as Aljović (2000, 104) observes, French prenominal adjectives (which I claim here only have a direct modification source) are rendered in Bosnian/Croatian/Serbian with long-form adjectives, while short-form adjectives correspond to those French postnominal adjectives that are interpreted as reduced relative clauses. It thus seems that Bosnian/Croatian/Serbian overtly distinguishes one of the two reduced relative clause sources of adnominal adjectives from direct modification adjectives.[19]

A.4 Romanian

Romanian is another language that appears to distinguish the two sources. Adjectives preceded by the article *cel/cea*/etc. only have the reduced relative clause source.[20] Evidence for this conjecture comes from a number of restrictions, noted in the literature, on the distribution of APs preceded by *cel*. First, they can only follow the N, even if the corresponding bare adjectives can either precede or follow it.[21] See (21b) and (22b):[22]

(21) a. bun*i*   prieteni/prieteni*i* buni
      good-the friends/friends-the good
      'the good friends'
   b. cei trei prieteni cei buni/*cei trei cei buni prieteni
      the three friends the good/the three the good friends
      'the three good friends'

(22) a. curajos*ul*   băiat/băiat*ul* curajos
      courageous-the boy/boy-the courageous
      'the courageous boy'
   b. băiat*ul* cel curajos/*cel   curajos   băiat
      boy-the the courageous/the courageous boy
      'the courageous boy'

If *cel* APs are in fact reduced relative clauses, their being limited to postnominal position simply follows from the fact that reduced relative clauses necessarily follow the N in Romanian (see (23a,b), from Dragăn 2002, 111, and (23c), from Carmen Dobrovie-Sorin, personal communication), a feature that Romanian shares with the other Romance languages (and that is not shared by the neighboring Balkan languages, Greek and Bulgarian):[23]

(23) a. cărţi*le*   citite/*citite*le*   cărţi
books-the read-FEM.PL/read-FEM.PL-the books
'the books read'
b. copac*ul* ars/*ars*ul*   copac
tree-the burnt-MASC.SG/burnt-MASC.SG-the tree
'the burnt tree'
c. cărţi*le* (deja) sosite/*(deja) sosite*le* cărţi
books-the (already) arrived/(already) arrived-the books
'the (already) arrived books'

A second property of *cel*, observed in Giusti 1993 and Cornilescu 2003, 2006, as noted, is that it can only appear before predicative adjectives. See:

(24) a. comedia   (*cea) musicală
comedy-the (the) musical
'the musical comedy'
b. literatura   (*cea) engleză
literature-the (the) English
'the English literature'
c. ordonanţa (*cea) judecătorească (Coene 1994, 18)
order-the (the) judicial
'the judicial order'
d. omul   (*cel) biet (Cornilescu 1992, 222)
man-the (the) pitiable
'the poor man'
e. demnitarul cel înalt (Cornilescu 1992, 222)
official   the tall/*high
'the tall/*high official'

These facts again follow directly if APs preceded by *cel* only have a reduced relative clause source.

Since the adjectives in (24) are nonpredicative, they cannot be the predicate of a (reduced) relative clause either, hence their ungrammaticality.

The conclusion that *cel* can only precede elements that are predicates of a reduced relative clause finds additional support in an observation found in Cornilescu 1992, 222: "A significant fact, which seems to have gone unnoticed is that, while with modifiers postnominal *cel* is grammatical, even if redundant, it is utterly ungrammatical with a PP or a DP which is theta-marked by the head noun or subcategorized by it." See (25) (= her (76)):

(25) a. *fratele   cel al Mariei
       brother-the the of Mary
       'Mary's brother'
    b. *grosimea   cea a zidurilor
       thickness-the the of the-walls
       'the thickness of the walls'
    c. *distrugerea   cea a orașului
       distruction-the the of the-city
       'the destruction of the city'
    d. *venirea   cea a musafirilor
       coming-the the of the-guests
       'the coming of the guests'
    e. *faptul   cel că   pleacă
       fact-the the that he-is-leaving
       'the fact that he is leaving'

This becomes understandable under a derivation of *cel* phrases from relative clauses because subcategorized PPs and DPs cannot constitute the predicate of a relative clause modifying the N that assigns them a theta-role (*fratele care e al Mariei* 'the brother who is of Mary'; *grosimea care e a zidurilor* 'the thickness that is of the walls', etc.).[24]

A.5 Greek

Another language that would seem at first sight to overtly distinguish the two sources of adjectives is Greek. In Greek definite DPs, adjectives have two options (see Androutsopoulou 1994, 1995, 1997, 2001; Kolliakou 1995, 1998, 1999, 2003, 2004; Stavrou 1995, 1996, 1999, forthcoming; Alexiadou and Wilder 1998; Alexiadou 2001, 2003; Campos and Stavrou 2004; among others). They can either be articleless, in which case they necessarily precede the Noun ((26)), or they can be preceded by an article, in which case they can either precede or follow the N ((27)):[25]

(26) a.   to megalo vivlio
          the big   book
    b. *to vivlio megalo
          the book big
          'the big book'
(27) a.   to megalo to vivlio
          the big   the book

b. to vivlio to   megalo
      the book (the) big
      'the big book'

Articulated adjectives like those in (27) (also referred to as adjectives in "Determiner Spreading"—Androutsopoulou 1994, 1995, 2001—or adjectives in polydefinite constructions—Kolliakou 1995, 1999, 2003, 2004, Campos and Stavrou 2004, and Lekakou and Szendrői 2007) seem to have all the characteristics of what I called above, following Sproat and Shih 1998, 1990, indirect modification (i.e., of reduced relative clauses).

First, articulated adjectives are necessarily restrictive (Mouma 1993, 86; Kolliakou 1999, 126; Manolessou 2000, 158; Campos and Stavrou 2004, 143) (Marinis and Panagiotidis 2006, 27, refer to them as "restrictive/predicative").[26] When the adjective is nonrestrictive, as in (28), it cannot have its own article (Manolessou 2000, 156; Alexiadou 2003, section 4.1):

(28) I   gigandeia (*i)   gafa (Manolessou 2000, 156)
     the gigantic (the) blunder
     'the gigantic blunder'

Second, articulated adjectives are interpreted intersectively (Kolliakou 1999, 123; Campos and Stavrou 2004, 144). So, for example, while (29a) is ambiguous between a nonintersective interpretation ("the singer sings beautifully") and an intersective one ("the singer is a beautiful woman"), (29b), the articulated variant, only has the intersective interpretation ("the singer is a beautiful woman"):

(29) a. Gnorises tin orea   tragudistria? (Campos and Stavrou
        meet-2SG the beautiful singer   2004, 144)
     b. Gnorises tin orea   tin tragudistria?
        meet-2SG the beautiful the singer
        'Did you meet the beautiful singer?'

Third, according to Alexiadou and Wilder (1998, 303ff.) and Alexiadou (2001, 232), articulated adjectives display free order among each other, while articleless adjectives have a rigid order.[27]

Fourth, articulated adjectives, as noted by Kolliakou (1999, 135), cannot be closer to the N than articleless adjectives. See (30):[28]

(30) a. *i   megali kenuria [i   kokkini] valitsa
        the big   new   the red   suitcase
        'the big new red suitcase'

b. i   megali i   kenuria kokkini valitsa
   the big the new   red   suitcase
   'the big new red suitcase'

Fifth, adjectives that cannot be articulated cannot be used as predicates either. However, as Androutsopoulou (1995, 25; 2001, 191) notes, the reverse is not true (pace Alexiadou and Wilder 1998, 306). While most adjectives that cannot appear in predicate position cannot be articulated either (see (31)–(36)), adjectives do exist that can be articulated even though they cannot appear in predicate position (as also noted in Leu 2009). See (37a,b), and the nonintersective reading of *o ftohos o anthropos* 'the poor/pitiable man' mentioned in note 29, all unexpected for Alexiadou and Wilder (1998):[29]

(31) o   ipotithemenos (*o) eglimatias (Tredinnick 1992, 203)
     the alleged   (the) convict
     'the alleged convict'
     (Cf. *o eglimatias itan ipotithemenos* 'the convict was alleged')

(32) o   proin (*o) ipurgos (Alexiadou 2001, 233)
     the former (the) minister
     'the former minister'
     (Cf. *o ipurgos itan proin* 'the minister was former')

(33) i   apli (*i) simptosi (Kolliakou 2004, 264)
     the mere (the) coincidence
     'the mere coincidence'

(34) o   monos tu (*o) erotas (cf. Campos and Stavrou 2004, 144)
     the only his (the) love
     'his only love'

(35) i   makedhoniki (*i) epithesi enadion ton
     the Macedonian (the) attack against the
     Person (Androtsopoulou 1995, 24)
     Persians
     'the Macedonian attack against the Persians'
     (cf. *i epithesi enadion ton Person itan makedhoniki* 'the attack on the Persian was Macedonian')

(36) o   Indikos (*o) Okeanos (Campos and Stavrou 2004, 163)
     the Indian (the) Ocean
     'the Indian Ocean'

(37) a. o   proighoumenos (o)   prothipourghos (Androutsopoulou
       the former   (the) prime minister   1995, 24)
       'the former prime minister'
       (cf. *o prothipourghos itan proighoumenos 'the prime minister
       was former')
    b. o   kaimenos o   mathitis (cf. Androutsopoulou 2001, 191)
       the pitiable   the student
       'the poor student'
       (cf. *Aftos o mathitis ine kaimenos 'this student is poor/pitiable')

Examples such as (37), and the nonintersective reading of *o ftohos o anthropos* 'the poor/pitiable man' of note 29, appear to rule out any derivation in which the articulated adjective is necessarily merged in predicate position (as in Alexiadou and Wilder 1998, and Alexiadou 2001, 2003). It is, however, still possible to derive articulated adjectives from a reduced relative clause if one assumes that the article and the adjective constitute a DP (with an elliptical N) that is the predicate of a reduced relative clause, as shown in (38) (alternatively, a DP (with an elliptical N) in "close apposition" to the DP containing the "modified N," as suggested in Stavrou 1995, Marinis and Panagiotidis 2006, and Lekakou and Szendrői 2007):

(38) to   vivlio [$_{IP}$ I° [$_{DP}$ to kokkino VIVLIO]]
     the book [$_{IP}$ I° [$_{DP}$ the red BOOK/ONE]]

This may account for the fact that articulated adjectives imply a contrast, as is the case for the remnant of a DP with N ellipsis: *I Theodora agorase to prasino Fiat ke i Maria agorase to kokkino* 'Theodora bought a green Fiat and Maria bought a red one' ("for a successful subdeletion there must be a contrast"; Giannakidou and Stavrou 1999, 304). The arguments against an elliptical DP given in Alexiadou and Wilder 1998, section 2.6, only apply to an appositive source, not to the restrictive one. Note that an elliptical DP analysis of articulated adjectives can also accommodate such cases as (37a,b) because the adjectives are merged as direct modifiers of the null noun (the same applies to the corresponding Slovenian and Bulgarian facts below). The fact that not all direct modifiers are possible in this construction can plausibly be attributed to its semantics (cf. '%the coincidence, the mere one', '%the ocean, the Indian one', etc.)[30]. The elliptical DP analysis may also be at the basis of a restriction that Melita Stavrou (personal communication) pointed out to me. For her only one articulated adjective is natural (which recalls the noniterability of articulated adjectives in Romanian; see note 21). This last property of Greek articulated adjectives is reminiscent (pace Leu 2008, 56) of the impossibility of recursion in German Restrictive Elliptic Appositives (Riemsdijk 1998).[31] To judge from Androutsopoulou's (1997, 25ff.) contrast between *to kokkino idha forema* ((lit.) the red saw.I dress 'It's the red dress that I saw') and **tin kathari miso adhikia* ((lit.) the pure hate.I injustice 'It's pure injustice that I hate'), adjective extraction may be one context in Modern Greek that distinguishes between the two sources of adjectives. Apparently, only indirect modification adjectives, not direct modification adjectives, can be extracted from DP, which recalls Nowak's (2000) observation on the extraction of adjectives from Polish DPs (cf. note 8 of chapter 2).

A.6 Some Notes on Russian and German

Russian, like Bosnian/Croatian/Serbian, also has short-form and long-form adjectives, but differs from the latter in two ways: first, it cannot use short-form adjectives in adnominal position (compare (39) with (12) above, repeated here as (40)) and second, it regularly utilizes long-form adjectives also in predicate position (compare (41) with (13) above, repeated here as (42)):[32]

(39) *Russian* (Pereltsvaig 2000, section 2)
 novyj/*nov dom stoit na gore
 new:nom (long form/*short form) house:nom stands on hill
 'The new house stands on a/the hill'

(40) *Bosnian/Croatian/Serbian*
 novi/nov kaput
 new (long form/short form) coat
 'the/a new coat'

(41) *Russian* (Pereltsvaig 2000, section 2)
 Dom nov/novyj
 house:nom new:nom (short form/long form)
 'The house is new'

(42) *Bosnian/Croatian/Serbian*
 Njegov kaput je nov/*novi
 his coat is new (short form/*long form)
 'His coat is new'

I submit that such differences ultimately stem from the fact that in Russian *all* adnominal adjectives, whether they are direct modification ones, or derive from the predicate of a (reduced) relative clause, *have to* take the long form, while in Bosnian/Croatian/Serbian adnominal adjectives deriving from the predicate of a (reduced) relative clause *can* retain the short form found in predicate position.[33]

Let's consider Siegel's (1976a, 1976b) analysis of Russian adjectives. She takes short-form adjectives to be exclusively predicative, semantically extensional, and intersective, and long-form adjectives to be exclusively attributive, semantically intensional, and nonintersective. The fact that long-form adjectives are apparently also found in predicate position (cf. (41)) is for her due to the fact that they can be the attribute of a predicate nominal with an empty noun reconstructed from context (an analysis originally proposed in Babby 1970).[34] Thus, according to this analysis *dom nov* means 'the house is new' and *dom novyj* roughly means 'the house is a new one'.

Siegel discusses some evidence in favor of this analysis. For one thing, the two options often differ semantically. So, for example, while both (43a) and (43b) are possible

(43) *Russian*
 a. studentka   umna
    student-fem intelligent-fem (short form)
    'The student is intelligent'
 b. studentka   umnaja
    student-fem intelligent-fem (long form)
    'The student is intelligent'

The former "means that the student is intelligent in general, absolute terms" while the latter "means that she is intelligent compared with other students; that is, 'The student is an intelligent one'" (Siegel 1976b, 297). This analysis also leads one to expect that, when the predicate nominal option that licenses the long form as a predicate is semantically inappropriate, only the short form should be possible. This appears confirmed by examples of general laws or with certain kinds of abstract subjects like the following (where such paraphrases as "the space is an infinite one," "everything is a clear one," and "to come home is a very pleasant one" are out of place):[35]

(44) *Russian*
 a. prostranstvo beskonečno/*beskonečnoe
    space   infinite (short form/*long form)
    'The space is infinite'

b. Vse   jasno/*jasnoe
   everything clear (short form/*long form)
   'Everything is clear'
c. prixodit' domoj očen' prijatno/*prijatnoe
   to-come home very pleasant (short form/*long form)
   'To come home is very pleasant'

Nonetheless, as is observed in Larson 1999, lecture 2, this analysis leads to certain expectations that do not seem to be fulfilled (and that are not discussed by Siegel). If long-form adjectives are only intensional and nonintersective, adnominal adjectives (which obligatorily come in the long form) should never show intersective interpretations, and should never display the systematic ambiguity that prenominal adjectives have in English between an intersective and a nonintersective interpretation in such phrases as *a beautiful dancer*. However, speakers of Russian consulted by Larson find that a phrase like *krasivyi tancor* '(a) beautiful dancer' has the same ambiguity that *a beautiful dancer* has in English between an intersective and a nonintersective reading.

In spite of these apparent problems, Siegel's analysis, with its desirable consequences mentioned above, can be retained, I think, if the following modification is introduced: long-form adjectives not only have the direct modification (intensional, nonintersective, individual-level, etc.) source, but can also derive from the other, relative clause, source (with its extensional, intersective, stage-level, etc., interpretations). What one has to assume is that an adjective that finds itself in an adnominal reduced relative clause necessarily takes on the long form. This is independently supported by the fact that participles unequivocally deriving from reduced relative clauses also take on the long form, which is different from the short form which they take in verbal contexts. See Siegel 1976b, 293, as well as Bailyn 1994, 28 n. 15:

(45) a. *Russian* (= (i) of note 15 of Bailyn 1994, 28)
        Ivan byl ubit
        Ivan was killed (short form)
     b. *Russian* (= (ii) of note 15 of Bailyn 1994, 28)
        Ubityj   soldat ležal na zemle
        killed (long-form) soldier lay on ground
        'A dead soldier lay on the ground'

A similar proposal seems appropriate for German, where adjectives in predicate position (and in postnominal position, apart from those in the Restrictive Elliptic Appositive construction; Riemsdijk 1998, 20) are invariant ((46)), while all prenominal adjectives necessarily show agreement with the N ((47)), whether they are of the direct modification type or are predicates of a reduced relative clause:

(46) *German*
   a. Der Vortrag war interessant/*interessanter
      the contribution (masc.sg.) was interesting (neuter/*masc.sg)
   b. Die Diskussion war
      The discussion (fem.sg) was
      interessant/*interessante (neuter/*fem.sg)
      interesting

(47) *German*
   a. ein interessant**er** Vortrag
      an interesting (masc.sg) contribution (masc.sg.)
   b. eine interessante Diskussion
      an interesting (fem.sg.) discussion (fem.sg.)

As in Russian, German participles, which have clear verbal properties, display the same behavior. They are invariant ((48)), except when they are part of a reduced relative clause in prenominal position, in which case they obligatorily show agreement with the head noun ((49)):[36]

(48) *German*
   Der Student/die Studentin, [sein/ihr Studium seit langem
   the student-MASC/FEM his/her studies for a long time
   hassend/*hassender/*hassende], fiel durch sein/ihr Examen
   hating-NEUT/MASC.SG/FEM.SG failed his/her exams
   'The student, because he/she had hated his/her studies for a long time, failed his/her exams'

(49) *German* (Riemsdijk 1983, 234)
   a. Ein [sein Studium seit langem hassender/*hassend]
      a his study for-a long-time hating (masc.sg/*neuter)
      Student...
      student (masc.sg.)...
      'a student hating his study for a long time'
   b. Eine [ihr Studium seit langem hassende/*hassend]
      a her study for-a long-time hating (fem.sg./*neuter)
      Studentin...
      student (fem.sg.)...
      'a student hating her study for a long time...'

Notes

Introduction

1. I concentrate here and below on the "alethic modal" reading of *possibile* ('which it is possible will occur/has occurred') rather than on the "root modal" reading ('which it is possible for someone to carry out'/'which is feasible').

2. This dual source was already utilized in Cinque 1994, although its implications were only partially explored there.

Chapter 1

1. In Cinque 1994 I tentatively suggested (p. 90) that the restriction would be understandable if thematic APs were to "compete with manner APs for one and the same position," but as (3) shows the restriction is more general (and the suggestion questionable in any case; see Bouchard 2002, 180–181, and Crisma 1993, 96).

2. See Cinque 1994, 98ff., for discussion.

3. Neither adjective is predicative in (4) and (5), as shown by the unacceptability of (i) and the corresponding Italian cases (ii):

(i) a. *The cause of his death is main
    b. *The main cause of his death is (most) probable

(ii) a. *La causa della sua morte è prima
     b. *La causa prima della sua morte è (la più) probabile

4. Similar facts hold in French (and in the other Romance languages). For example, according to Bouchard 2002, 122, (i) shows the only natural order of the adjectives *français* and *possible*:

(i) Le seul fournisseur français possible d'armes   nucléaires, c'est
    the only supplier   French possible of-weapons nuclear,   is
    l'Etat   français
    the-state French
    'The only possible French supplier of nuclear weapons is the French state'

5. For the other possible readings of *les présumés professeurs chinois malhonnêtes*, and their derivations, which are not necessarily the ones attributed by Bouchard (forthcoming) to cartographic analyses, see chapter 6, note 7.

Chapter 2

1. Alexiadou, Haegeman, and Stavrou (2007, 329–330, 374) surprisingly claim that in Italian the postnominal position of nonpredicative adjectives like *principale* is ungrammatical.

2. While Bolinger (1967, 4) appears to claim that when both positions are available for a given adjective, the adjective is interpreted as an enduring or characteristic property in prenominal position, and as an occasional, temporary, property in postnominal position ("*the only river navigable* is unambiguously occasion, *the only navigable river* unambiguously characteristic"), Sadler and Arnold (1994, 193) observe that temporary (for them, stage-level) readings "are not totally excluded in prenominal position—one can speak of *currently navigable rivers*, for example, where *currently navigable* is presumably a stage-level predicate." Similarly, though postnominal adjectives are more often interpreted as stage-level (see Larson 1998, 2000b, and Larson and Marušič 2004), the individual-level interpretation does not seem to be entirely excluded (for some adjectives). See the discussion and the examples in Ferris 1993, 45, 48.

3. "Bolinger (1967) notes that prenominal adjectives can be ambiguous between a restrictive and a non-restrictive interpretation, whereas postnominal adjectives can only be understood restrictively" (Larson and Marušič 2004, 275).

For the observation that prenominal adjectives in Italian are unambiguously nonrestrictive while postnominal ones are ambiguous between a restrictive and a nonrestrictive interpretation, see Giorgi and Longobardi 1991, 123. This can also be seen with proper names in appropriate contexts. Differently from what is claimed in Ticio 2003, 123, *Il Mozart geniale del periodo viennese* 'the engenious Mozart of the Viennese period' does not necessarily contrast one (stage of) Mozart of the Viennese period with another.

Bolinger (1972), Luján (1980, 87–89), Demonte (1982, 271, 278ff.), Martín (1995, 187), Morzycki (2006, 2008, 103–104), citing Mackenzie (2004), note that postnominal adjectives in Spanish, in addition to a restrictive reading, can also have a nonrestrictive one. The same is true of Romanian ("In Romanian, the pre-nominal position mostly accomodates evaluative non-restrictive readings.... The post-nominal allows both readings"; Cornilescu 2006, 60) and French. See, for example, *le coiffeur a peigné ses cheveux soyeux* 'the hairdresser combed her silky hair (lit. hair silky)' (Vergnaud and Zubizarreta 1992, 603). It has been claimed (Blinkenberg 1969, 113) that with proper names even a prenominal adjective may have a restrictive reading: *J'aime mieux le jeune Renan que le vieux Renan* 'I prefer the young Renan to the old Renan' (the same appears true of Italian: *Ho letto il giovane Goethe, non il vecchio Goethe* 'I read the young Goethe, not the old Goethe'). That conclusion is dubious, however. The inappropriateness of (ia) and (iia) in opposition to (ib) and (iib) (where the adjective is postnominal) seems to indicate that the prenominal positioning is not genuinely restrictive (what the examples above compare, it seems, are two unanalyzable "stages" of Renan and Goethe):

(i) a. ??Ho letto solo il giovane Goethe, non i suoi ultimi lavori
   b. Ho letto solo il Goethe giovane, non i suoi ultimi lavori
      'I read only the young Goethe, not his last works'

(ii) a. *?Ho letto il giovane ma non il vecchio Goethe
      'I have read the young but not the old Goethe'
    b. Ho   letto il   Goethe giovane, ma non il   Goethe vecchio
       I-have read the Goethe young,   but not the Goethe old
       'I have read the young, but not the old Goethe'

4. For reasons that are not entirely clear, omission of the genitive PP *di Ferri* renders the nonrestrictive reading in (8a) virtually impossible, and (7a), for which a restrictive reading is unavailable, virtually ungrammatical. A similar effect is noted for Spanish in Morzycki 2008, note 2, where the observation is attributed to Violeta Demonte. See Demonte 2008, 74.

5. An analogous pattern is shown by the adjective *wrong*. Larson (2000a) takes the ambiguity of (*We discussed*) *the wrong answer* to stem from the possibility of interpreting *wrong* either as an attributive modifier (= 'incorrect'), or (pace Schwarz 2006) as a predicative adjective in the predicate position of a reduced relative clause with Antecedent Contained Deletion (= the [wrong for us to discuss] answer). This seems confirmed by the possibility of having two occurrences of the adjective:

(i) We discussed the wrong wrong (= incorrect) answer

Gengel (2008, 36) claims that in French the implicit relative clause reading with Antecedent Contained Deletion is also available pre-nominally, but this was judged impossible by my linguists informants. Her claim that French is much freer than the other Romance languages in the distribution of adjectives also finds no clear base.

6. A similar contrast is found between (ia), which has both the intersective and nonintersective interpretations, and (ib), which only has the intersective interpretation:

(i) a. I've never met quite so beautiful a dancer as Mary
    b. I've never met a dancer quite so beautiful as Mary

For an interesting refinement of Larson's analysis of the ambiguity of *beautiful dancer* that may account for the loss of the nonintersective reading of the adjective in such contexts as *a beautiful young dancer*, see Saba 2008.

Also note that in other languages an adjective like 'beautiful' may not be similarly ambiguous. *Bello* 'beautiful' in Italian is not, though *meraviglioso* 'wonderful', or *buono* 'good', are. Similarly, *schön* 'beautiful' and *wunderbar* 'wonderful' in German are not, though *groß* 'big', is, as pointed out to me by Waltraud Paul. What is crucial is that there be adjectives, not necessarily the same ones across languages, that are ambiguous in the relevant way.

7. The same holds for Spanish and French. See, for example, Demonte 1982, 280 ("La differencia de posición no correlaciona con la oposición intersectivo–no intersectivo.... En realidad, el único principio que puede formularse con alguna certeza es que los adjetivos que aparecen 'exclusivamente' antes del nombre son exclusivamente no-intersectivos.... No puede formularse ningún principio equivalente para los adjetivos pospuestos"; also see Demonte 2008, 72–73); Abeillé and Godard 1999, note 12 ("Avec les subsectives qui ont naturellement les deux positions, comme *immense*, les deux interprétations sont disponibles pour le A postposé; *C'est un artiste immense* (en tant qu'homme/par sa taille/ou en tant qu'artiste/par son talent)").

Morzycki (2006, 2009), in analyzing the nonintersective use of size adjectives as adverbial, or degree, modifiers (like in the reading of *big drinker* that corresponds to 'someone who drinks a lot'), claims that such a reading is available in Spanish only prenominally. From such cases as (i), and from the Italian case in (ii), it seems however that in Romance that reading is not entirely excluded from the postnominal position:

(i) ?Un fumador grande de cigarrillos (tiene riesgos de sufrir enfermedades
    a smoker big of cigars (has risks to suffer diseases
pulmonares) (Maria Martinez Atienza, personal communication)
of-the-lungs)
'A big cigar smoker (risks suffering from lung deseases)'

(ii) ?Gianni è un ammiratore grandissimo di Gorbaciov
    Gianni is an admirer very-big of Gorbachev
'Gianni is a very big admirer of Gorbachev (= Gianni admires Gorbachev very much')

If idiomatic readings of a noun plus an adjective are only possible when the adjective allows for a nonintersective interpretation, the fact that in Romance postnominal adjectives can induce an idiomatic reading (see section 7.2) provides further evidence that postnominal adjectives in Romance can be nonintersective.

8. Also see Ludlow 1989 and the references cited there. Adjectives relative to a comparison class are referred to as "subsective" in Chierchia and McConnell-Ginet 1990, 370ff., in that, contrary to intersective adjectives (*Pavarotti is a pink tadpole*), they (*Pavarotti is a large tadpole*) do not allow the inference N_{proper} is A and an N_{common} (*Pavarotti is large and a tadpole*) but only the weaker N_{proper} is an N_{common} (*Pavarotti is a tadpole*). For the standard semantic classification of adjectives see Partee 1995 and Kamp and Partee 1995. In Partee 2003a, 2003b, 2007, partly redressing her own earlier analyses, she points out that the "NP/PP Splitting" phenomenon of Polish (Nowak 2000) and other Slavic languages (Gouskova 2000; Mehlhorn 2001) casts doubt on the standard semantic classification into intersective, subsective, privative, and modal adjectives. The main divide, as shown by the "NP/PP Splitting" phenomenon, appears rather to be between intersective ('carnivorous', etc.), subsective ('skillful', etc.), and privative ('fake', etc.), on the one hand, which allow splitting in Polish, and such adjectives as 'poor' in the sense of 'pitiful' and modal adverbial adjectives (like 'former', 'alleged', etc.) on the other, which do not. Crucially, she also points out that the adjectives "that cannot split also cannot occur predicatively." This semantic gen-

eralization seems to converge with the conclusion reached here that the main syntactic divide is between "adverbial" direct modification adjectives and those that derive from (reduced) relative clauses (as a consequence of their being able to occur in predicate position). On the possible double nature of 'fake, false' in Italian (and English), see section 6.1.

9. I thank Chris Kennedy for calling my attention to this ambiguity. For detailed discussion of the syntactic and semantic conditions licensing the relative and the absolute readings of superlatives, see Szabolcsi 1986, Farkas and Kiss 2000, and the references cited there. The ambiguity was apparently first noted in Ross 1964. Also see Stateva 1999, 2000, Sharvit and Stateva 2002, and Schueler 2005.

10. Subjunctive relatives in indefinite DPs in Italian induce a nonspecific interpretation of the indefinite DP (*Cercano una segretaria che sappia tradurre in cinese* 'They are looking for a secretary who can translate into Chinese'). However given that such relatives are only possible if embedded in a modal (*irrealis*) context, the presence of a prenominal adjective does not give rise to a conflict of interpretation, because the adjective in that context does not force a specific reading of the indefinite DP: *Cercano una brava segretaria che sappia tradurre in cinese* 'They are looking for an expert secretary who can translate into Chinese'.

11. Given that extraction is blocked from specific DPs (see Fiengo and Higginbotham's (1981) Specificity Condition), there should be a contrast between the following two cases (in Italian):

(i) a. Non ho   che una foto   piccola di tutti i   miei figli
       not I-have but a   photo small   of all   the my children
       'I only have a small photo of all my children'
    b. Non ho   che una piccola foto   di tutti i   miei figli
       not I-have but a   small   photo of all   the my children
       'I only have a small photo of all my children'

Indeed, (ia), where the adjective is postposed, allows both the reading where *tutti i miei figli* 'all my children' scopes over *una foto* 'a photo' ('I only have different small photos, one for each of my children'), arguably as a consequence of its extraction from the DP, and the reading where there is only one small photo depicting all of my children together (one > all). Example (ib), on the other hand, only allows the second reading (one > all). We can attribute this effect to the prenominal position of the adjective, which forces a specific interpretation of the indefinite DP, and thus prevents the extraction of *tutti i miei figli* from it, forcing the other reading (all > one). Examples with "LF" extractions like (i) are clearer than examples of overt extractions of *di* 'of' phrases because of the interfering factor of base-generated *di* phrases in sentence-initial position (Barbaud 1976).

12. Other adjectives showing a similar semantics are *undisclosed, unexpected, unspecified*, and so on. See Abusch and Rooth 1997.

13. I abstract away from a third reading of *different* (the "reciprocal" one, for which see Moltmann 1992; Beck 2000, 104). I also abstract away from an additional distinction that Beck (2000) draws within the class of NP-dependent readings between plural and universal quantifier NP-dependent readings (which happen to be rendered by two distinct adjectives in German), for which also see

Tovena and Van Peteghem 2003. On French *différent* see Laca and Tasmowski 2001, 2003, 2004, as well as Tovena and Van Peteghem 2003. Also see Alrenga 2006 and Brasoveanu 2008, 2009.

14. The inappropriateness of this reading is brought out more clearly in the following context, which provides a discourse-salient item of comparison for 'different':

(i) a.   Piero vive a Roma, ma...
    b. #Gianni e Mario vivono in **differenti** città
    c.   Gianni e Mario vivono in città **differenti**
        'Piero lives in Rome, but... Gianni and Mario live in different cities'

15. The fact that for some of these properties the postnominal interpretation cannot be tested in English (because of the limited availability of the postnominal position) should not be seen as a problem. The situation is still compatible with the generalization that the postnominal position in English is limited to interpretations available to adjectives in the predicate position of a relative clause. There would only be a problem if the postnominal position were available to a certain adjective and its interpretation were not that of the adjective in the predicate position of a relative clause.

16. This should not be taken to mean that prenominal adjectives in Italian (Romance) are never ambiguous. They are whenever they belong to two (or more) of the classes of adjectives that can occur prenominally with the properties associated to the prenominal position seen above. Consider, for example, the ambiguity of *grande* 'great or big' in (i):

(i) De Laurentiis è stato un grande   produttore cinematografico
    De Laurentiis was   a   great-or-big producer   film
    'De Laurentis was a great/big film producer'

That the ambiguity is a function of the structural position that the adjective occupies (rather than of a simple lexical ambiguity) is shown by the fact that the two readings can co-occur (in the order 'great' > 'big'):

(ii) De Laurentiis è stato un grandissimo grande   produttore
     De Laurentiis was   a   really great big/*really big great producer
     cinematografico
     film
     'De Laurentis was a really great big film producer'

(Also see Abeillé and Godard 1999, 13, for the similar case of French *un gros fumeur* 'someone who smokes a lot or a fat smoker'). Another structural ambiguity is that of *vecchio* 'old' (*la vecchia bicicletta di Gianni* 'Gianni's old bicycle') between what Larson and Cho (1999, 2003) call the N-modifying ('the bicycle is old') and the POSS-modifying ('the bicycle that Gianni formerly possessed') readings. If both are prenominal, with some degree of cumbersomeness (*la vecchia vecchia bicicletta di Gianni* 'Gianni's old old bicycle'), the first *vecchia* is necessarily interpreted as POSS-modifying and the second *vecchia* as N-modifying, just as in English. The better alternative is with the higher (POSS-modifying) *vecchia* in prenominal position and the lower (N-modifying) *vecchia* in postnominal position (*la vecchia bicicletta vecchia di Gianni*). Differently from their note 5, I cannot easily have the POSS-modifying *vecchia* in postnominal position. On the ambiguity of French *vieux* and English *old*, see Bouillon 1999 and Taylor 1992.

17. The same is true for the absolute interpretation of superlatives. Szabolcsi (1986, 255ff.) makes the interesting observation that absolute superlatives pattern with definite/specific noun phrases (the absolute and the specific interpretations are also found, as noted above, with adjectives in prenominal position in Romance), whereas comparative superlatives pattern with indefinite/nonspecific ones (again the relative and the nonspecific interpretations are found together with adjectives in postnominal position in Romance).

18. One of the reviewers doubts "that all properties enumerated under *direct modification* hold at once," adding that "it is semantically not possible for an adjective to be non-restrictive and non-intersective at the same time (e.g. *noiose* is nonrestrictive and very clearly intersective in (7))." While it may be difficult to tell apart the nonintersective reading of *noioso* in (7) ('he lectured in a boring way') from the intersective one ('events that were lectures and were boring', which I would still take not to be available prenominally), it is certainly true that an adjective can be nonrestrictive and nonintersective at the same time. See for example (i), in the 'dance beautifully' reading:

(i) Ieri abbiamo avuto modo di ammirare una meravigliosa ballerina
    'Yesterday, we had the opportunity to admire a beautiful dancer'

Following Siegel (1976a), Alexiadou, Haegeman, and Stavrou (2007, 336) claim that the restrictive/nonrestrictive and the intersective/nonintersective distinctions are independent of one another because *beautiful* in *Olga is the beautiful dancer on stage* can also be interpreted as nonintersective and restrictive. But this appears dubious, since one cannot easily contrast the adjective in the nonintersective interpretation as is normally possible with adjectives used restrictively. See *I want to hire the beautiful dancer, not the lousy one!*

19. There are only a few exceptions to this generalization. Adjectives like *akimbo, aplenty*, and *galore* can only be postnominal, yet cannot be found in predicate position (Ferris 1993, 49). A potential problem of a different kind is provided by *sinistro* 'left' and *destro* 'right', which are nonpredicative (**questa mano è sinistra/ destra* 'this hand is left/right') and yet seem to be restrictive and intersective (properties that were seen to go together with the possibility of occupying the predicate position of a relative clause). Perhaps they are syntactically complex modifiers incorporating a silent locative phrase (AT THE left/right SIDE), and directly modify the NP. Interestingly, Anna Cardinaletti tells me that her son, at the age of four and a half, also used these two adjectives in prenominal position (which for him too was exclusively reserved for direct modification adjectives).

20. This ordering is confirmed by the contrast between (ia) and (ib), observed by Barbara Citko (as reported in Larson 1998, 155):

(i) a. The INVISIBLE visible stars include these
    b. *The VISIBLE invisible stars include these

The first is coherent, because it refers to intrinsically visible stars that happen to be invisible at the moment; (ib) is not, under normal conditions (it refers to a situation in which intrinsically invisible stars are said to be visible at the moment). Of course, it too would become coherent if, for example, the stars were invisible with the naked eye, but contingently visible using a telescope.

21. Also see the case of *wrong* mentioned in note 5 in this chapter.

22. This order is also shown by other adjectives that are ambiguous between an intersective and a nonintersective reading—for example, *old*, which is ambiguous, among other readings, between 'aged' (intersective), and 'of long standing' (nonintersective). See *he is an old* (aged) *old* (of long standing) *friend* (DeGraff and Mandelbaum 1993; Scott 2002, note 43), which finds an exact parallel in the German *Er ist ein alter alter Freund* (Sauereisen 2005, section 3). Also see the case of *the good* (= morally good) *good* (= fast, efficient) *typist* discussed in Jackendoff 1997, 62, and Scott 2002, 112. English may also have, like Italian (see note 16), a nonintersective usage of old 'aged', which however is more difficult to tease apart in English from its predicative intersective usage.

23. Boucher (2006, 52) also notes that postnominally, in French, individual-level adjectives are closer to the noun than stage-level ones, the mirror image of the English prenominal case observed by Larson (1998):

(i) a.   Les étoiles visibles invisibles
         the stars   visible invisible
         'The visible stars invisible'
    b. *Les étoiles invisibles visibles
         the stars   invisible visible
         'The invisible stars visible'

24. Also compare the double occurrence of *sbagliato* 'wrong' in postnominal position in Italian with that of prenominal *wrong* in English (note 5 in this chapter). In Italian the readings are reversed:

(i) Abbiamo discusso   la risposta sbagliata (= incorrect)
    we-have discussed the answer   wrong
    sbagliata (= which it was wrong for us to discuss)
    wrong
    'We discussed the wrong wrong answer'

25. Although the present work corroborates Sproat and Shih's fundamental insight of the existence of two different types of modification, and of the presence of ordering restrictions for only one of them, it differs from their work in a number of respects. For example, I do not take a "direct modification" adjective in combination with the noun to behave as a syntactic word (see chapter 4, especially section 4.1.2); nor do I follow Sproat and Shih in analyzing all Chinese adjectives followed by *de* as (reduced) relative clauses, and all *de*-less ones as compounds (see the appendix, section A.1). I would also give a different analysis to some of the facts of some of the languages discussed by them, even though their work has in general been greatly inspiring.

26. I have omitted in (64) (and (65)) the case where the two readings are in conflict with each other (as is the case with the specificity- and non-specificity-inducing readings).

27. On the basis of crosslinguistic evidence, in Cinque 2005 it is actually suggested that head movement within DP is unavailable, and that only movement of phrases containing the (pronounced) NP are possible (within a unique UG structure of Merge). See section 3.6 for some discussion of this point.

Chapter 3

1. This idea rests in fact on a long tradition. See Bolinger 1967, Siegel 1976a, 1976b, Sproat and Shih 1988, 1990, as well as Cinque 1994 and Alexiadou and Wilder 1998, among many others. Also see Kayne 2008b, note 8.

2. In this connection, see Lehmann's (1984, 201–203) and Hawkins's (1990, 241–243; 1994, 269–274) typological generalization that adjectives are found closer to the head noun than relative clauses. They note that while (ia) and (ib) (as well as (ie) and (if)) are all attested orders, no language appears to have as its basic word order adjectives further away from the N than relative clauses ((ic) and (id)):

(i) a. RC Adj N   c. *Adj RC N   (also e. Adj N RC)
    b. N Adj RC   d. *N RC Adj   (also f. RC N Adj)

Rijkhoff (1998, 362) claims that relative clauses in Dargwa (North East Caucasian) and Finnish follow "all other prenominal modifiers, yielding [dem num A [Rel] N]." No clear indication of this is to be found in Sumbatova and Mutalov 2003, 161–162, 183ff., or in Sulkala and Karjalainen 1992, 87–88, respectively. But Dal Pozzo (2007, 26) explicitly states that in Finnish, APs can either precede or follow prenominal reduced relative clauses, giving (ii) as an example:

(ii) nämä kolme (komeaa)   toimistossaan työskentelevää (komeaa)   miestä
     these three (fascinating) office-INESS working   (fascinating) men
     'these three fascinating men working in the office'

Interestingly, however, it seems that only indirect modification adjectives can precede reduced relative clauses. Direct modification ones are only possible *after* the reduced relative clause, as the following contrasts (kindly provided by Lena Dal Pozzo, personal communication) show:

(iii) a. tuo   huomenna kilpaileva mahdollinen   voittaja
         that-NOM tomorrow playing   probable-NOM winner-NOM
         'the probable winner that is playing tomorrow'
      b. ?*tuo   mahdollinen   huomenna kilpaileva voittaja
         that-NOM probable-NOM tomorrow playing   winner-NOM

(iv) a. tuo   toimistossani   työskentelevä kova
        that-NOM office-INESS+POSS1sg working   hard-NOM
        that   in-my-office   working   heavy
        tupakoitsija
        smoker-NOM
        smoker
        'that heavy smoker that works in my office'

b. ?*tuo   kova   toimistossani   työskentelevä
   that-NOM hard-NOM office-INESS+POSS1sg working
   that   heavy   in-my-office   working
   tupakoitsija
   smoker-NOM
   smoker

The (b) examples become better, as Lena Dal Pozzo also observed, if the reduced relative clause is pronounced with a parenthetical intonation, a situation that has a perfect analogue in German and English (see note 32 in the next chapter).

3. I consider only reduced relative clauses here. As noted in Cinque 2003, 2008a, the prenominal origin of relative clauses allows both raising and matching derivations in accord with antisymmetry. In the present framework, Rubin's (1994, 1997, 2002) Mod head, which he proposes in order to reduce adnominal intersective modification to the function composition needed for predicative adjectives, may perhaps be directly identified with the INFL of the reduced relative clause. At the same time, given the existence of direct modification adjectives, it is not clear whether adnominal modification can be reduced entirely to function composition.

4. Although it seems that the two readings cannot easily obtain simultaneously (#*who bought the tallest* (comparative) *most expensive* (absolute) *building*?), the relative ordering of the two readings can be indirectly inferred from the interpretive patterns characterizing Italian and English, plus the fact that prenominally, in Italian, only the absolute reading is possible.

5. The same considerations brought up in the previous note hold for the relative order of the two readings, specific and nonspecific.

6. I differ here from Alexiadou (2003, section 2.2) and Laenzlinger (2005a, 654), who assume that nonpredicative adjectives occur higher in DP (more distant from the N) than predicative ones.

7. Other languages that, like English, are reported to have a preferred, or unmarked, rather than a rigid, order of adjectives are Arabic (both Standard and regional; Fassi Fehri 1998a, 1998b, 1999), Finnish and Ibibio (Scott 2002, 99), Russian (Pereltsvaig 2007, section 2), as well as Bosnian/Croatian/Serbian and Greek (see the appendix, sections A.3 and A.5).

8. I abstract away here from the important, but distinct, questions of what the precise order of adjectives is (see for discussion Barrit 1952; Lance 1968; Quirk et al. 1972, 925; Dixon 1982; Fries 1986; Adamson 2000; Scott 2002; and the references cited there), and what the ultimate cause of that order is. Of the many attempts to derive it from external, mostly semantic, cognitive, or pragmatic, principles, none seems entirely convincing (see, for example, Vendler 1968; Hetzron 1978; Seiler 1978; Dixon 1982; Risselada 1983; Posner 1986; Sproat and Shih 1988, 1990; Frawley 1992, section 10.3; Zuber 1996; Dirven 1999; Adamson 2000; Muromatsu 2001; Vandelanotte 2002; Wulff 2003; Kiefer 2004; Bouchard 2005; Matushansky 2005a, section 5.4; Champollion 2006; Teodorescu 2006; Bakker 2007; and for an overview Feist 2008). On the latter question also see the discussion in Scott 2002, section 2.2, and in Alexiadou, Haegeman, and Stavrou

2007, part III, chapter 1, section 3. Whether adjective order should be encoded syntactically via merger in dedicated functional projections (see section 4.1.1) remains an open question. But leaving the merger of adjectives entirely free, with the illegitimate orders filtered out in the semantics (Bošković 2009, section 2), begs the question of why UG avails itself of the semantic classes of adjectives that it has rather than of other conceivable ones. Thinking of the many "adverbial" adjectives that there are, the existence of remarkable gaps (*a just(ly) departure 'an event of having just left', *an already winner 'an individual who has already won', a luck(il)y survivor 'an individual who has luckily survived', etc.) may in fact be taken to suggest that the syntax/numeration of UG is so built as to specify which actual classes as well as members (and corresponding projections) are admitted, and which are not.

9. In (10a), *heavy drinker* can be understood nonintersectively, as 'someone who (allegedly) drinks a lot'; in (10b), it is understood intersectively only, as 'an (alleged) drinker who weighs a lot'. Similarly in (11). Posner (1986, 312 n. 8) observes that *a light heavy drinker* is interpreted as 'a light person that drinks heavily' and *a heavy light drinker* as 'a heavy person that drinks lightly', and not the other way round. Similar effects are observable in other Germanic languages. See for example the German case in (i), given in Sauereisen 2005, section 2:

(i) a. ein arroganter großer   Idiot
       an arrogant   big (degree) idiot
    b. ein großer arroganter Idiot
       a   tall   arrogant   idiot
    (cf. *Der idiot ist groß* 'The idiot is tall/*big (degree)')

10. For the original discussion of this ambiguity and for different accounts of it, see Partee [1983] 1997, Partee and Borschev 2000, and Larson and Cho 1999, 2003. Also see note 16 in chapter 2 above. The same ambiguity is found in Guaraní with the nominal tense suffix *-kue* (Tonhauser 2006, 159).

11. It is also possible that *alleged* has a usage as a focusing adjective, much like the corresponding evidential (and epistemic) adverbs (see Cinque 1999, section 1.6), thus giving the impression (like *allegedly*, cf. ⟨*Allegedly*⟩ *he quickly left his office* ⟨*allegedly*⟩ *at 5 o'clock*) that it has no fixed position. As with the corresponding adverbs in their focusing usage (see Kayne 1998), *alleged* could then be taken to attract what falls under its narrow scope, apparently reversing its position relative to the adjective *former* (which should be *alleged* > *former*):

(i) a. [former [thief]] → merger of a focus head and attraction of NP
    b. [thief F° [former t]] → merger of *alleged* (in the Spec of a head)
    c. [alleged X° [thief F° [former t]]] → merger of a head and attraction of the remnant
    d. [[former t] Y° [alleged X° [thief F° [t]]]]

In this respect, *alleged* would behave much like the focusing adjective *unico* 'only' in Demonte's (1999b, 51) pair *mi unica divertida amica* 'my only funny colleague', and *mi divertida unica amica* 'my funny unique colleague'. The viability of this conjecture needs to be further checked, however, just as possible factors limiting it need to be. For example, certain direct modifiers of the NP cannot easily be "stranded" by the NP, to be later moved within a remnant, as the meaning of (10b), and the ungrammaticality of *A fréquent alleged flier* discussed in section 5.1, seem to show. In other contexts, however, this may be marginally possible. Taking (i) to represent the canonical order of *occasional* and *heavy*, it seems that (iib) is marginally acceptable in the context of (iia) (thanks to Megan Rae for pointing this fact out to me):

(i) (I am) an occasional heavy smoker

(ii) a. Speaker A: I'm only an occasional smoker
 b. Speaker B: But you are a fairly heavy occasional smoker

12. For nondefinite superlatives, see the discussion in Teodorescu 2006 and the references cited there.

13. The sentence was suggested to me by one of the reviewers, who also pointed out that superlatives are not interpreted intersectively ("the highest mountain is not the highest object and a mountain"; cf. Heim 1999). Larson and Cho (2003, note 19) observe that a prenominal adjective that is otherwise under the scope of a relative clause (like *old* in example (ia)) necessarily takes scope over the relative clause when it is made superlative (see (ib)):

(i) a. the old antique that was rotten with age
 b. the oldest antique that was rotten with age

This suggests once more that, to become superlative, an adjective must move to a scope position higher than that of relative clauses, which may also be at the basis of the fact, noted by Kayne (2008b, note 15), that "in Persian (Moshiri 1988, 24) superlatives end up prenominal, while ordinary adjectives and even comparatives are generally postnominal." Kayne, in the same note, also observes that adjectives, when superlative, can be higher than numerals too (*the blackest two dogs that I've ever seen*), which are higher than direct modification adjectives (and arguably lower than the Merge position of restrictive relative clauses (cf. Cinque 2008b, note 35; 2008a). Megan Rae (personal communication) tells me that for her the superlative adjective can license negative polarity *any* even if it follows the numeral (*the two blackest dogs that anyone ever owned*).

14. To judge from Saxon 2000, 99, the same is true of the related Athapaskan language Dogrib. In both languages attributive adjectives are expressed through relative clauses (Keren Rice, personal communication; Saxon 2000, 99), nonpredicative ones (*former, future,* etc.) being rendered with periphrases ('the one who used to be..., etc.'; Keren Rice, personal communication). But Rice informs me that there are a few adjectival meanings ('new', 'flat', 'old') "that are uninflected stems that, at least phonologically, are part of the same word as the noun that they modify." It is thus not entirely clear whether (direct modification) attributive adjectives are entirely missing in the language, or are just a closed class of very few items. The same may be true of Ika (Chibchan, Colombia), in which most adnominal adjectives occur inside a (head-internal) relative clause (Frank 1990, 20; Baker 2003a, 207), yet a few occur in direct attribution (Frank 1990, 19–20, 32–33). Baker (2003a, 240, n. 34; 2003b) claims that adjectives in Japanese (at least those of the *utsukushi* class) can enter the DP only as predicates of (reduced)

relative clauses (hence their free ordering, their necessarily intersective interpretation, etc.).

15. They "fall into four distinct semantic classes, and show ordering restrictions [Color > Dimension > Quality > Quantity]." Ajíbóyè (2001; 2005, chapter 1, section 1.2.4) also notes that the rigid order of the adjectives in Yoruba is the mirror image of the English order, which is consistent with the fact that the head N is initial and the demonstrative final: N > A_{Color} > $A_{Dimension/size}$ > $A_{Quality}$ > Numeral/Quantifier > Demonstrative.

16. Madugu (1976, 93) gives similar pairs (see (i)), also pointing out (pp. 89ff.) that one can have 'Olu has wisdom' instead of 'Olu is wise':

(i) a. Olú jé ọmọ rere b. *Olú rere
  Olu is child good Olu good
  'Olu is a good child' 'Olu is good'

Savosavo (Papuan; Wegener 2008, section 4.3.1) and Iká (Niger-Congo; Maho 1998, 9) present a similar picture, though the latter also has adjectives that can be used both attributively and predicatively. Attributive-only adjectives show in Iká a rigid order, which is the same as the English (unmarked) order, for size and color adjectives, even if all other modifiers show an inverse order after the N (N A_{size} A_{color} Num Dem Rel.Cl) (Maho 1998, 21):

(i) a. *ŋkitɛ ogi uku
  dog black big
 b. ŋkitɛ uku ogi
  dog big black
  'a big black dog'

17. Other languages appear to be like Yoruba and Gbaya Mbodómó in having a closed class of "adnominal-only" adjectives. Welmers and Welmers (1969) as well as Welmers (1973, 258–262) mention Igbo, Siegel (1976a) mentions Ngamambo, Koopman (1984, 64–66) mentions Vata and Gbadi (all Niger-Congo languages), Osumi (1995, 77–78) mentions Tinrin (Austronesian), Dutta Baruah and Bapui (1996, 56) mentions Hmar (Tibeto-Burman), Wetzer (1996, 77–78) mentions Kassena and Babungo (Niger-Congo). To express adjectival predications Kassena and Babungo utilize a strategy still different from that of Yoruba or Gbaya Mbodómó. As Wetzer (1996, 77) points out, a sentence like *This man is tall* is rendered as *This man is a tall man*, where "the head of the predicative noun phrase is usually some kind of dummy noun, such as "man", "child", or "thing"." The same appears to be true of the Dravidian language Tamil, in which "a sentence like English 'this is good' is not possible [...and] must have the form 'this thing is a good thing'..." (Schiffman 1999, 141), as well as the Papuan languages Yagaria (Baker 2003a, 206–207) and Hua (Haiman 1978, 567; Haiman 1980, 268; Schachter 1985, 16), which also have a closed class of adnominal-only adjectives. See, for example, (ia,b), from Haiman 1978, 567:

(i) a. *Bura fu nupa baie b. Bura fu nupa fu baie
  that pig black is   that pig black pig is
  'That pig is black'   'That pig is a black pig'

This strategy also appears to be available in Korean (see Kang 2007, 131).

18. See for example Cinque 2000, Shlonsky 2000, 2004, and Sichel 2000a, 2000b, 2002, 2003, on Semitic, as well as Cinque 2005 for a more general claim that only NP movement (with or without pied piping) is available within the DP crosslinguistically. Laenzlinger (2000, 2005a, 2005b), Alexiadou (2001, 2003), Mallén (2001, 2002), Alexiadou, Haegeman, and Stavrou (2007, 364ff.), and Knittel (2005, 216) also assume the presence of certain DP-internal phrasal movements, though their analysis differs from the one developed here in a number of respects (see notes 1 and 18 in chapter 2, note 6 in this chapter, the last paragraph of section 5.1, notes 3 and 7 in chapter 6, and the appendix, A.5, and notes 27, 29). If head movement is to be abandoned in DP in favor of phrasal movement (pace Dehé and Samek-Lodovici 2007), Longobardi's (1994, 2001) results based on N-to-D movement should perhaps be rethought of in terms of NP movement to Spec,DP (for which also see Giusti 2002, section 3.4).

19. For the apparent problem raised for the phrasal movement analysis by the fact that complement and adjunct PPs are not dragged along by the NP, or a larger phrase containing it, when these move, see section 6.2.

20. This line of argumentation is developed within a broader context in Cinque 2009. Abels and Neeleman (2009), without doing away with movement entirely, propose returning to a direct "base generation" of orders excluded by Kayne's 1994 Linear Correspondence Axiom. I would like to keep to that axiom and still feel that a system that minimizes base generation (to one structure/order for all languages), deriving all other structures/orders via independently needed types of movement, is more interesting. Abels and Neeleman's (2009) system, in deriving certain orders either via base generation or via movement, appears to me to introduce a redundancy that should perhaps be avoided ("For example, (1biii) can be base-generated as above or derived on the basis of, for example, (1bii) by short movement of N as in (10)" (p. 9)).

21. In certain languages, (only) one of these elements, if it bears a focus feature, can apparently move to an initial focus position. See note 4 in chapter 5 and Cinque 2009, note 20, for relevant references.

Chapter 4

1. Bernstein (1993b, 75–76) and Kayne (2005b, section 2.1) also postulate the existence of (certain) "functional adjectives." This section draws substantially from the introduction to Cinque 2006.

2. In the wake of Lyons (1968, section 9.5.2), and a much earlier tradition, I take "lexical" categories to be distinguished from "functional," or "grammatical," ones in being *open* classes (classes with open membership) in opposition to the latter, which are *closed*. See Cinque 2004a, section 1, for the parallel claim that adverbs too should be considered functional elements, because there are languages where they constitute a closed and quite limited class (Dixon 1982, 40; Schachter 1985, 21ff.; Reesink 1990). Richard Kayne has recently advanced the very interesting conjecture that if most "lexical" verbs are derived from the incorporation of a noun into a "light" verb (à la Hale and Keyser 1993), possibly nouns are

the only truly open class. Interestingly, Dixon (1982, 225), reports that "some languages from North Australia and some from New Guinea have only a small set of monomorphemic verbs (varying from about six to around 100 members)." Also see Pawley 2006.

3. Dixon 2004, 36ff.

4. Backhouse 1984.

5. Lindsey and Scancarelli 1985.

6. This is not necessary, though. They will still be a closed class if in the language in question most "adjectival predication" is expressed by verbs and/or nouns. Dixon (2004, 29) reports two north Carib languages (Hixkaryana and Tiriyó) as having a closed class of *predicate-only* adjectives (on the order of thirty/forty).

7. A neurolinguistic study (Kemmerer 2000) would seem to suggest that knowledge of the grammatically relevant semantic features that influence prenominal adjective order (categories like 'size', 'color', etc.) can be selectively impaired, while knowledge of grammatically irrelevant aspects of adjective meaning (like, for example, perceptual and conceptual features distinguishing 'brown' from 'black') is not. This may perhaps be construed as additional evidence for the functional nature of (direct modification) adjectives.

8. Nonetheless exceptions exist even in English (and Germanic, more generally, for which see Holmberg and Rijkhoff 1998, 97, and Kester 1996, 168). One is provided by *easy-to-please* constructions (see (i)); another by comparative cases like those in (ii), but other types exist as well (see (iii)):

(i) a. a difficult to please child (Sadler and Arnold 1994, 190)
  b. a hard to pronounce name (Sadler and Arnold 1994, 190)

(ii) a. a bigger than usual ice-cream cone (Svenonius 1992, note 15)
  b. (He showed) a larger than average capacity for inaptitude (Radford 1989, example (45a))
  c. Linguists are showing a greater than ever fascination for functional fantasies (Radford 1989, example (45b))
  d. a larger than expected profit (Pullum and Huddleston 2002, 551)

(iii) the much talked about new show (Sadler and Arnold 1994, 190)

Even if they are quite restricted, most such cases become productive if extraposition of the complement or adjunct takes place. See Berman 1974, especially chapters 1 and 6; Riemsdijk 2001; Matushansky 2005a, section 5.2; and Fleisher 2008.

9. Among the other Slavic languages, Czech, Slovak, Sorbian, Bosnian/Croatian/Serbian, and Slovene obligatorily place complements before the prenominal adjective, while Macedonian, Polish, and Ukrainian, like Bulgarian and Russian, place them after it (see Siewierska and Uhlířová 1998, 135–136).

10. For it could be claimed, at least in the present framework, that the nonphrasal nature of direct modification adjectives is simply obscured by the presence on the same side of the noun of phrasal indirect modification adjectives with their different properties.

11. Danish is similar. See Julien 2005, 6.

12. The impossibility for a complement (or adjunct) to follow the head, which still defies proper understanding, is generally attributed to a ban on right recursion for phrases found on (certain) left branches. For discussion and different proposals, see Zwarts 1974; Emonds 1976, 18–19; Williams 1981, 1982; Giorgi and Longobardi 1991, 95–100; Escribano 2004; among others. It also follows from Biberauer, Holmberg, and Roberts's (2008) Final-over-Final Constraint (FOFC), which rules out head final over head initial orders, although examples like (6) are unexpected. In English, preposed participles, arguably reduced relative clauses (see section 5.4), cannot take complements preceding the participle either, just as adjectives cannot take complements preceding the adjective (cf. (i) and (ii)):

(i) *a to me recently sent book

(ii) *an of his children proud father

13. The exceptions mentioned in note 8 to the ban on complements and adjuncts for English prenominal adjectives extend to nonpredicative adjectives, which thus provides evidence that they too are (may be) phrasal. See, for example,

(i) a. He is a *bigger than usual* pasta eater

14. A similar case is provided by the synthetic absolute superlatives of Italian, at least if -*issim*- (and -*o*) betray the presence of separate functional heads above AP. See, for example, (ia) and (ib) in the nonpredicative interpretation of *buono* as 'considerable', and *vecchio* as 'longtime':

(i) a. questi sono in   buonissima   parte inutilizzabili
       these are   to-a very-considerable extent nonutilizable
   b. lui è un mio   vecchissimo   collaboratore
      he-is a   longtime collaborator of mine.

For the analogous possibility of superlative modification of (direct modification) *de*-less adjectives in Chinese, see Paul 2005, section 4.2.

15. *AP enough* arguably has a trace of the AP to the right of *enough*: [[AP$_i$ [enough t$_i$]] NP] (see Kayne 2005b, 32).

16. The presence of *of* (*how old of a friend*) renders fronting of nonpredicative adjectives quite marginal if not ungrammatical (which may indicate the presence of predicate inversion in such cases). The well-formedness of (9) instead suggests (pace Troseth 2004) that the construction without *of* does not involve predicate inversion (before A-bar movement). The loss of the 'pitiable' reading of *poor* in *Bill Bradley is too poor of a man* arguably depends on the presence of *of*, and in addition, as Troseth (2004, note 1) herself notes, on the presence of the degree word *too*. For a nonmovement analysis of the construction, see Abney 1987, chapter 4, 3.2a.

17. The evidence reviewed in this section also seems to argue against the weaker hypothesis (Bernstein 1991, 1993b; DeGraff and Mandelbaum 1993; Zamparelli 1993) that exclusively prenominal adjectives in Romance (like *vecchio* 'old' in the sense of 'longtime', and *mero* 'mere' in Italian) are heads, while postnominal ones are phrases.

18. In section 3.2, Santorini and Mahootian (1995) discuss evidence that they take to suggest that some adjectives may be heads after all. Although English adjectives, as one would expect, are overwhelmingly postnominal in Irish-English code switching when the language of the head is Irish, there are few expletive adjectives (*bloody, fucking,...*) that precede the Irish noun. This fact, however, can hardly be interpreted as evidence for their head status, given that some other high adjectives are also prenominal in Irish (see Stenson 1981, 30, 161 n. 7, as well as Stenson 1990, 177–178, and 195 n. 9).

19. In the present analysis, after the "roll-up" of the NP (shells) around the APs, the noun is plausibly more deeply embedded with respect to specifiers found after it than (the head of) a prenominal specifier is with respect to a lower specifier, or the NP (also see Laenzlinger 2005a, note 36).

20. The fact that even "ergative" (or "unaccusative") adjectives (i.e., those whose subject is merged in complement position; Cinque 1989, 1990b; Stowell 1991; Bennis 2000, 2004; Bentley 2004; Baker 2008, section 3.1.1) can occur prenominally (see (i)) also casts doubt on the pure head status of prenominal adjectives:

(i) Le [PRO note t]   vicende   giudiziarie di Gianni
    the PRO well-known vicissitudes judicial   of Gianni
    'Gianni's well-known judicial vicissitudes'

What I indicated as PRO in (i) (more generally the unpronounced subject of all direct modification adjectives) is possibly smaller than a DP, in that it corresponds only to an NP plus any inner direct modifiers ('[$_{XP}$ [$_{NP}$ vicende] giudiziarie]' in (i)). It remains to be seen whether the highly articulated structure of adjunct modifiers uncovered by Fults (2006, chapter 2) for gradable adjectives in predicate position ([than DP [compared to DP [PP complement [for DP [A]]]]]) is also present silently in their attributive use.

21. Other adjectives for which the preposing operation would have to be blocked include *ill, right* (in one of its readings), *present* (in its locative reading), *glad* (Pullum and Huddleston 2002, 529), and all the adjectives mentioned in section 5.2.2, which begin with the aspectual prefix *a-*. Also see Borsley 1997, note 3.

22. Note that (11) becomes grammatical if a demonstrative is used in place of the article (a demonstrative can also be used in (12)). Spanish is different in that all of the forms corresponding to (11) are possible, though certain other possibilities are blocked (see Kester and Sleeman 2002, Cabredo Hofherr 2005, and the references cited there).

23. For a comparison with other Romance languages, see Brucart and Gràcia 1986, Sleeman 1993, 1996, chapter 2, and the references cited there.

24. Note that the same adjective without the complement is instead possible with the article:

(i) (?)Le persone testarde e   le orgogliose...
    the persons stubborn and the proud....
    'The stubborn people and those proud...'

25. Interestingly, only the locative interpretation of *presenti*, the one found in postnominal position in English, gives unacceptable results. The temporal one is

instead possible: *le condizioni passate, e le presenti, sono tutt'altro che rosee* 'the past conditions, and the present, are all but favorable'.

26. An exception is represented by direct modification adjectives like *solo* 'only', *mero* 'mere', *puro e semplice* 'pure and simple', etc. (see Bernstein 1993b, 70–71).

27. Other Romance languages do not share the same paradigm. See Brucart 1994 for some discussion.

28. Also see Vendler 1968, chapter 6, for many other putative sources one would have to adopt in order to derive nonpredicative adjectives from relative clauses.

29. Also see Berman 1974, section 3.1. A derivation of classificatory adjectives (the other main class of nonpredicative adjectives) from relative clauses raises comparable difficulties. See Levi 1973, 1975, 1978, and Berman 1974, section 3.2.

30. Arguments against deriving attributive adjectives in Spanish, Polish, Japanese, and Korean, from relative clauses are presented in Contreras 1981; Fedorowicz-Bacz 1977; Yamakido 2000, 2007; and Kang 2005, 2006, 2007, respectively. Also see Alexiadou, Haegeman, and Stavrou 2007, 295–306. See, however, Leu 2008, section 4.5, for an attempt at reconciling an approach like that taken here with one involving relativization even for nonpredicative adjectives.

31. Also, nonrestrictive adjectives (in Italian) appear compatible with *only* (see (i)), while nonrestrictive relative clauses are not (see Kayne 1994, 163 n. 65).

(i) I   soli industriosi greci   di Megara (riuscirono a sopravvivere)
    the only industrious Greeks of Megara (managed   to survive)

Further reasons for not deriving nonrestrictive adjectives from nonrestrictive relative clauses (in Chinese) are discussed in Del Gobbo 2004.

32. See Rijkhoff 1998, 362: "In Dutch (as well as e.g. in German and Frisian) the preposed participial construction follows the demonstrative and the numeral." As Martina Witschko (personal communication) pointed out to me, the (b) example in (20) becomes better if the reduced relative clause (*kürzlich angekommene*) has a parenthetical intonation (cf. note 2 in chapter 3). Of course, indirect modification adjectives, which are also reduced relative clauses, should be able to precede participial reduced relative clauses. A case in point may be (i), from Kafka, cited in Koch 2005, section 3:

(i) kleine, unter dem Strassenniveau liegende, durch   paar Treppen
    small under the street-level   lying   through a-few stairs
    erreichbare Läden
    reachable   stores
    'small stores that lie below the level of the street that are reachable by (walking down) a few stairs'

The same situation appears to hold in English. See (ii) versus (iii):

(ii) that beautiful recently arrived letter (Kayne 2005a, 66)

(iii) *That former recently arrived ambassador (barring a parenthetical intonation)

33. The argument that follows is based on Fanselow 1986.

34. The arguments against the presence of PRO in Italian (and French) reduced relative clauses given in Siloni 1995, section 3.2, do not seem to me to be cogent. For example, reduced relative clauses like *Gianni era l'unico tornato contento* '(lit.) Gianni was the only (one) returned happy' are embedded in a DP, hence islands, independently of the status of their subject, and contrast with infinitival clauses like *Gianni era l'unico a tornare contento* '(lit.) Gianni was the only (one) to return happy', which are not so embedded, hence not islands. This is shown by the contrast in (i), where the infinitival clause, but not the reduced relative clause, appears preposable:

(i) a.   A tornare contento, non era l'unico
         'To return happy, he was not the only (one)'
    b.   *?Tornato contento, non era l'unico
         'Returned happy, he was not the only (one)'

Chapter 5

1. *Possible*, in its reduced relative clause reading with Antecedent Contained Deletion (see section 2.3) actually appears to occupy a position even higher than that of ordinary indirect modification adjectives derived from relative clauses, because it has to precede (ordinal and cardinal) numerals (which are higher than reduced relative clauses). See the contrast between (ia) and (ib):

(i) a.   She always goes to see every póssible first two games
    b.   She always goes to see every first two possible games

Only in the former can *possible* have the reduced relative clause reading with Antecedent Contained Deletion. To judge from Schmitt 1996, 115–116, the same may be true of the adjective *wrong* in its reduced relative clause reading with Antecedent Contained Deletion (see chapter 2, note 5):

(ii) a. We discussed the wrong two answers (= which it was wrong for us to discuss)
     b. We discussed the two wrong (= incorrect) answers

If the adjective *wrong* in its reduced relative clause reading with Antecedent Contained Deletion is merged higher than numerals, Schwarz's (2006, 365) argument against Larson's syntactic analysis is weakened.

2. See the references in note 8 of chapter 3, and especially Scott 2002.

3. As noted, size adjectives normally precede color adjectives: *a small black dog* (Bloomfield 1933, 202). Yet their order can be reversed if one wishes to distinguish different groups of individuals of the same size (*I've shown you my black small dogs; now, these are my two brown small dogs*), in which case "some contrastive stress [on the color adjective] is necessary" (Sproat and Shih 1988, 469–470).

4. Also compare (6c) and (i):

(i) the most fréquent alleged flier

Movement of (even direct modification) APs to a focus position seems to be possible in certain languages. See Giusti 1996, 2006, section 3.2, for Albanian;

Demeke 2001, 211 and note 18, for Amharic; Demonte 2008, section 4.4.1.3, for Spanish. The predemonstrative position of nonpredicative adjectives with *de* in Mandarin Chinese (Aoun and Li 2003, 150) may be another case in point (though *de*-less adjectives cannot; cf. Cheung 2005 and Yang 2005, 211). For further relevant references see Cinque 2005, note 23, and Campos 2009, section 2.3.1.8.

5. One way to obtain this (and avoid the recursion restriction) without losing their attributive status could be to assume that their "heavy" character allows them to raise to the Spec of some higher focus projection, with subsequent movement of the entire remnant to their left. That is (omitting previous steps of the derivation),

(i) a. [Focus [proud of their children young fathers]] →
   b. [proud of their children Focus [t young fathers]] →
   c. [[t young fathers] X [proud of their children Focus [t]]]

The fact that such derivations are not available, for the empirical considerations that follow in the text, suggests that no direct modification adjective in English can move to a DP internal focus projection.

6. I have slightly adapted Williams's examples. It should be noted, however, that (6) could involve the passive participle of *allege* rather than the adjective *alleged*.

7. This contrasts with *He is a heavier drinker than his father*, which can retain the nonintersective interpretation. See section 2.4.

8. This is essentially true of Germanic in general. For German, see Riemsdijk 1998, 20, Cinque 1994, 94–95, and the references cited there (though some differences with English exist; see König 1971, 49–50). For Dutch, see Kester 1996, 71–72. For Scandinavian, see Delsing 1993b, 9: "Attributive adjectives in Scandinavian are normally prenominal. However they can also be used postnominally, and then they are referred to as *predicative attributes*.... They are only allowed if the adjective has a complement or an adjunct, or if it is part of a coordination.... As can be seen in [(i)], predicative attributes always take the strong form, just like ordinary predicative adjectives, regardless of the definiteness of the phrase."

(i) en låda försedd/*försedda   med lock
   a box equipped[str/*weak] with lid

Why reduced participial relative clauses in German cannot occur postnominally (see (19) in chapter 4), and why restrictive postnominal bare adjectives are unavailable in Germanic other than English, remains to be understood.

9. But see note 15 on one (expected) restriction on their postnominal position. Napoli (1993, 183) gives examples like those in (ia,b), where the adjective seems to have an interpretation close to a reduced *if/when* clause (but other speakers find them dubious):

(i) a. A lion hungry is a danger to all
   b. A man unhappy is seldom in control of his emotions

10. Larson and Marušič (2004, note 2) note that the impossibility of the prenominal position for adjectives formed with the prefix *a-* (but see Jacobsson 1961 and

Blöhdorn 2009, 80, already mentioned in section 2.10.2 for certain limited exceptions) could be related to Williams's (1981, 1982) Righthand Head Rule (a version of the right recursion restriction mentioned in note 12 in chapter 4) if the head of such adjectives were the prefix *a-* itself. Keenan (2002) contains a brief discussion of the historical derivation of the prefix (from the preposition *on*). Also see Coulter 1983, 118, and Leu 2008, 78 n. 13.

11. When the term *extraposition* is used, here and below, it should be understood as an abbreviation for its antisymmetrical counterpart of leftward attraction followed by further leftward movement of the remnant.

12. In section 4.2, we saw some suggestive evidence that reduced relative clauses are lower than numerals. Cinque (in preparation) reviews some crosslinguistic evidence that full finite restrictive relative clauses are instead merged higher than numerals (and below demonstratives). For evidence that nonrestrictive relative clauses are merged even higher, see Cinque 2008b, note 35.

13. In Italian (more generally, Romance) all kinds of relative clauses—finite, participial, and complex or bare AP, reduced relative clauses—are subject to obligatory "extraposition" (except for highly formal registers, as noted). A comparison between English and Italian may suggest the presence of an implicational scale (itself to be derived): if some relative clause type (of those shown in (14)) obligatorily "extraposes," all those merged higher do likewise, but not necessarily those merged lower. In Italian, for example, bare AP reduced relative clauses (those merged the lowest) obligatorily "extrapose," and so do all higher relative clauses. In English bare AP reduced relative clauses do not "extrapose," the immediately higher participial reduced relative clauses "extrapose" only optionally, and only the highest finite restrictive (and nonrestrictive) relative clauses obligatorily "extrapose."

14. Larson and Takahashi (2007) extend this idea to the (prenominal) relative clauses of Japanese/Korean and other rigid OV languages. For a similar extension to Chinese relative clauses (also prenominal), see Del Gobbo 2005.

The apparent outlier position of stage-level relative clauses w.r.t individual-level relative clauses in these languages, as opposed to English, Italian, and other languages with full finite relative clauses, may indicate that the former are reduced nonfinite relative clauses. Larson and Takahashi (2007) in fact suggest that the apparently free ordering of stage- and individual-level relative clauses in languages like English may be due to the fact that a full finite relative clause contains independent existential and generic operators.

15. The same must hold of *nearby* when occurring postnominally as an indirect modification adjective. When it is used nonrestrictively (i.e., as a direct modification adjective) it expectedly cannot occur postnominally. See (ia,b):

(i) a. The big airbase at nearby Mildenhall
    b. *The big airbase at Mildenhall nearby

On the role of nonpronounced elements, see many of the chapters in Kayne 2005a.

16. This of course does not exclude the possibility that certain participles will be the input to a morphological rule that turns them into adjectives (in which case

they will be compatible with *very*, and not with *very much*). Prenominal present participles in *-ing* appear, for example, to always behave like adjectives (as originally suggested by Borer 1990) since they systematically resist modification by *very much* (*a very much inspiring thought*, *a very much debilitating climate*, etc.). For a detailed analysis of *very, much, well*, and so on and the classes of adjectives and participles with which they combine, see Kennedy and McNally 2005.

17. For additional evidence that not all prenominal active or passive participles are categorially simple adjectives in English see Fabb 1984, section 4.2, Laskova 2006b, as well as the references cited there.

18. This portion of the extended projection of the NP (the ZP of (20)) corresponds, I submit, to a "small" indefinite dP, which is the (external) Head of "matching" relative clauses, the "internal" Head of "raising" relative clauses, and the Head of those Head Internal relative clauses that show an indefiniteness restriction (Williamson 1987). Some evidence to this effect is discussed in Cinque 2008a and in preparation.

19. Slavic languages pattern with English in having "bare" AP reduced relative clauses in prenominal position only. All of their adjectives precede the N, with Polish being exceptional w.r.t. classificatory and nationality adjectives. See for example Sussex 1975; Willim 2000, 2001; Rutkowski 2007; Rutkowski and Progovac 2005, 2006; Cetnarowska, Pysz, and Trugman 2008; and the references cited there. Also see Trugman 2005, forthcoming, on Russian, and Rutkowski 2007 for differences between Polish and Russian, where the phenomenon is apparently optional and is only found in generic contexts. Slavic languages also pattern like English in the behavior of indefinite pronouns, which precede reduced relative clause APs. See Larson and Marušič 2004 on Slovenian, and the Bulgarian minimal pair *nesto interesno* 'something interesting' versus *interesno nesto* 'an interesting thing', *nesto* being ambiguous between an indefinite pronoun and a common noun (Iliyana Krapova, personal communication).

20. As we saw above, French and Italian (more generally, Romance) differ from English (Germanic) in requiring even reduced relative clause "bare" APs to "extrapose" (more accurately, to undergo the attraction/remnant movement derivation of (21). This is possibly at the basis of the preposition *de/di* appearing in front of the adjective (*quelq'un d'intéressant* 'someone interesting'):

(i) a. [[*quelq'un*] *intéressant*] → (merge of C and attraction of the AP to Spec,C)
   b. [*intéressant* C [t [*quelq'un*]]] → (merge of *de* (C) and attraction of the remnant to Spec,*de*)
   c. [[*quelq'un*] *d'* [*intéressant* C [t t]]] → (merge of Q and attraction of *quelq'un* to its Spec)
   d. [[*quelq'un*] Q [t *d'* [*intéressant* C [t t]]]]

If *autre* 'else' is also present, [*quelq'un*], on its way to Spec,Q, is apparently attracted to the Spec of another *de* merged above *autre* (*quelq'un d'autre d'intéressant* 'someone else interesting'). In Italian, the presence of *di* is sometimes optional (?*qualcos'altro interessante*, *qualcos'altro di interessante*, *qualcosa d'altro di interessante*, ??*qualcosa d'altro interessante*), sometimes impossible (*qualcun/nessun altro* (*di*) *interessante*, **qualcuno/nessuno d'altro* (*di*) *interessante*), in ways that need to be understood.

Chapter 6

1. See note 13 of the previous chapter. This Germanic/Romance contrast can be construed as an additional piece of evidence that the prenominal position in English cannot be taken as a diagnostic for adjectivehood, because it can also host reduced relative clauses (see the discussion in section 5.4 of the previous chapter).

Certain present and past participle can apparently occur before the noun in Italian (Romance) (*la restante somma* 'the remaining sum'; *le agognate vacanze* 'the craved for holidays'). There is, however, evidence that such prenominal forms are categorially adjectives (derived from participles). A clitic can be found enclitic to a participle, but not to an adjective (as originally noted by Luigi Rizzi). The fact that a clitic cannot be enclitic to these forms when they are prenominal (**Questa è la restantemi somma* 'This is the remaining-to-me sum'), if not in very formal styles of Italian (see below) shows that they are adjectives. Note that the clitic can be enclitic to these forms when they are postnominal where past participles are indeed possible (*Questa è la somma restantemi* 'This is the sum remaining-to-me'). Apparent past participles like *agognate* can bear the adjectival suffix *-issimo* of absolute degree (*le agognatissime vacanze* 'the extremely craved for holidays'), and can be made superlative (*le più agognate vacanze* 'the most craved for holidays'), options open to adjectives but not to verbal participles. It is only in very formal styles, apparently, that reduced relative clauses may precede the noun in Romance (cf. Giorgi 1988, 307–308). See, for example, *il da poco restaurato museo atestino* 'the recently renovated museum of Este' (adapted from F. Sartori *Dall'Italia all'Italia*, vol. 2 (Padua: Editoriale Programma, 1992, 281), with the adverb *da poco* favoring the participial reading. In such cases, quite expectedly, the adjectival suffix -*issimo* is impossible. Compare the otherwise acceptable *il restauratissimo museo atestino* 'the much renovated museum of Este' (where, because of the absence of the adverb *da poco*, *restaurato* can be a (deverbal) adjective) with **il da poco restauratissimo museo atestino* 'the recently much renovated museum of Este'. Also see Cornilescu 2006, section 4.1, on the comparable possibility of prenominal stative participles in Romanian.

2. The adjectives of these two classes (which actually comprise further subclasses) are also called "pseudo-adjectives" Postal 1972; Bartning 1976, "relational" (Giorgi and Longobardi 1991), or "associative" (Giegerich 2005). Those in (9) have also been called "thematic" (Cinque 1994 and the references cited there), "ethnic" (Alexiadou and Wilder 1998), and "group" adjectives (Oersnes and Markantonatou 2002; Van de Velde 2006). On relational adjectives, also see Valassis 2001 and Fábregas 2007.

3. This is of course true for the direct modification reading. For example, the prenominal position of the color adjective in (10a) (this position is unavailable with invariant color adjectives like *rosa* 'pink', *blu* 'blue', etc.; Zamparelli 1993, 156) only has the individual-level, nonrestrictive, nonintersective, etc., readings (hence, its interpretation that all Tuscan hills are characteristically green). This reading

(unexpectedly for Bouchard 1998, 2002, and Alexiadou 2001, 2003) is preserved in postnominal position, though of course the stage-level, restrictive, intersective, etc., readings also become available (given the possible alternative derivation of the postnominal adjective from a reduced relative clause). With the same classes of adjectives, the postnominal position retains the interpretations found prenominally also in French (see chapter 2, notes 3 and 7, and Aljović 2000, 102), in Spanish (see Bolinger 1972; Luján 1980, chapter 3; Contreras 1981, 151; Demonte 1999a, 208), in Catalan (see Picallo 2002, 1655ff.), in Romanian (see Cornilescu 2003, 5; 2006, 60), and in Portuguese (see Gonzaga 2004, section 2.1.3). Finally, I should note that the NP (or a larger phrase containing it) may fail to raise above color and shape adjectives in Italian only in noncolloquial styles of the language, giving to such cases as (10a) and (11a) their characteristic literary or 'poetic' flavor.

4. For example, as Brito (1993, 49) points out, color adjectives can precede the N in French (under the same conditions noted for Italian; cf. Blinkenberg 1969, 113ff.), but not in Portuguese. For further (limited) differences, see below in this section.

5. And presumably the lower classificatory ones. This means that the NP fails to raise over direct modification adjectives except for nationality (and classificatory) ones, *as well as* over all indirect modification adjectives (in reduced relative clauses), which remain prenominal. Related to this, Walloon also shows for the occurrence prenominally of participial reduced relative clauses, which was seen not to be ordinarily possible in the Romance languages considered so far. See (i):

(i) a. dès r'tchâfés crompîres (Bernstein 1991, 106) (cf. French: *des pommes de terre réchauffées*)
   some reheated potatoes
   b. du l'corante êwe (Bouchard 2002, 194) (cf. French: *de l'eau courante*)
   of the-running water
   c. lès cuts pans (Bouchard 2002, 194) (cf. French: *les pains (bien) cuits*)
   the baked loaves

6. Similarly, I would interpret the "direct" (or "English") order of (ii) in Hebrew, which Siloni (2001, note 15) finds possible alongside the unmarked mirror-image order of (i) given by Shlonsky (2000, 2005), to involve a relative clause source for the second AP (on the mirror-image order in Hebrew of what she calls "light" adjectives versus the free order of what she calls "heavy" adjectives, arguably derived from relative clauses, see Pereltsvaig 2006b, 280; 2006a):

(i) para švecarit xuma
   cow swiss brown
   'a brown Swiss cow'

(ii) ?para xuma švecarit
   cow brown swiss
   'a Swiss brown cow'

As in Italian, the expectation is that with nonpredicative adjectives only one order—the mirror-image one—should be possible.

7. Bouchard (1998, section 6.2) and Knittel (2005, 198) take such cases as (i), parallel to (14) and (16) in Italian, to indicate that no rigid order is found postnominally in French, but this conclusion is not warranted. It stems from a failure to distinguish the two sources of adjectives:

(i) a. le lignes parallèles colorées
       the lines parallel colored
       'the colored parallel lines'
    b. les lignes colorées parallèles
       the lines colored parallel
       'the parallel colored lines'

The possibility for certain adjectives to access either one of the two sources can also account for the ambiguity of cases like *les présumés professeurs chinois malhonnêtes* noted in Bouchard 2009, section 2.2. In addition to the reading represented by (7) in chapter 1, repeated here as (ii), where all adjectives are direct modification adjectives and the NP raises above the AP *chinois* and pied pipes it when raising around the higher *malhonnêtes*, there is another possible derivation, in which *présumés* and *chinois* are direct modification adjectives and *malhonnêtes* is an indirect modification AP, as shown in (iii):

(ii) les [présumés [[[professeurs] chinois] malhonnêtes]]

(iii) a. les [malhonnêtes [présumés [chinois [professeurs]]]] → raising of NP
     b. les [malhonnêtes [présumés [[professeurs] chinois [ ]]]] → raising of the NP plus direct modification APs around the indirect modification AP *malhonnêtes*
     c. les [présumés [professeurs [chinois t]] malhonnêtes t]

For the more marked reading that has *malhonnêtes* and *chinois* taking scope over *présumés* (*les [[[présumés professeurs] chinois] malhonnêtes]*) see the discussion in note 11 of chapter 3 and the related text. If N-movement is unavailable and only movement of NP and pied piping of the *whose*-picture type (Cinque 2005) are allowed in Romance, no undesired readings (and orders) are derived and perhaps less motivation is left for Bouchard's (2009) skepticism.

Here I also differ from Laenzlinger (2005a, 2005b), who takes the direct ("English") order of (16) and the mirror-image order of (14) to be alternative options derived either by moving the NP from Spec to Spec (without pied piping) or by moving the NP with subsequent pied piping of the node that dominates the Spec's. The reason for not assuming the two orders to be on a par is the obligatory mirror-image order found when both adjectives are direct modification adjectives, as in (17) and (18).

8. This is, for example, the position taken in Cinque 1994 and in other works.

9. These adjectives also appear to be exclusively prenominal in Spanish (Demonte 1999b, 48; Ticio 2003, 114), in Catalan (McNally and Boleda 2004, 181; Ana Bartra and Maria Luisa Hernanz, personal communication), in Portuguese (Gonzaga 2004, 23), and in French (Bouchard 1998, 2002, 63; Aljović 2000, 103), although *présumé* is for Christopher Laenzlinger (personal communication) only postnominal.

10. *Perfetto* 'perfect/total' seems to belong to an entire class of exclusively prenominal adjectives that indicate the way a certain description fits. See *un completo sconosciuto* 'a complete stranger', *un vera menzogna* 'a true lie', *una semplice/mera/pura coincidenza* 'a simple/mere/pure coincidence', and so on, and corresponding adjectives in the other Romance languages. They can be postnominal (with no change in meaning) only if coordinated. See the text around (10a,b) in section 4.1.2 for Italian, and the text below for French.

11. The same seems true of English. See (ia–c) and (iia–c):

(i) a. past presidents/*presidents past
 b. future presidents/*presidents future
 c. past and future presidents/presidents past and future

(ii) a. my old friends/*my friends(,) old
 b. my new friends/*my friends(,) new
 c. my old and new friends/my friends, old and new (cf. Taylor 1992, 34 n. 11)

12. For some reason, neither stress nor the presence of complements or adjuncts (the other ways of becoming "heavy"; Kayne 1975) are sufficient to make such adjectives "heavy."

13. Also see the distinct oddness of *Quel problema è falso* 'that problem is false' in the sense of 'that is a false problem'. The Spanish adjective *falso* appears to be similarly ambiguous. See Demonte 2008, 82.

14. As noted in Cinque 2005, note 34, (PP) complements of the N in OV languages interestingly appear in DP-initial position, normally before the Demonstrative. This is for example the case in Turkish (Jaklin Kornfilt, personal communication) and Tatar (cf. Laenzlinger, forthcoming, section 4), in Hindi (Anoop Mahajan, personal communication), in Armenian (Sona Haroutyunian, personal communication), and in Malayalam (K. A. Jayaseelan, personal communication). In other words, as VO languages, OV languages seem to involve attraction to the P, merged higher up (normally above the demonstrative) but without further movement of the remnant.

15. In Cinque 1994, section 3, it was noted that bare adjectives cannot follow a PP complement ((ia)) unless they are either heavily stressed ((ib)), modified ((ic)), coordinated ((id)), or followed by a complement or adjunct ((ie)). (See Di Sciullo 1980, 79–80, and Giurgea 2009, section 2.6, for corresponding facts in French and Romanian, respectively):

(i) a. *I sostenitori di Gianni fedeli
 the supporters of Gianni faithful
 b. I sostenitori di Gianni fedéli
 the supporters of Gianni faithful (stressed)
 c. I sostenitori di Gianni più fedeli
 the supporters of Gianni more faithful
 d. I sostenitori di Gianni fedeli o presunti tali
 the supporters of Gianni faithful or presumed so
 e. I sostenitori di Gianni fedeli al loro leader
 the supporters of Gianni faithful to their leader

These conditions, however, are not required, apparently, for those adjectives that can be postnominal in English, and that can follow *celui* in French. See the last part of this section and sections 6.3 and 6.4 for further discussion.

16. From the existence of PP and relative clause extraposition, we know that both Ps and Cs can be merged at different heights (see Kayne 1994, 2000, 2002).

17. I would thus take Lamarche's (1991, 219) example (ia) to necessarily involve an indirect modification adjective, and his (ib) to involve either a direct or an indirect modification one:

(i) a. un groupe de femmes important
       a group of women important
  b. un groupe important de femmes
       a group important of women
       'an important group of women'

Direct modification adjectives like *principale* 'main' can instead only appear to the left of the PP (see Cinque 1994, section 3). Cases like *des lunettes de soleil rouges* 'red sunglasses', where the adjective need not be "heavy" and can only appear after the PP (**des lunettes rouges de soleil*; Lamarche 1991, 219) possibly involve an N P N compound.

18. Brugè (2002, 20) observes that in Spanish adjectives precede the postposed demonstrative, which she argues occupies the same position of the demonstrative reinforcer (*el chico ⟨alto⟩ este ⟨*alto⟩* '(lit.) the boy ⟨tall⟩ this ⟨tall⟩'), unless a pause separates the demonstrative from the adjective, which she shows is necessarily predicative (see her note 5). As Stefania Chèvre (personal communication) pointed out to me, French appears to be like Italian (and Spanish).

19. Leu (2007, 2008) takes the demonstrative to arise via incorporation of an adjectival demonstrative HERE/THERE (distinct from reinforcer *here/there*) into the determiner. This may be at the basis of Afrikaans *hierdie* (*hier*) (from [*die* [*hier* (*hier*)]]) and of languages that have (the equivalent of) *the book here*. I will abstract away here from this and other finer-grained decompositions.

20. (Nonstandard) English *these here (four) (nice) books* (see Kayne 2008a, section 7), and corresponding sentences in other Germanic languages, could be taken to involve only this movement. The Romance pattern is however not absent from Germanic. See Norwegian *denne boka mi her* (lit. 'this book my here'), from Vangsnes 2004, section 7. As also pointed out there (also see the discussion in Leu 2008, chapter 2), (Eastern) Norwegian can display up to three reinforcers, the first of which must carry (adjectival) inflection: *den **herre** her populære boka mi (**her**)* (lit. 'this here here popular book my (here)'). This suggests that the structure in (43) may be too simple.

21. In Spanish, the demonstrative may be missing (or nonpronounced), yielding *el libro de aquí*, not possible in Italian (Brugè 2002, note 13). The other option, also unavailable in Italian, of *el libro este de aquí*, perhaps involves merger of the head attracting *aquí* and merger of *de* inside the XP constituent of (43) ([*este aquí*]), yielding: Det [*este de aquí*] *libro*, followed by attraction of [*este de aquí*] above Det, followed by attraction of the remnant *el libro* above it.

Chapter 7

1. The epithet with the postnominal adjective in (1) is of course fine if *angry at his constituents* is interpreted as an appositive, or parenthetical, modification of *the man*.

2. For numerous examples of idiomatic AN and NA sequences in Italian, see Jamrozik 1996. Also see the appendix, sections A.1 and A.3, for the parallel fact that only *de*-less adjectives in Mandarin Chinese and only long-form adjectives in Bosnian/Croatian/Serbian allow for idiomatic readings.

3. The impression that the prenominal adjective in (10), and similar cases, modifies both singular nouns is plausibly due to the deletion (nonpronunciation) of an identical instance of the adjective in the second conjunct: *con grande amore e GRANDE affetto*. For a different analysis, see Androutsopoulou and Español-Echevarría 2006 as well as Androutsopoulou, Español-Echevarría, and Prévost 2008, section 2.3.

Conclusion

1. See Knittel 2005, 213ff., on the noncompound status of the corresponding French collocation *roman noir* ('thriller', '(lit.) novel black').

2. Also see the case of the adjectives *grande* and *vecchio* in chapter 2, note 16. In its classificatory usage, a color adjective will appear closer to the N than a nationality/provenance adjective, thus apparently contradicting what was taken in section 3.6 and the references cited there to be the canonical order color > nationality > N. See *la mela verde canadese* (*è la mela più buona in assoluto*) 'the Canadian green apple (is absolutely the best apple)', and Yang 2005, chapter 6, section 4.1, for the corresponding Chinese case.

Appendix

1. This seems clearly true of Chinese, as already claimed in Sproat and Shih 1988, 1990 (section A.1), Maltese (section A.2), Bosnian/Croatian/Serbian (section A.3), and possibly Romanian (section A.4). The case of Greek may instead be spurious if the analysis sketched in section A.5 for the polydefinite construction (in terms of an elliptical DP with an adnominal adjective in apposition to another DP) is correct.

Other languages that will not be discussed here that seem to distinguish the two sources overtly are American Sign Language (MacLaughlin 1997, chapter 4), (the Ganja dialect of) Balanta (Fudeman 2004), the Ladin dialects studied in Rasom 2006, 2008 and Javanese (Vander Klok 2009). If nonrestrictive adjectives are only direct modifiers and restrictive ones only indirect modifiers derived from a reduced relative clause source (see chapters 2 and 3 above), then Icelandic and Western Jutlandic also distinguish the two sources overtly. As observed in Delsing 1993b, 132 n. 25, Icelandic marks the nonrestrictive interpretation with the strong form of the adjective (cf. (i)), and Western Jutlandic with the æ rather than with the *de* article (cf. (ii)) (also see the discussion in Roehrs 2006, 132ff.):

(i) a. guli   bíllinn
       yellow [wk] car.the
       'the yellow car'
   b. gulur   bíllinn
       yellow [str] car.the
       'the car, which by the way is yellow'

(ii) a. de gul   bil
        the yellow car
        'the yellow car'
    b. æ gul   bil
        the yellow car
        'the car, which by the way is yellow'

2. As will be apparent from the text below, which draws on Mui's (2002) and Sio's (2006) analyses, Cantonese represents a similar case.

3. Rigidity of order, however, is not per se a necessary diagnostic of the compound status of a certain A A N sequence. See Paul 2005, notes 16 and 24, Paul 2009, and the text below. Not all Chinese dialects appear to allow for two adjectives with *de*. Yang (2005, 218ff.) reports that for Taiwanese speakers the second of the two adjectives in (1) must be without *de*.

4. As Aoun and Li (2003, chapter 5, note 15) and Paul (2005, note 7) observe, Sproat and Shih's conclusion was based on the impossibility of *de* with *qian* (the shorter form of *yiqian* 'former'. See *qian de zongtong* versus *qian-zongtong* 'former president), which is plausibly a bound morpheme. Aoun and Li (2003, 148ff.), Cheung (2005), and Sio (2006, chapter 5, section 6.2.2) also argue that not all adjectives followed by *de* can be analyzed as relative clauses since nonpredicative adjectives like *zhuyao* 'main', *weiyi* 'only', etc. can also be followed by *de*:

(i) a. zhuyao de daolu (cf. *daolu (hen/bu) zhuyao 'the road is (very/not) main')
       main   DE road
       'the main road'
   b. weiyi de daolu (cf. *daolu weiyi 'the road is only')
       only DE road
       'the only road'

5. Arguments for the phrasal nature of many A N sequences in Chinese are also presented in Wang 1995. Among the considerations supporting the existence of phrasal [A N] sequences, is the fact that the adjective can itself be modified, if not by *hen* 'very', *tebie* 'especially', *feichang* 'extremely' etc., at least by the superlative adverb *zui* 'most' (although, as Chi Fung Lam points out, modification by *zui* is not entirely productive). This fact is reminiscent of what happens in Italian, where prenominal adjectives cannot be modified by *molto* 'very', *specialmente* 'especially', *estremamente* 'extremely', etc., but can be by the superlative morpheme *più* 'most' (see (7) in chapter 4):

(i) zui gao shuiping
most high level
'the highest level'

Adjectives modified by *hen* 'very', reduplicated, or derived (what Huang 2006 calls "complex adjectives") can be used as predicates (see (i)), but not as adnominal attributes without *de* (see (iib)). Instead, bare adjectives (what Huang 2006 calls "simple adjectives") can be used without *de*, but not as predicates (compare (iia) with (i)):

(i) Zhangsan *(hen) gao (Huang 2006, 345)
 Zhangsan very tall
 'Zhangsan is very tall'

(ii) a. zang shui (Huang 2006, 345)
 dirty water
 b. hen zang *(de) shui (Huang 2006, 345)
 very dirty (DE) water

Also see Paul 2006, Cheng and Sybesma 2009, and Schäfer 2009.

6. Reversals of the rigid order are possible only if *de* follows the first of the two adjectives—that is, if the relative clause source is accessed:

(i) yi-tiao hei de da gou
 1-CL black DE big dog
 'one black big dog'

In this case, *da* 'big' is "conceived of as [a] defining propert[y] and as a result, *da gou* 'big dog' [...is] interpreted as constituting [a] particular type of dogs. It is this newly created type as a whole that [is] subsequently modified."

7. See Sio 2006, chapter 5, section 2.2.3, for a finer analysis. Sproat and Shih (1990, 574) note that the nonintersective adjective *wèi* 'fake', which is also nonpredicative (*nèifu yào wèi* 'that medicine (is) fake') cannot be followed by *de*: *wèi* (**de*) *yào* 'a fake medicine'. Aoun and Li (2003, chapter 5, note 15), however, observe that this behavior of *wei* may be due to its prefix nature in Modern Chinese. If so, perhaps only direct modification adjectives can be prefixes in Modern Chinese. On the Italian and English adjectives *falso, finto* (*fake, false*), see section 6.1. Yang (2005, 253) notes that without *de* an adjective like *lao* 'old' is ambiguous between the meaning of 'longtime, of long standing' (*lao pengyou* 'old friend', *lao tongxue* 'old classmate') and that of 'aged' (*lao xiansheng* 'old gentleman') (like the case of prenominal *vecchio* in Italian: *un vecchio amico* 'a friend of long standing', and *un vecchio signore* 'an aged gentleman'. Interestingly, when followed by *de* the meaning of 'longtime, of long standing' disappears (Tong Wu, personal communication): *lao de pengyou*. Again, compare the case of *vecchio* in Italian in a predicative position (*quel mio amico è vecchio* 'that friend of mine is aged'). This may be taken to suggest that when a direct modification adjective can be *de*-less (like *lao* 'old' versus *yiqian* 'former') it must, so that the *de* that follows it is the relative *de* (which forces an intersective reading of *lao*). Sio (2006, 123ff.) notes the same for Cantonese. In a sentence like (i) the adjective *old* followed by the

subordination marker *ge* can only mean 'aged', while the bare adjective *old* following it can be interpreted as 'longtime, of long standing':

(i) jat^1 go^3 lou^5 ge^3 lou^5 pang^4-jau^5
    one CLF old MARKER old   friend
    'an old old friend'

As Wang also observes, "It is natural to say *xian yan* '(salty) salt' and *suan cu* '(sour) vinegar', but odd to say *xian de yan* and *suan de cu* because there is usually no other choice for *yan* and *cu* except to be *xian* and *suan*" (p. 310); but see Paul 2009 for different judgments and a different interpretation. The fact, noted in Paul 2009, section 3, that such direct modifiers as *yiqian* 'former', *janglai* 'future', etc., require the presence of *de* does not seem to be a problem for the present analysis if, as just conjectured, direct modification adjectives are either with *de* or obligatorily without *de* (in which case whenever they appear with *de*, that *de* must be the relative clause *de*, with its associated properties).

8. The same is true of adjectives with *ge* in Cantonese, which have to precede bare adjectives (Sio 2006, 114). What remains to be understood is why this also holds, apparently, of combinations of two potentially nonpredicative adjectives, like those in (i) of the previous note, one of which is with *ge*, and the other without.

9. Aoun and Li (2003, chapter 5, note 11), Yang (2005, 165 note 12), Simpson (2005, 810), and Wang and Liu (2007, section 2.2) note that adjectives like *big* or *small* may also occur in Chinese between the numeral and the classifier (if they are not followed by *de*). Apparently these are two out of a handful of adjectives that can appear there, in semantic agreement with mass or sortal classifiers indicating size, shape, length, thickness, thinness, and so on (Tong Wu and Liejiong Xu, personal communications), perhaps in the specifier position of the classifier projection.

10. For a critique of den Dikken and Singhapreecha's (2004) Predicate Inversion analysis of Chinese adjectives with *de*, see Sio 2006, 138–141. Kang (2005) shows that the adjectival -*n* suffix of Korean should likewise not be necessarily identified with the relative clause suffix -*n*, and that not all Korean adnominal adjectives derive from relative clauses. Also see Yamakido 2000 on Japanese adjectives.

11. Adjectives generally follow the N. The few that can precede it (like *allegat* 'alleged'; Müller 2009, section 4) bear the article, which cannot be repeated in front of the N (Plank and Moravcsik 1996, 189). In indefinite noun phrases, the indefinite article is never repeated in front of the adjective (Plank and Moravcsik 1996, 187).

12. I thank Ray Fabri for discussion on this point.

13. Special thanks go to Nadira Aljović, Nedžad Leko, and an anonymous reviewer for their judgments and comments. The distinction between the two forms is typically marked by an additional morpheme in the nominative masculine singular (mlad (short form)—mladi (long form) 'young'), but depends on vowel length, and/or stress, and/or tone in other cases. For a discussion of the morphological complexities of the two forms, see Leko 1999 and Aljović 2000, 2002. For

arguments that the relevant distinction is specific/nonspecific rather than definite/indefinite, see Aljović 2000, 2002, as well as Trenkić 2004.

14. Aljović (2000, 85) states that the long form is only acceptable in predicate position if it is "interprété comme un SN où l'adjectif précède un nom elliptique" (i.e., again in attributive position):

(i) Goran je mudri
'Goran is the wise (long form) one'

For Nedžad Leko the long form with ellipsis of the head noun in predicate position is only possible if a demonstrative is also present: *Goran je onaj mudri* 'Goran is that wise (long-form) one' (I have a similar preference in Italian: (dei miei amici, Gianni è quello saggio/??il saggio '(lit.) Of my friends, Gianni is that wise one/??the wise one')). This usage may be related (pace Pereltsvaig 2000) to the predicative usage of the long form of the adjective in Russian, which has also been analyzed as occurring in an elliptical NP (Babby 1970, 1973, 1975; Siegel 1976a, 1976b; Bailyn 1994). See section A.6 below for discussion.

15. Nadira Aljović (personal communication) tells me that the restrictive interpretation of short-form adjectives and the implicit relative reading of the short form of *moguć* 'possible' are, however, extremely difficult to obtain, possibly owing to the fact that short-form adjectives cannot easily combine with universal quantifiers, demonstratives, possessives, and so on. Nonetheless, she says that to the extent that it is possible to use the short form of the adjective in examples like (i) with a universal quantifier, then the interpretation is exclusively restrictive:

(i) ?(?)Svi naši vrijedni i   pametni studenti vole sintaksu
    all our diligent and clever   students like syntax
    'all of our students that are diligent and clever like syntax'

16. Short-form As > long-form As > N. Those speakers (generally younger speakers) who find the combination short form followed by long form marginal still find the opposite order (long form followed by short form) totally impossible. See Aljović 2002, note 14. Leko (1992) takes this order to follow from the fact that short-form adjectives are base-generated higher than long-form adjectives. This is also the position taken here. The fact that short-form adjectives have to precede long-form adjectives even when the latter have a reduced relative clause source, as discussed in the text immediately below, may perhaps be understood if they are merged in the higher reduced relative clause slot that in English contains nonbare AP reduced relative clauses, and that is higher than the reduced relative clause slot containing bare APs. See (14) of chapter 5, and the relevant discussion.

17. Nadira Aljović (personal communication) tells me that, differently from what she claimed in Aljović 2000, 147; 2002, 34, she now thinks that their order is indeed only a matter of (strong) preference. Bašić (2004, 83) gives the following (partial) order as the natural order of adjectives in Serbian: evaluating > size > color > referential > denominal (e.g., *ogromna bela srpska svadbena torta* 'a huge white Serbian wedding cake').

18. This strikingly recalls the specificity-inducing property of the prenominal position of the adjective in Romance indefinite DPs noted in chapter 2.

19. As Leko (1992, 624) notes, short- and long-form adjectives cannot be coordinated together:

(iv) a. siromašan i bolestan dječak
 'a/the-poor (short-form) and sick (short-form) boy'
 b. siromašni i bolesni dječak
 'a/the-poor (long-form) and sick (long-form) boy'
 c. *siromašan i bolesni dječak
 'a/the-poor (short-form) and sick (long-form) boy'
 d. *siromašni i bolestan dječak
 'a/the-poor (long-form) and sick (short-form) boy'

He also notes (pp. 225–226) that only short-form adjectives can be separated from the N by parenthetical material or preposed to the beginning of the DP.

20. But I do not exclude the possibility that (postnominal) adjectives not preceded by *cel* may also be derived from reduced relative clauses.

Giusti (1993, 75ff.; 2006) notes that co-occurrence with *cel* is only possible with adjectives that can be found in predicate position, and Cornilescu (2003, 2006) explicitly suggests that postnominal adjectives preceded by *cel* are (reduced) relative clauses. For comparative remarks on nominal modification in Romanian and in the Arvantovlaxika dialect of Aromanian, see Campos 2005.

21. Unless they are in the superlative form: *cei mai buni prieteni* 'the best friends', *cel mai curajos băiat* 'the most courageous boy'. Lombard (1974, 177) notes that another exception is the ordinal adjectival phrase *din urmă* 'last' (*cea din urmă pagină* 'the last page'). For a possible reason why no more than one adjective can be preceded by *cel* (**băiatul cel înalt cel curajos* 'the courageous tall boy'), see Grosu 1994, section 6.5.2. A similar restriction on Greek articulated adjectives is noted at the end of section A.5 below.

22. Note that in the well-formed variant of (22b) there are two instances of determination, one on the N (*băiatul*) and one in front of the adjective (*cel*). The latter is comparable to the "adjectival determiner" that can also occur with Greek APs in the so-called Determiner Spreading, or Polydefinite, construction, which as will be noted in the next section many authors analyze as deriving from a (reduced) relative clause.

23. Apparent counterexamples such as *conoscutele romane* 'the well-known novels' and *iubitul/apreciatul cântăreţ* 'beloved/appreciated singer' arguably involve adjectives, derived from past participles of "transitive verbs denoting states and evincing a marked imperfective reading" (Dragăn 2002, 111). Also see note 1 in chapter 6 for comparable cases in Italian. As in Italian some prenominal participles are possible in higher registers.

24. *Cel* can instead unproblematically precede PPs that are not subcategorized by the N (hence can be predicates of a (reduced) relative clause) (Cornilescu 1992, 222):

(i) a. palatul   cel de argint
 palace-the the of silver
 'the silver palace'

b. ?romanul cel despre care ai vorbit cel mai mult
novel-the the about which (you)-have talked most
'the novel which you talked about most'

25. Melita Stavrou tells me that with articulated adjectives, the postnominal order is the unmarked one, the prenominal being necessarily contrastively focused. Postnominal adjectives in *indefinite* DPs can also be taken to be possible only under Determiner Spreading, if one assumes that what is occasionally taken to be an indefinite article is in fact just the numeral "one" (in view of their homophony) and that the indefinite article in Greek is null. *Ena vivlio oreo* '(lit.) one/a book nice' would thus be *ena Ø vivlio Ø oreo*, parallel to *to vivlio to oreo* '(lit.) the book the nice' (this recalls Alexiadou and Wilder's (1998, section 3.6) position, modulo their taking *ena* to be an article and to follow, rather than precede, an abstract indefinite determiner). Detailed syntactic and semantic evidence for this treatment of indefinite DPs (redressing Horrocks and Stavrou's (1987), Karanassios's (1992, 53), and Stavrou's (1996, 1999, section 4.3.2) N-raising analysis of indefinite DPs) has in fact been presented by Melita Stavrou in classes at the University of Venice in the spring of 2005. See, now, Stavrou, forthcoming.

26. Campos and Stavrou (2004, section 3.3) also point out that in the Determiner Spreading construction the N may never be stressed and the adjective unstressed.

27. The latter claim should in fact be redressed. As Melita Stavrou (personal communication) pointed out to me, articleless adjectives only show a preferred order. As in English, their order can be reversed under special pragmatic conditions if heavy stress is put on the first of the two adjectives. Compare *I megali dermatini tsanta* 'the big leather bag' with *I DERMATINI megali tsanta* 'the LEATHER big bag'. This is expected given the further similarity of English prenominal adjectives and Greek articleless adjectives that she notes. Both English prenominal adjectives and Greek articleless adjectives are systematically ambiguous between the two sets of interpretations seen in chapter 2 above, suggesting for Greek too the existence prenominally of a reduced relative clause source independent of Determiner Spreading. Interestingly, verbal reduced relative clauses can also be prenominal in Greek (see (5c) in chapter 4). For the ambiguity of articleless adjectives also see Marinis and Panagiotidis 2005, section 2.2. Greek, then, is closer to English than to Italian. In prenominal position, it allows adjectives derived from relative clauses to precede adjectives merged as direct modifiers. In contrast to English, however, it does not allow for (articleless) postnominal adjectives (Alexiadou, Haegeman, and Stavrou 2007, 287). Alexiadou and Wilder (1998, 317) claim that in prenominal position even articulated adjectives have an unmarked order (size > color > N vs. (*) color > size > N), but not all speakers appear to share this judgment. See Ramaglia 2007, 163 n. 1.

28. Recall the analogous cases of Bosnian/Croatian/Serbian ((19) and (20) above), where short-form adjectives (which only have a relative clause source) cannot be closer to the N than long-form adjectives, and of Chinese *de* and *de*-less adjectives ((6) and (7) above).

29. Alexiadou and Wilder (1998) claim that "it is predicted that adjectives that cannot be used predicatively (in copula sentences etc.) should not permit deter-

miner spreading in attributive use" (p. 306), and that those readings of an adjective that are unavailable in predicate position, like the reading 'unfortunate'/'pitiable' for the adjective *ftohos* ('poor'), cannot be articulated (pp. 314–315). However, Androutsopoulou (1995, 24; 2001, 191) gives examples such as (37) below, and Melita Stavrou (personal communication) tells me that *o ftohos o anthropos* can (for speakers like her) mean 'the pitiable man'. Arhonto Terzi (personal communication) tells me that Determiner Spreading is in fact obligatory with *kaimenos* 'pitiable'. Those adjectives, or readings of an adjective, that are unavailable in predicate position are typically found in Romance in prenominal position, but Alexiadou's (2001, 222) claim that "those adjectives which do not participate in D[eterminer] S[preading] in Greek occur strictly in prenominal position in Romance" (cf. also Alexiadou 2003, section 5.1) is not accurate. Thematic and classificatory adjectives corresponding to those in (35) and (36), which do not participate in DS, appear in Romance obligatorily in postnominal position, like many other nonpredicative adjectives (e.g., *L'/Il* ⟨*medio⟩ americano ⟨medio⟩* 'the average American' (on the adjective 'average' see Carlson and Pelletier 2000, and Kennedy and Stanley 2008), *un* ⟨*unico⟩ figlio ⟨unico⟩* 'an only child', ⟨*stretti⟩ parenti ⟨stretti⟩* 'close relatives'. Romance nonrestrictive adjectives corresponding to the Greek example (28), which does not participate in Determiner Spreading, can also be postnominal.

30. This analysis recalls the Bosnian/Croatian/Serbian case discussed in note 14 (and that of Russian long-form adjectives to be discussed in section A.6 below). More directly it recalls the analysis given by Marušič and Žaucer (2006, 2007, 2009) and Laskova (2006a) for the articulated adjective constructions of colloquial Slovenian and Bulgarian, respectively, in terms of an elliptical DP. See, for example, (i) from Slovenian and (ii) from Bulgarian:

(i) a. tá [ta zelen [e]] svinčnik (Marušič and Žaucer 2006, 189)
   this the green   pencil
   'this green pencil'
   b. moj [ta bivši   [e]] mož je pjanc (Marušič and Žaucer 2006, 201)
   my the former   husband is drunkard
   'My former husband is a drunkard'

(ii) a. onaia [zelena*ta* [e]] bluza (Laskova 2006a, 72)
    that   green-*the*   blouse
    'that green blouse'
    b. onaia [predišna*ta* [e]] magazinerka (Laskova 2006a, 79)
    that   previous-*the* shop-clerk
    'That previous shop clerk'

As Marušič and Žaucer (2006, 201) point out, only the presence of *ta* in (ib) (which is otherwise optional) implies that I have a new husband (as it would, it seems, to say in English 'my husband, the former one' versus 'my former husband'). Exactly the same holds of the corresponding Bulgarian sentence (Vesselina Laskova, personal communication).

If one adds the case of Romanian presented above, the phenomenon of reduced relative clauses with a DP in predicate position containing an elliptical N appears to represent a Balkan feature (although the case of articulated adjectives in Albanian may be different—see, for discussion, Androutsopoulou 2001; Turano 2002; Alexiadou 2003, section 6.3). It remains to be seen whether the differences pointed out in Marchis and Alexiadou 2008 between Greek Determiner Spreading and the Romanian *cel* construction can be explained away under an essentially unified analysis in terms of a reduced relative clause appositional DP with an elliptical N.

31. It is not clear whether the other two differences pointed out by Leu (2008, 55–56) between Greek Determiner Spreading and German Restrictive Elliptic Appositives are real differences. If what is proposed in note 25 above and in Stavrou, forthcoming (namely that Determiner Spreading of null indefinite articles is also possible in Greek), German and Greek would be similar in this respect. The fact that in Greek Determiner Spreading is also possible prenominally while Restrictive Elliptic Appositives in German are not might instead depend on a separate difference: the existence of DP internal focus movement in Greek but not in German.

32. On Russian long- and short-form adjectives there is a rich literature (see Babby 1970, 1973, 1975, 1999, 2010; Sussex 1971; Siegel 1976a, 1976b; Bailyn 1994; Groen 1998; Pereltsvaig 2000, 2001; Corbett 2004; Matushansky 2006, 2008; and the references cited there).

33. See note 16, where it was conjectured that only those adjectives that are merged as predicates of the higher reduced relative clause can retain the short form, while those merged as predicates of the lower reduced relative clause have to take the long form.

34. See Pereltsvaig 2000, sections 4.1, 4.2, for some complications in the agreement properties of such null nouns. Even though she shows that some of the arguments for the presence of a null noun are not cogent, I take the overall evidence in favor of the null noun analysis to be sound.

35. For similar examples, see Corbett 2004, 206. Siegel (1976b) discusses additional evidence in favor of her analysis. For example, she notes (pp. 294–295) that long-form adjectives ((ia)) behave like predicate nouns ((ib)), and unlike short-form adjectives ((ic)) and verbs ((id)), in taking singular agreement with the second-person plural pronoun *vy* used for second-person singular in nonintimate speech:

(i) a. Ivan, vy   molodoj/*molodye
       Ivan, you-(are) young (long form sg/*pl)
   b. Ivan, vy   artist/*artisty
       Ivan, you-(are an) artist (sg./*pl)
   c. Ivan, vy   *molod/molody
       Ivan, you-(are)   young (short form *sg/pl)
   d. Ivan, vy   *govoril/govorili
       Ivan you-were speaking (*sg/pl)

(ia) and (ib) reduce to one and the same property if long-form adjectives are taken to agree with a null predicate noun. (Also see Bailyn's (1994, 12ff.) discussion on this point.) She also notes (p. 293 n. 1) that those adjectives that cannot be used as predicates (like *byvshij* 'former') have no short form. For careful discussion of the traditional arguments and additional arguments that long-form adjectives in Russian are only attributive, see Matushansky 2006; 2008, section 6.

Pereltsvaig (2000, section 5.1) notes that short-form adjectives often differ from the corresponding long-form ones in a systematic way, with short forms denoting temporary (or stage-level) properties, and long forms more enduring (or individual-level) properties (also see Siegel 1976b, 295, and Groen 1998). Pereltsvaig also points out that in some short-form/long-form pairs, the long forms have additional meanings. So for example the short-form *beden* means 'penniless' while the long-form *bednyj* means either 'penniless' or 'pitiable', which recalls the situation found in Romance, where the adjective 'poor' means 'penniless' when used in predicate position, but is ambiguous between 'penniless' and 'pitiable' in adnominal position.

36. Also see Krause 2001, section 2.1.1, and 85ff. A similar situation holds in Dutch:

(i) a. het boek is moeilijk (Corver 1997, 345)
       the book is difficult
    b. het moeilijk-e   boek (Corver 1997, 345)
       the difficult-INFL book

(ii) a. De vrouw kwam huilend de kamer binnen (Corver, p.c.)
        The woman came crying the room into
        'The woman entered the room crying/while she was crying'
     b. de huilend-e   vrouw (Corver, p.c.)
        the crying-INFL woman

On adjective inflection in Dutch, also see Kester 1996, section 2.3.1.3.

References

Abeillé, Anne, and Danièle Godard. 1999. La position de l'adjectif épithète en français: Le poid des mots. *Recherches linguistiques de Vincennes* 28: 9–32. http://rlv.revues.org/docannexe.html?id=1220.

Abeillé, Anne, and Danièle Godard. 2000. French word order and lexical weight. In R. Borsley, ed., *Syntactic Categories*, 1–27. New York: Academic Press.

Abels, Klaus, and Ad Neeleman. 2009. Universal 20 without the LCA. In J. M. Brucart, A. Gavarró, and J. Solà, eds., *Merging Features*, 60–80. Oxford: Oxford University Press.

Abney, Steven. 1987. *The English Noun Phrase and Its Sentential Aspect*. Doctoral dissertation, MIT.

Abusch, Dorit, and Mats Rooth. 1997. Epistemic NP Modifiers. In A. Lawson, ed., *Proceedings from Semantics and Linguistic Theory (SALT) VII*, 1–18. Ithaca, NY: CLC Publications, Cornell University.

Adamson, Sylvia. 2000. A lovely little example: Word order options and category shift in the premodifying string. In O. Fischer, A. Rosenbach, and D. Stein, eds., *Pathways of Change: Grammaticalization in English*, 39–66. Amsterdam: Benjamins.

Ajíbóyè, Ọládiípọ̀. 2001. The internal structure of Yorùbá DP. Ms., University of British Columbia (presented at ACAL 32, UC Berkeley, March 25, 2001).

Ajíbóyè, Ọládiípọ̀. 2005. *Topics in Yoruba Nominal Expressions*. Doctoral dissertation, University of British Columbia.

Albro, Daniel M. 1998. Some investigations into the structure of DPs in Nawdm. Ms., UCLA. http://www.linguistics.ucla.edu/people/grads/albro/squib1.pdf.

Alexiadou, Artemis. 2001. Adjective syntax and noun raising: Word order asymmetries in the DP as the result of adjective distribution. *Studia Linguistica* 55: 217–248.

Alexiadou, Artemis. 2003. Adjective syntax and (the absence of) noun raising in the DP. In A. Mahajan, ed., *Syntax at Sunset 3: Head Movement and Syntactic Theory (UCLA Working Papers in Linguistics No. 10, 1–39)*.

Alexiadou, Artemis, Liliane Haegeman, and Melita Stavrou. 2007. *Noun Phrase in the Generative Perspective*. Berlin: Mouton de Gruyter.

Alexiadou, Artemis, and Chris Wilder. 1998. Adjectival modification and multiple determiners. In A. Alexiadou and C. Wilder, eds., *Predicates and Movement in the DP*, 303–332. Amsterdam: Benjamins. http://ifla.uni-stuttgart.de/institut/mitarbeiter/artemis/aacwfin.pdf.

Aljović, Nadira. 2000. *Recherches sur la morpho-syntaxe du groupe nominal en serbo-croate*. Doctoral dissertation, Université de Paris VIII.

Aljović, Nadira. 2002. Long adjectival inflection and specificity in Serbo-Croatian. *Recherches Linguistiques de Vincennes* 31: 27–42. http://rlv.revues.org/docannexe.html?id=1340.

Aljović, Nadira. 2010. Syntactic positions of attributive adjectives: In P. Cabredo Hofherr and O. Matushansky, eds., *Adjectives: Formal analyses in syntax and semantics*, 29–52. Amsterdam: Benjamins.

Alrenga, Peter. 2006. Scalar (non-)identity and similarity. In D. Baumer, D. Montero, and M. Scanlon, eds., *Proceedings of the 25th West Coast Conference on Formal Linguistics*, 49–57. Somerville, MA: Cascadilla Press. http://www.lingref.com/cpp/wccfl/25/index.html.

Androutsopoulou, Antonia. 1994. The distribution of the definite determiner and the syntax of Greek DPs. In K. Beals, J. Denton, R. Knippey, L. Melnar, H. Suzuki, and E. Zeinfeld, eds., *Papers from the 30th Regional Meeting of the Chicago Linguistic Society*, vol. 1, 16–29. Chicago: Chicago Linguistic Society.

Androutsopoulou, Antonia. 1995. The licensing of adjectival modification. In J. Camacho, L. Choueiri, and M. Watanabe, eds., *Proceedings of the Fourteenth West Coast Conference on Formal Linguistics*, 17–31. Stanford, CA: CSLI Publications.

Androutsopoulou, Antonia. 1997. Reduced relatives in DPs: Evidence from adjective extraction in Modern Greek. *MIT Working Papers in Linguistics* 31: 19–40 (*Papers from the Eighth Student Conference in Linguistics*).

Androutsopoulou, Antonia. 1998. Split DPs, Focus, and Scrambling in Modern Greek. In E. Curtis, J. Lyle, and G. Webster, eds., *Proceedings of the Sixteenth West Coast Conference on Formal Linguistics* (*WCCFL*) 16: 1–16. Stanford, CA: CSLI Publications.

Androutsopoulou, Antonia. 2000. On the (in)ability of prenominal attributive adjectives to take complements. In R. Billerey and B. D. Lillehaugen, eds., *Proceedings of the Nineteenth West Coast Conference on Formal Linguistics*, 29–42. Stanford, CA: CSLI Publications.

Androutsopoulou, Antonia. 2001. Adjectival determiners in Albanian and Greek. In M. L. Rivero and A. Ralli, eds., *Comparative Syntax of Balkan Languages*, 161–199. New York: Oxford University Press.

Androutsopoulou, Antonia, and Manuel Español-Echevarría. 2006. Degree modifiers and DP-internal agreement. Ms., Université Laval.

Androutsopoulou, Antonia, Manuel Español-Echevarría, and Philippe Prévost. 2008. On the acquisition of the prenominal placement of evaluative adjectives in L2 Spanish. In J. Bruhn de Garavito and E. Valenzuela, eds., *Selected Proceed-*

ings of the 10th Hispanic Linguistics Symposium, 1–12. Somerville, MA: Cascadilla Press. http://www.lingref.com/cpp/hls/10/paper1781.pdf.

Aoun, Joseph, and Yen-hui Audrey Li. 2003. *Essays on the Representational and Derivational Nature of Grammar: The Diversity of Wh-Constructions.* Cambridge, MA: MIT Press.

Authier, J.-Marc 1988. *The Syntax of Unselective Binding*. Doctoral dissertation, University of Southern California.

Babby, Leonard H. 1970. *A Transformational Grammar of Russian Adjectives.* Doctoral dissertation, Harvard University.

Babby, Leonard H. 1973. The deep structure of adjectives and participles in Russian. *Language* 49: 349–360.

Babby, Leonard H. 1975. *A Transformational Grammar of Russian Adjectives.* The Hague: Mouton.

Babby, Leonard H. 1999. Adjectives in Russian: Primary vs. secondary predication. In K. Dziwirek, H. Coats, and C. M. Vakareliyska, eds., *Annual Workshop on Formal Approaches to Slavic Linguistics: The Seattle Meeting 1998*, 1–16. Ann Arbor: Michigan Slavic Publications.

Babby, Leonard H. 2010. The syntactic differences between long and short forms of Russian adjectives. In P. Cabredo Hofherr and O. Matushansky, eds., *Adjectives: Formal analyses in syntax and semantics*, 53–84. Amsterdam: Benjamins.

Bach, Emmon. 1968. Nouns and noun phrases. In E. Bach and R. T. Harms, eds., *Universals in Linguistic Theory*, 90–122. New York: Holt, Rinehart and Winston.

Bache, Carl. 1978. *The Order of Premodifying Adjectives in Present-Day English.* Odense: Odense University Press.

Backhouse, A. E. 1984. Have all the adjectives gone? *Lingua* 62: 169–186.

Bailyn, John. 1994. The syntax and semantics of Russian long and short adjectives: An X'-theoretic account. In J. Toman, ed., *Annual Workshop on Formal Approaches to Slavic Linguistics: The Ann Arbor Meeting*, 1–30. Ann Arbor: Michigan Slavic Publications.

Baker, Mark C. 2003a. *Lexical Categories: Verbs, Nouns, and Adjectives.* Cambridge: Cambridge University Press.

Baker, Mark C. 2003b. "Verbal adjectives" as adjectives without phi-features. In Y. Otsu, ed., *Proceedings of the Fourth Tokyo Conference on Psycholinguistics*, 1–22. Keio University. http://www.rci.rutgers.edu/~mabaker/verbal-adjs.pdf.

Baker, Mark C. 2008. *The Syntax of Agreement and Concord.* Cambridge: Cambridge University Press.

Bakker, Stéphanie J. 2007. Adjective ordering in Herodotus: A pragmatic explanation. In R. Allan and M. Buijs, eds., *The Language of Literature*, 188–210. Leiden: Brill.

Barbaud, Philippe. 1976. Constructions superlatives et structures apparentées. *Linguistic Analysis* 2: 125–174.

Barkaï, Malachi. 1972. On the shiftability of past participles in English. *Linguistic Inquiry* 3: 377–378.

Barrit, Carlyle W. 1952. *The Order Classes of English Modifiers*. Doctoral dissertation, University of Virginia.

Bartning, Inge. 1976. *Remarques sur la syntaxe et la sémantique des pseudo-adjectifs denominaux en français*. Stockholm: Almquist & Wiksell.

Bartsch, Renate. 1972. Relative adjectives and comparison in a Montague Grammar. Appendix to Renate Bartsch and Theo Vennemann, *Semantic Structures*, 157–186. Frankfurt am Main: Athenäum Verlag.

Bartsch, Renate, and Theo Vennemann. 1972. *Semantic Structures*. Frankfurt am Main: Athenäum Verlag.

Bašić, Monika. 2004. *Nominal Subextractions and the Structure of NPs in Serbian and English*. Master's thesis, University of Tromsø. http://www.ub.uit.no/munin/bitstream/10037/238/1/thesis.pdf.

Beck, Sigrid. 1998. NP dependent readings of *different*. In D. Strolovitch and A. Lawson, eds., *Proceedings from Semantics and Linguistic Theory (SALT) VIII*, 19–35. Ithaca, NY: CLC Publications, Cornell University.

Beck, Sigrid. 2000. The semantics of *different*: Comparison operator and relational adjective. *Linguistics and Philosophy* 23: 101–139.

Benincà, Paola, and Guglielmo Cinque. 2008. La frase relativa. To appear in G. Salvi and L. Renzi, eds., *Grammatica dell'italiano antico*. Bologna: il Mulino.

Bennis, Hans. 2000. Adjectives and argument structure. In P. Coopmans, M. Everaert, and J. Grimshaw, eds., *Lexical Specification and Insertion*, 27–69. Amsterdam: Benjamins.

Bennis, Hans. 2004. Unergative adjectives and psych verbs. In A. Alexiadou and M. Everaert, eds., *Studies in Unaccusativity: The Syntax-Lexicon Interface*, 84–113. Cambridge: Cambridge University Press. http://www.meertens.nl/medewerkers/hans.bennis/unacc.pdf.

Bentley, Delia. 2004. *Ne*-cliticization and split intransitivity. *Journal of Linguistics* 40: 219–262.

Berg, René van den. 1989. *A Grammar of the Muna Language*. Dordrecht: Foris.

Berman, Arlene. 1974. *Adjectives and Adjective Complement Constructions in English*. Report No. NSF-29 to the National Science Foundation. Cambridge, MA: Department of Linguistics, Harvard University.

Bernstein, Judy. 1991. DPs in French and Walloon: Evidence for parametric variation in nominal head movement. *Probus* 2: 1–26.

Bernstein, Judy. 1993a. The syntactic role of word markers in null nominal constructions. *Probus* 5: 5–38.

Bernstein, Judy. 1993b. *Topics in the Syntax of Nominal Structure across Romance*. Doctoral dissertation, CUNY.

Bernstein, Judy. 1997. Demonstratives and reinforcers in Romance and Germanic languages. *Lingua* 102: 87–113.

Biberauer, Theresa, Anders Holmberg, and Ian Roberts. 2008. Disharmonic word-order systems and the Final-over-Final-Constraint (FOFC). In A. Bisetto and F. E. Barbieri, eds., *Proceedings of the XXXIII Incontro di Grammatica Generativa*, 86–105. University of Bologna: Department of Modern Languages and Literatures. http://amsacta.cib.unibo.it/archive/00002397/01/PROCEEDINGS_IGG33.pdf.

Blackwell, Aleka. 2001. On the acquisition of the syntax of English adjectives. In A. Okrent and J. P. Boyle, eds., *Proceedings from the Panels of the Thirty-Sixth Regional Meeting of the Chicago Linguistic Society*, vol. 36-2, 361–375. Chicago: Chicago Linguistic Society.

Blackwell, Aleka. 2005. Acquiring the English adjective lexicon: Relationships with input properties and adjectival semantic typology. *Journal of Child Language* 32: 535–562.

Blinkenberg, Andreas. 1969. *L'ordre des mots en français moderne. Deuxième partie*. Copenhagen: Munksgaard.

Blöhdorn, Lars M. 2009. *Postmodifying attributive adjectives in English*. Frankfurt am Main: Lang.

Bloomfield, Leonard. 1933. *Language*. Chicago: University of Chicago Press.

Bolinger, Dwight. 1967. Adjectives in English: Attribution and predication. *Lingua* 18: 1–34.

Bolinger, Dwight. 1972. Adjective position again. *Hispania* (Amherst) 55: 91–94.

Borer, Hagit. 1990. V+*ing*: It walks like an adjective. It talks like an adjective. *Linguistic Inquiry* 21: 95–103.

Borer, Hagit. 2005. *Structuring Sense, Volume 1: In Name Only*. Oxford: Oxford University Press.

Borg, Albert J. 1996. The structure of the noun phrase in Maltese. In A. J. Borg and F. Plank, eds., *The Maltese Noun Phrase Meets Typology* (*Rivista di linguistica* 8(1): 5–28).

Borg, Albert J., and Marie Azzopardi-Alexander. 1997. *Maltese*. London: Routledge.

Borillo, Andrée. 2001. Quelques adjectifs de référence temporelle du français. *Cahiers de Grammaire* 26: 37–53.

Borroff, Marianne L. 2006. Degree phrase inversion in the scope of negation. *Linguistic Inquiry* 37: 514–521.

Borsley, Robert D. 1997. Relative clauses and the theory of phrase structure. *Linguistic Inquiry* 28: 629–647.

Bošković, Željko. 2005. On the locality of left branch extraction and the structure of NP. *Studia Linguistica* 59: 1–45. http://web2.uconn.edu/boskovic/papers/leftbranch.pdf.

Bošković, Željko. 2009. More on the no-DP analysis of article-less languages. *Studia Linguistica* 63: 187–203. http://web2.uconn.edu/boskovic/papers/StudiaLing.Pereltsvaig.Format.pdf.

Bosque, Ignacio. 1993. Degree quantification and modal operators in Spanish. Paper presented at the 1993 "Going Romance" meeting, Utrecht.

Bosque, Ignacio. 1996. On Specificity and adjective position. In J. Gutiérrez-Rexach and L. Silva-Villar, eds., *Perspectives on Spanish Linguistics*, vol. 1, 1–13. Los Angeles: Department of Linguistics, UCLA.

Bosque, Ignacio. 2001. Adjective position and the interpretation of indefinites. In J. Gutiérrez-Rexach and L. Silva-Villar, eds., *Current Issues in Spanish Syntax and Semantics*, 17–63. Berlin: Mouton de Gruyter.

Bosque, Ignacio, and Violeta Demonte, eds., 1999. *Gramática Descriptiva de la Lengua Española*. Madrid: Espasa Calpe.

Bosque, Ignacio, and Carme Picallo. 1996. Postnominal adjectives in Spanish DPs. *Journal of Linguistics* 32: 349–385.

Bouchard, Denis. 1998. The distribution and interpretation of adjectives in French: A consequence of Bare Phrase Structure. *Probus* 10: 139–183.

Bouchard, Denis. 2002. *Adjectives, Number and Interfaces: Why Languages Vary*. Elsevier: Amsterdam.

Bouchard, Denis. 2005. Sériation des adjectives dans le SN et formation de concepts. *Recherches Linguistiques de Vincennes* 34: 125–142.

Bouchard, Denis. 2009. A solution to the conceptual problem of cartography. In J. van Craenenbroeck, ed., *Alternatives to Cartography*, 245–274. Berlin: Mouton de Gruyter.

Boucher, Paul. 2006. Mapping function to form: Adjective positions in French. *Lingvisticae Investigationes* 29: 43–60.

Bouillon, Pierrette. 1999. The adjective "vieux": The point of view of "generative lexicon." In E. Viegas, ed., *Breadth and Depth of Semantic Lexicons*, 148–166. Dordrecht: Kluwer. http://citeseer.ist.psu.edu/307780.html.

Bouldin, John M. 1990. *The Syntax and Semantics of Postnominal Adjectives in English*. Doctoral dissertation, University of Minnesota.

Boyd, Virginia Lee. 1997. *A Phonology and Grammar of Mbodómó*. MA thesis, University of Texas at Arlington. http://www.sil.org/Africa/Cameroun/bydomain/linguistics/phonology/Mbodomo1-2-3-4nn1-21-98.pdf.

Brasoveanu, Adrian. 2008. Sentence-internal readings of *same/different* as quantifier–internal anaphora. In N. Abner and J. Bishop, eds., *Proceedings of the 27th West Coast Conference on Formal Linguistics*, 72–80. Somerville, MA: Cascadilla. http://www.lingref.com/cpp/wccfl/27/paper1818.pdf.

Brasoveanu, Adrian. 2009. Sentence-internal *different* as quantifier–internal anaphora. Ms., UC Santa Cruz. http://abrsvn.googlepages.com/different_2009.pdf.

Bresnan, Joan. 1978. A realistic transformational grammar. In M. Halle, J. Bresnan, and G. A. Miller, eds., *Linguistic Theory and Psychological Reality*, 1–59. Cambridge, MA: MIT Press.

Bresnan, Joan. 1982. The passive in lexical theory. In J. Bresnan, ed., *The Mental Representation of Grammatical Relations*, 3–86. Cambridge, MA: MIT Press.

Bresnan, Joan. 2001. *Lexical-Functional Syntax*. Oxford: Blackwell.

Brito, Ana Maria. 1993. Aspects de la syntaxe du SN en portugais et en français. *Linguas e Literaturas* (*Revista da Faculdade de Letras do Porto*), II série, vol. X, 25–53.

Brucart, José M. 1994. Sobre una incompatibilidad entre posesivos y relativas especificativas. In V. Demonte, ed., *Gramática del español*. México (D.F.): El Colegio de México.

Brucart, José M., and Lluïsa Gràcia. 1986. I sintagmi nominali senza testa: Uno studio comparato. *Rivista di grammatica generativa* 11: 3–32.

Brugè, Laura. 1996. Demonstrative movement in Spanish: A comparative approach. *University of Venice Working Papers in Linguistics* 6(1): 1–53. http://dspace-unive.cilea.it/bitstream/10278/436/1/6.1.1.pdf.

Brugè, Laura. 2002. The positions of demonstratives in the Extended Nominal Projection. In G. Cinque, ed., *Functional Structure in DP and IP: The Cartography of Syntactic Structures*, vol. 1, 15–53. New York: Oxford University Press.

Brugè, Laura, and Gerhard Brugger. 1996. On the accusative *a* in Spanish. *Probus* 8: 1–51.

Brugè, Laura, and Giuliana Giusti. 1996. On demonstratives. Paper presented at the 19th GLOW Colloquium, Athens, April 17–19, 1996 (abstract in *GLOW Newsletter* 36: 24–25).

Brunot, Ferdinand. 1922. *La Pensée et la Langue*. Paris: Masson.

Cabredo Hofherr, Patricia. 2005. Les sequences determinant défini + adjectif en français et en espagnol: Une comparaison. *Recherches linguistiques de Vincennes* 34: 143–164.

Camacho, José. 2003. *The Structure of Coordination: Conjunction and Agreement Phenomena in Spanish and Other Languages*. Dordrecht: Kluwer.

Campos, Héctor. 2005. Noun modification, pseudo-articles, and last resort operations in Arvantovlaxika and in Romanian. *Lingua* 115: 311–347.

Campos, Héctor. 2009. Some notes on adjectival articles in Albanian. *Lingua* 119: 1009–1034.

Campos, Héctor, and Melita Stavrou. 2004. Polydefinite constructions in Modern Greek and in Aromanian. In O. M. Tomić, ed., *Balkan Syntax and Semantics*, 137–173. Amsterdam: Benjamins.

Cardinaletti, Anna, and Giuliana Giusti. 2006. The syntax of Quantified Phrases and Quantitative Clitics. In M. Everaert and H. van Riemsdijk, eds., *The Blackwell Companion to Syntax*, vol. 5, 23–93. Oxford: Blackwell.

Cardinaletti, Anna, and Giuliana Giusti. 2007. The acquisition of adjectival ordering in Italian. To appear in M. Anderssen, K. Bentzen, and M. Westergaard, eds., *Variation in the Input: Studies in the Acquisition of Word Order*. Dordrecht: Springer. http://dspace-unive.cilea.it/bitstream/10278/351/1/Cardinaletti_Giusti_May_2008.pdf.

Carlson, Greg. 1987. *Same* and *different*: Some consequences for syntax and semantics. *Linguistics and Philosophy* 10: 531–566.

Carlson, Greg, and F. Jeffrey Pelletier. 2000. Average noun phrases. In B. Jackson and T. Matthews, eds., *Proceedings from Semantics and Linguistic Theory (SALT)* X, 17–26. Ithaca, NY: CLC Publications, Cornell University.

Carlson, Greg, and F. Jeffrey Pelletier. 2002. The average American has 2.3 children. *Journal of Semantics* 19: 1–32. http://www.ling.rochester.edu/people/carlson/download/generics/jos-Carlson.pdf.

Cetnarowska, Bożena, Agnieszka Pysz, and Helen Trugman. 2008. Accounting for some flexibility in a rigid construction: On the position of classificatory adjectives in Polish. Paper presented at Generative Linguistics in Poland 6, Warsaw, April 5–6, 2008.

Champollion, Lucas. 2006. A game-theoretic account of adjective ordering restrictions. http://www.ling.upenn.edu/~champoll/adjective-ordering.pdf.

Cheng, Lisa Lai-Shen. 1986. De in Mandarin. *Canadian Journal of Linguistics* 31: 313–326.

Cheng, Lisa Lai-Shen, and Rint Sybesma. 2009. De as an underspecified classifier: first explorations. Unpublished manuscript, University of Leiden.

Cheung, Candice Chi-Hang. 2005. Adjective modification in Chinese. Ms., University of Southern California.

Chierchia, Gennaro, and Sally McConnell-Ginet. 1990. *Meaning and Grammar: Introduction to Semantics*. Cambridge, MA: MIT Press.

Chomsky, Noam. [1955] 1975. *The Logical Structure of Linguistic Theory*. New York: Plenum Press.

Chomsky, Noam. 1957. *Syntactic Structures*. The Hague: Mouton.

Chomsky, Noam. 1965. *Aspects of the Theory of Syntax*. Cambridge, MA: MIT Press.

Cinque, Guglielmo. 1989. On embedded verb second clauses and ergativity in German. In *Complementation and the Lexicon: A Festschrift for Wim de Geest*, 77–96. Dordrecht: Foris.

Cinque, Guglielmo. 1990a. Agreement and head-to-head movement in the Romance NP. Paper presented at the *20th Linguistic Symposium on Romance Languages*, University of Ottawa.

Cinque, Guglielmo. 1990b. Ergative adjectives and the Lexicalist Hypothesis. *Natural Language and Linguistic Theory* 8: 1–39.

Cinque, Guglielmo. 1994. On the evidence for partial N movement in the Romance DP. In G. Cinque, J. Koster, J.-Y. Pollock, L. Rizzi, and R. Zanuttini, eds., *Paths Towards Universal Grammar: Studies in Honor of Richard S. Kayne*, 85–110. Washington, DC: Georgetown University Press. http://dspace-unive.cilea.it/handle/10278/508.

Cinque, Guglielmo. 1996. The Antisymmetric Programme: Theoretical and typological Implications. *Journal of Linguistics* 32: 447–464.

Cinque, Guglielmo. 1999. *Adverbs and Functional Heads: A Cross-linguistic Perspective*. New York: Oxford University Press. (A prepublication version is available at http://dspace-unive.cilea.it/handle/10278/440.)

Cinque, Guglielmo. 2000. On Greenberg's Universal 20 and the Semitic DP. *University of Venice Working Papers in Linguistics* 10(2): 45–61. http://lear.unive.it/bitstream/10278/492/1/10.2.2c.pdf. (An abridged version appears in L.-O. Delsing, C. Falk, G. Josefsson, and H. Sigurðsson, eds., *Grammar in Focus: Festschrift for Christer Platzack 18 November 2003*, vol. 2, 243–251. Lund: Publications of the Department of Scandinavian Languages, 2003. http://dspace-unive.cilea.it/bitstream/10278/123/1/Semitic_DP.pdf.)

Cinque, Guglielmo. 2003. The prenominal origin of relative clauses. Paper presented at the Workshop on Antisymmetry and Remnant Movement, New York University, October 31–November 1, 2003.

Cinque, Guglielmo. 2004a. Issues in adverbial syntax. *Lingua* 114: 683–710. http://dspace-unive.cilea.it/handle/10278/120.

Cinque, Guglielmo. 2004b. A phrasal movement analysis of the Romanian DP. In A. Minuţ and E. Munteanu, eds., *Studia Linguistica et Philologica in honorem D. Irimia*, 129–142. Iaşi: Editura Universităţii "A. I. Cuza." http://dspace-unive.cilea.it/handle/10278/121.

Cinque, Guglielmo. 2005. Deriving Greenberg's Universal 20 and its exceptions. *Linguistic Inquiry* 36: 315–332. http://dspace-unive.cilea.it/handle/10278/91.

Cinque, Guglielmo. 2006. *Restructuring and Functional Heads: The Cartography of Syntactic Structures*. Vol. 4. New York: Oxford University Press.

Cinque, Guglielmo. 2008a. More on the indefinite character of the Head of restrictive relatives. In P. Benincà, F. Damonte, and N. Penello, eds., *Selected Proceedings of the 34th Incontro di Grammatica Generativa*. Padua: Unipress. (Special issue of the *Rivista di grammatica generativa* 33: 3–24. http://dspace-unive.cilea.it/handle/10278/880.)

Cinque, Guglielmo. 2008b. Two types of nonrestrictive relatives. In O. Bonami and P. Cabredo Hofherr, eds., *Empirical Issues in Syntax and Semantics*, vol. 7, 99–137. Paris: CNRS. http://www.cssp.cnrs.fr/eiss7.

Cinque, Guglielmo. 2009. The fundamental left-right asymmetry of natural languages. In S. Scalise, E. Magni, and A. Bisetto, eds., *Universals of Language Today*, 165–184. Berlin: Springer. (A prepublication version is available at http://dspace-unive.cilea.it/handle/10278/214.)

Cinque, Guglielmo. In preparation. A unified analysis of relative clauses. Ms., University of Venice.

Cinque, Guglielmo, and Iliyana Krapova. 2009. The two "possessor raising" constructions of Bulgarian. In S. Franks, V. Chidambaram, and B. Joseph, eds., *A Linguist's Linguist: Studies in South Slavic Linguistics in Honor of E. Wayles Browne*, 123–148. Bloomington, IN: Slavica. http://dspace-unive.cilea.it/handle/10278/997.

Coene, Martine. 1994. Some reflections on the position of the adjective in Romanian. *Cahiers de linguistique théorique et appliquée* 31: 9–26.

Cole, Peter, Gaby Hermon, and Y. N. Tjung. 2005. How irregular is WH in situ in Indonesian? *Studies in Language* 29: 553–581.

Contreras, Heles. 1981. The case for base-generated attributive adjectives in Spanish. In W. W. Cressey and D. J. Napoli, eds., *Linguistic Symposium on Romance Languages*, 147–163. Washington, DC: Georgetown University Press.

Corbett, Greville. 1979. Adjective movement. *Nottingham Linguistic Circular* 8: 1–10.

Corbett, Greville. 2004. The Russian adjective: A pervasive yet elusive category. In R. M. W. Dixon and A. Aikhenvald, eds., *Adjective Classes: A Cross-Linguistic Typology*, 199–221. Oxford: Oxford University Press.

Cornilescu, Alexandra. 1992. Remarks on the determiner system of Rumanian: The demonstrative *al* and *cel*. *Probus* 4: 189–260.

Cornilescu, Alexandra. 2003. The adjectival phrase inside the DP. Ms., University of Bucharest. http://www.linguist.jussieu.fr/~mardale/Volume_1.htm.

Cornilescu, Alexandra. 2005. Romanian adjectives and the stage level / individual level contrast. In M. Coene and L. Tasmowski, eds., *On Space and Time in Language*, 75–91. Cluj-Napoca: Clusium.

Cornilescu, Alexandra. 2006. Modes of semantic combinations: NP/DP adjectives and the structure of the Romanian DP. In J. Doetjes and P. González, eds., *Romance Languages and Linguistic Theory 2004*, 43–69. Amsterdam: Benjamins.

Corver, Norbert. 1997. The internal syntax of the Dutch extended adjectival projection. *Natural Language and Linguistic Theory* 15: 289–368.

Coulter, Jane McKenna. 1983. *Prenominal Adjectival Modifiers*. Doctoral dissertation, University of Washington.

Crisma, Paola. 1993. On adjective placement in Romance and Germanic event nominals. *Rivista di grammatica generativa* 18: 61–100.

Dal Pozzo, Lena. 2007. *The Finnish Noun Phrase*. Master's thesis, University of Venice. http://dspace-unive.cilea.it/handle/10278/881.

Dayley, Jon P. 1989. *Tümpisa (Panamint) Shoshone Grammar*. Berkeley: University of California Press.

DeGraff, Michel, and Deborah Mandelbaum. 1993. Why is my old friend not old? In K. Beals, G. Cooke, D. Kathman, S. Kita, K.-E. McCullough, and D. Testen, eds., *Papers from the 29th Regional Meeting of the Chicago Linguistic Society*, 121–136. Chicago: Chicago Linguistic Society.

Dehé, Nicole, and Vieri Samek-Lodovici. 2007. On the prosody and syntax of DPs: Evidence from Italian noun adjective sequences. *UCL Working Papers in Linguistics* 19: 93–127. http://www.langsci.ucl.ac.uk/linguistics/publications/WPL/uclwpl19.php.

Del Gobbo, Francesca. 2004. On prenominal relative clauses and appositive adjectives. In V. Chand, A. Kelleher, A. J. Rodríguez, and B. Schmeiser, eds., *Proceedings of the 23rd West Coast Conference on Formal Linguistics* (*WCCFL*). Somerville, MA: Cascadilla Press.

Del Gobbo, Francesca. 2005. On the interpretation of Chinese relative clauses. Unpublished ms., University of Venice.

Delomier, Dominique. 1980. La place de l'adjectif en français: Bilan des points de vue et théories du XXe siècle. *Cahiers de Lexicologie* 37: 5–24.

Delsing, Lars-Olof. 1993a. On attributive adjectives in Scandinavian and other languages. *Studia Linguistica* 47(2): 105–125.

Delsing, Lars-Olof. 1993b. *The Internal Structure of Noun Phrases in the Scandinavian Languages*. Doctoral dissertation, University of Lund.

Demeke, Girma. 2001. N-final relative clauses: The Amharic case. *Studia Linguistica* 55: 191–215.

Demonte, Violeta. 1982. El falso problema de la posición del adjetivo: Dos análisis semánticos. *Boletín de la Real Academia Española* 62: 453–485. (A revised version appeared as chapter 8 in Violeta Demonte, *Detrás de la palabra: Estudios de grámatica del espãnol* (Madrid: Alianza Editorial).)

Demonte, Violeta. 1991. *Detrás de la palabra: Estudios de grámatica del español*. Madrid: Alianza Editorial.

Demonte, Violeta. 1999a. El adjetivo. Clases y usos. La posición del adjetivo en el sintagma nominal. In I. Bosque and V. Demonte, eds., *Gramática Descriptiva de la Lengua Española*, 129–215. Madrid: Espasa Calpe.

Demonte, Violeta. 1999b. A minimal account of Spanish adjective position and interpretation. In J. Franco, A. Landa, and J. Martín, eds., *Grammatical Analyses in Basque and Romance Linguistics: Papers in Honor of Mario Saltarelli*, 45–76. Amsterdam: Benjamins.

Demonte, Violeta. 2008. Meaning-form correlations and adjective position in Spanish. In L. McNally and C. Kennedy, eds., *Adjectives and Adverbs: Syntax, Semantics, and Discourse*, 71–100. Oxford: Oxford University Press.

Dikken, Marcel den, and Pornsiri Singhapreecha. 2004. Complex noun phrases and linkers. *Syntax* 7: 1–54.

Dimitrova-Vulchanova, Mila. 2003. Modification in the Balkan nominal expression. In M. Coene and Y. D'hulst, eds., *From NP to DP*, vol. 1, 91–118. Amsterdam: Benjamins.

Dirven, René. 1999. The cognitive motivation for adjective sequences in attribution. *Journal of English Studies* 1(1): 57–67.

Di Sciullo, Anna Maria. 1980. N and X-bar theory. In J. T. Jensen, ed., *Cahiers Linguistiques d'Ottawa* (NELS X), 73–87. Ottawa: University of Ottawa.

Dixon, Robert M. W. 1982. *Where Have All the Adjectives Gone?* The Hague: Mouton.

Dixon, Robert M. W. 1994. Adjectives. In R. E. Asher, ed., *The Encyclopedia of Language and Linguistics*, 29–35. New York: Pergamon Press.

Dixon, Robert M. W. 2004. Adjective classes in typological perspective. In R. M. W. Dixon and A. Aikhenvald, eds., *Adjective Classes: A Cross-Linguistic Typology*, 1–49. Oxford: Oxford University Press.

Dobrovie-Sorin, Carmen. 1987. A propos de la structure du groupe nominal en Roumain. *Rivista di grammatica generativa* 12: 123–152.

Dragăn, Ruxandra. 2002. Issues with adjectival participles in English and Romanian. *Bucharest Working Papers in Linguistics* 4(1): 107–112.

Duanmu, San. 1998. Wordhood in Chinese. In J. Packard, ed., *New Approaches to Chinese Word Formation: Morphology, Phonology and the Lexicon in Modern and Ancient Chinese*, 135–196. Berlin: Mouton de Gruyter.

Duffield, Nigel. 1995. *Particles and Projections in Irish Syntax*. Dordrecht: Kluwer.

Duffield, Nigel. 1999. Adjectival modifiers and the specifier-adjunct distinction. In D. Adger, S. Pintzuck, B. Plunkett, and G. Tsoulas, eds., *Specifiers: Minimalist Approaches*, 126–145. Oxford: Oxford University Press.

Dumitrescu, Domniţa, and Mario Saltarelli. 1998. Two types of predicate modification: Evidence from the articulated adjectives of Romanian. In J. Lima and E. Treviño, eds., *Theoretical Analyses on Romance Languages: Selected Papers from the 26th Linguistic Symposium on Romance Languages (LSRL XXVI), Mexico City, 28–30 March 1996*, 175–192. Amsterdam: Benjamins.

Emonds, Joseph. 1976. *A Transformational Approach to English Syntax*. New York: Academic Press.

Emonds, Joseph. 1985. *A Unified Theory of Syntactic Categories*. Dordrecht: Foris.

Escribano, José Luis González. 2004. Head-final effects and the nature of modification. *Journal of Linguistics* 40: 1–43.

Escribano, José Luis González. 2005. "Discontinuous" APs in English. *Linguistics* 43: 563–610.

Ewert, Manfred, and Fred Hansen. 1993. On the linear order of the modifier-head-position in NPs. In G. Fanselow, ed., *The Parametrization of Universal Grammar*, 161–181. Amsterdam: Benjamins.

Fabb, Nigel A. J. 1984. Syntactic affixation. Doctoral Dissertation, MIT.

Fabian, Grace, Edmund Fabian, and Bruce Waters. 1998. *Morphology, Syntax and Cohesion in Nabak, Papua New Guinea*. Canberra: Pacific Linguistics (Australian National University), Series C-144.

Fábregas, Antonio. 2007. The internal syntactic structure of relational adjectives. *Probus* 17: 1–36.

Fabri, Ray. 1993. *Kongruenz und die Grammatik des Maltesischen*. Tübingen: Niemeyer.

Fabri, Ray. 2001. Definiteness marking and the structure of the NP in Maltese. In M. L. Knittel, ed., *Du nom au syntagme nominal* (*Verbum* 23(2): 153–172).

Fanselow, Gisbert. 1986. On the sentential nature of prenominal adjectives in German. *Folia Linguistica* 20: 341–380.

Farkas, Donka F., and Katalin É. Kiss. 2000. On the comparative and absolute readings of superlatives. *Natural Language and Linguistic Theory* 18: 417–455.

Fassi Fehri, Abdelkader. 1998a. Layers in the distribution of Arabic adverbs and adjectives and their licensing. In E. Benmamoun, M. Eid, and N. Haeri, eds., *Perspectives on Arabic Linguistics* 11: 303–332. Amsterdam: Benjamins.

Fassi Fehri, Abdelkader. 1998b. Typological ingredients of Mediterranean adjectives. Paper presented at the Terza Mostra Mediterranea dell'innovazione tecnologica, Naples, December 9–12, 1998.

Fassi Fehri, Abdelkader. 1999. Arabic modifying adjectives and DP structures. *Studia Linguistica* 52: 105–154.

Fedorowicz-Bacz, Barbara. 1977. Are exclusively attributive adjectives "transpositional"?—some comments on the nature of lexical rules as opposed to syntactic transformations. In J. Fisiak, ed., *Papers and Studies in Contrastive Linguistics*, 33–48. Poznań: Adam Mickiewicz University. http://eric.ed.gov/ERICDocs/data/ericdocs2sql/content_storage_01/0000019b/80/2e/f4/9e.pdf.

Feist, James Murray. 2008. *The Order of Premodifiers in English Nominal Phrases*. Doctoral dissertation, University of Auckland. http://researchspace.auckland.ac.nz/bitstream/2292/3301/7/02whole.pdf.

Feist, James Murray. 2009. Premodifier order in English nominal phrases: A semantic account. *Cognitive Linguistics* 20: 301–340.

Felber, Sarah, and Dorian Roehrs. 2004. *So weird a baffling construction. *Snippets* 8: 7–9. http://www.ledonline.it/snippets/allegati/snippets8002.pdf.

Ferris, Connor. 1993. *The Meaning of Syntax: A Study in the Adjectives of English*. London: Longman.

Fiengo, Robert, and James Higginbotham. 1981. Opacity in NP. *Linguistic Analysis* 7: 395–421.

Fleisher, Nicholas. 2008. A crack at a hard nut: Attributive-adjective modality and infinitival relatives. In C. B. Chang and H. J. Haynie, eds., *Proceedings of the 26th West Coast Conference on Formal Linguistics*, 163–171. Somerville, MA: Cascadilla Press. http://www.lingref.com/cpp/wccfl/26/paper1669.pdf.

Forsgren, Mats. 2004. La place de l'adjectif épithète: Une solution globale est-elle possible? In Jacques François, ed., *L'adjectif en français et à travers les langues*, 257–277. Caen: Presses Universitaires de Caen.

François, Jacques, ed., 2004. *L'adjectif en français et à travers les langues*. Caen: Presses Universitaires de Caen.

Frank, Paul. 1990. *Ika Syntax*. Arlington: Summer Institute of Linguistics and University of Texas.

Frawley, William. 1992. *Linguistic Semantics*. Hillsdale, NJ: Erlbaum.

Freidin, Robert. 1975. The analysis of passives. *Language* 51: 384–405.

Fries, Peter H. 1986. Towards a discussion of the ordering of adjectives in the English noun phrase. In B. l. Elson, ed., *Language in Global Perspective: Papers in Honor of the 50th Anniversary of the Summer Institute of Linguistics 1935–85*, 123–133. Dallas: Summer Institute of Linguistics.

Fu, Jingqi. 1987. *La structure du syntagme nominal en chinois*. Doctoral dissertation, Université de Paris III.

Fudeman, Kirsten. 2004. Adjectival agreement vs. adverbial inflection in Balanta. *Lingua* 114: 105–123.

Fults, Scott. 2006. *The Structure of Comparison: An Investigation of Gradable Adjectives*. Doctoral dissertation, University of Maryland, College Park. http://www.lib.umd.edu/drum/bitstream/1903/3932/1/umi-umd-3783.pdf.

Gengel, Kirsten. 2008. Local dislocation in the distribution of French adjectives. In F. Schäfer, ed., *Working Papers of the SFB 732 (Incremental Specification in Context)* 1: 33–51. http://elib.uni-stuttgart.de/opus/volltexte/2008/3547/pdf/SinSpeC1_3_Gengel.pdf.

Giannakidou, Anastasia, and Melita Stavrou. 1999. Nominalization and ellipsis in the Greek DP. *Linguistic Review* 16: 295–331.

Giegerich, Heinz J. 2005. Associative adjectives in English and the lexicon-syntax interface. *Journal of Linguistics* 41: 571–591.

Giorgi, Alessandra. 1988. La struttura interna dei sintagmi nominali. In L. Renzi, ed., *Grande Grammatica Italiana di Consultazione*, vol. 1, 273–314. Bologna: il Mulino.

Giorgi, Alessandra. Forthcoming. Struttura del sintagma nominale. In G. Salvi and L. Renzi, eds., *Grammatica dell'italiano antico*. Bologna: il Mulino.

Giorgi, Alessandra, and Giuseppe Longobardi. 1991. *The Syntax of Noun Phrases*. Cambridge: Cambridge University Press.

Giry-Schneider, Jacqueline. 1997. Sur quoi peut porter un adjectif épithète? L'expression du temps et de l'aspect dans les groupes nominaux. *Langages* 126 (*La description syntaxique des adjectifs pour les traitements informatiques*), 11–38.

Giurgea, Ion. 2005. La linéarisation des adjectifs en roumain: Mouvement ou contraintes sémantiques? In M. Coene and L. Tasmowski, eds., *On Space and Time in Language*, 51–73. Cluj-Napoca: Clusium.

Giurgea, Ion. 2009. Adjective placement and linearization. In J. van Craenenbroeck, ed., *Alternatives to Cartography*, 275–323. Berlin: Mouton de Gruyter.

Giusti, Giuliana. 1993. *La sintassi dei determinanti*. Unipress: Padova.

Giusti, Giuliana. 1996. Is there a FocusP and a TopicP in the noun phrase structure? *University of Venice Working Papers in Linguistics* 6(2): 105–128. http://dspace-unive.cilea.it/bitstream/10278/471/1/6.2.4.pdf.

Giusti, Giuliana. 2002. The functional structure of noun phrases: A bare phrase structure approach. In G. Cinque, ed., *Functional Structure in DP and IP: The Cartography of Syntactic Structures*, vol. 1, 54–90. New York: Oxford University Press.

Giusti, Giuliana. 2005. At the left periphery of the Romanian noun phrase. In M. Coene and L. Tasmowski, eds., *On Space and Time in Language*, 23–49. Cluj-Napoca: Clusium. http://lear.unive.it/handle/10278/734.

Giusti, Giuliana. 2006. Parallels in clausal and nominal periphery. In M. Frascarelli, ed., *Phases of Interpretation*, 163–184. Berlin: Mouton de Gruyter.

Giusti, Giuliana. Forthcoming. Il sintagma aggettivale. In G. Salvi and L. Renzi, eds., *Grammatica dell'italiano antico*. Bologna: il Mulino.

Givón, Talmy. 1970. Notes on the semantic structure of English adjectives. *Language* 46: 816–837.

Givón, Talmy. 1980. *Ute Reference Grammar*. Ignacio, CO: Ute Press.

Goes, Jan. 1999. *L'adjectif: entre nom et verbe*. Paris: De Boek et Larcier.

Gonzaga, Manuela. 2004. The structure of DP in European Portuguese—Evidence from adjectives and possessives. *Harvard Working Papers in Linguistics* 10: 19–49.

Gould, Drusilla, and Christopher Loether. 2002. *An Introduction to the Shoshoni Language*. Salt Lake City: University of Utah Press.

Gouskova, Maria. 2000. The interaction of topic, focus and constituency in Russian. Ms., Amherst College.

Greenberg, Joseph H. 1963. Some universals of grammar with particular reference to the order of meaningful elements. In J. H. Greenberg, ed., *Universals of Grammar*. 73–113. Cambridge, MA: MIT Press.

Groen, B. M. 1998. The use of the long and short adjectival forms in contemporary standard Russian. In A. A. Barentsen, B. M. Groen, J. Schaeken, and R. Sprenger, eds., *Dutch Contributions to the Twelfth International Congress of Slavists: Cracow, August 26–September 3, 1998: Linguistics*, 151–173. Amsterdam: Rodopi.

Grosu, Alexander. 1994. *Three Studies in Locality and Case*. London: Routledge.

Grune, Dick. 1997. Hopi: Survey of an Uto-Aztecan language. http://www.cs.vu.nl/~dick/Summaries/Languages/Hopi.pdf.

Hagège, Claude. 1974. The "adjective" in some African languages. In *Studies in African Linguistics*, supplement 5, 125–133.

Haiman, John. 1978. Conditionals are topics. *Language* 54: 564–589.

Haiman, John. 1980. *Hua: A Papuan Language of the Eastern Highlands of New Guinea*. Amsterdam: Benjamins.

Hale, Ken, and Jay S. Keyser. 1993. On argument structure and the lexical expression of syntactic relations. In K. Hale and J. S. Keyser, eds., *The View from Building 20: Essays in Linguistics in Honor of Sylvain Bromberger*, 53–109. Cambridge, MA: MIT Press.

Hamann, Cornelia. 1991. Adjectives. In A. von Stechow and D. Wunderlich, eds., *Semantik: Ein internationales Handbuch der zeitgenössischen Forschung*, 657–673. Berlin: Walter de Gruyter.

Haspelmath, Martin. 1994. Passive participles across languages. In B. Fox and P. J. Hopper, eds., *Voice: Form and Function*, 151–177. Amsterdam: Benjamins.

Hawkins, John A. 1983. *Word Order Universals*. New York: Academic Press.

Hawkins, John A. 1990. A parsing theory of word order universals. *Linguistic Inquiry* 21: 223–261.

Hawkins, John A. 1994. *A Performance Theory of Order and Constituency*. Cambridge: Cambridge University Press.

Heim, Irene. 1999. Notes on superlatives. Ms., MIT.

Hendrick, Randall. 1990. Operator movement within NP. In A. Halpern, ed., *Proceedings of the Ninth West Coast Conference on Formal Linguistics*, 249–264. Stanford, CA: CSLI Publications.

Hetzron, Robert. 1978. On the relative order of adjectives. In H. Seiler, ed., *Language Universals*, 165–184. Tübingen: Gunter Narr.

Higginbotham, James. 1985. On semantics. *Linguistic Inquiry* 16: 547–593.

Holmberg, Anders, and Jan Rijkhoff. 1998. Word order in the Germanic languages. In A. Siewierska, ed., *Constituent Order in the Languages of Europe*, 75–104. Berlin: Mouton de Gruyter.

Horrocks, Geoffrey, and Melita Stavrou. 1987. Bounding theory and Greek syntax: Evidence from *wh*-movement in NP. *Journal of Linguistics* 23: 79–108.

Huang, C. T. James. 1982. *Logical Relations in Chinese and the Theory of Grammar*. Doctoral dissertation, MIT.

Huang, Shi-Zhe. 2006. Property theory, adjectives, and modification in Chinese. *Journal of East Asian Linguistics* 15: 343–369.

Hulk, Aafke, and Els Verheugd. 1992. "Something funny" in French. In R. Bok-Bennema and R. van Hout, eds., *Linguistics in the Netherlands* 9: 87–100. Amsterdam: Benjamins.

Ihsane, Tabea. 2003. Demonstrative reinforcers in Arabic, Romance, and Germanic. In J. Lecarme, ed., *Research in Afroasiatic Grammar*, vol. 2, 263–285. Amsterdam: Benjamins.

Jackendoff, Ray S. 1972. *Semantic Interpretation in Generative Grammar*. Cambridge, MA: MIT Press.

Jackendoff, Ray. 1997. *The Architecture of the Language Faculty*. Cambridge, MA: MIT Press.

Jacob, Daniel. 2006. Adjective position, specificity, and information structure in Spanish. In Klaus von Heusinger, Georg A. Kaiser, and Elisabeth Stark, eds., *Proceedings of the Workshop "Specificity and the Evolution/Emergence of Nominal Determination Systems in Romance."* Working Paper No. 119, Fachbereich Sprachwissenschaft der Universität Konstanz. http://w3.ub.uni-konstanz.de/v13/volltexte/2006/1718//pdf/AP_119.pdf.

Jacobsson, Bengt. 1961. An unexpected usage: *Ahead, alive*, and the like, before nouns. *Moderna Språk* 55: 240–247.

Jacobsson, Bengt. 1996. A new look at "predicative-only" adjectives in English. *Journal of English Linguistics* 24: 206–219.

James, Deborah. 1979. Two semantic constraints on the occurrence of adjectives and participles after the noun in English. *Linguistics* 17: 687–705.

Jamrozik, Elzbieta. 1996. L'adjectif dans les expressions figées en italien. In G. Groos, P. Lerat, and C. Molinier, eds., *L'adjectif: Une catégorie hétérogène* (*Studi Italiani di Linguistica Teorica e Applicata* 25(3): 641–665).

Jespersen, Otto. 1924. *The Philosophy of Grammar*. London: Allen and Unwin.

Jones, Michael A. 1993. *Sardinian Syntax*. London: Routledge.

Jones, Michael A. 1996. *Foundations of French Syntax*. Cambridge: Cambridge University Press.

Julien, Marit. 2005. *Nominal Phrases from a Scandinavian Perspective*. Amsterdam: Benjamins.

Kamp, Hans. 1975. Two theories about adjectives. In E. Keenan, ed., *Formal Semantics of Natural Language*, 123–155. Cambridge: Cambridge University Press.

Kamp, Hans, and Partee, Barbara. 1995. Prototype theory and compositionality. *Cognition* 57: 129–191.

Kang, Soon Haeng. 2005. On the adjective in Korean. *University of Venice Working Papers in Linguistics* 15: 153–169. http://dspace-unive.cilea.it/bitstream/ 10278/199/1/2005-4s-Haeng_Soon.pdf. (Also published in *Rivista di grammatica generativa* 30 (2005): 3–15.)

Kang, Soon Haeng. 2006. The two forms of the adjective in Korean. *University of Venice Working Papers in Linguistics* 16: 137–163. http://dspace-unive.cilea.it/ bitstream/10278/206/1/2006-4s-Haeng_Soon.pdf.

Kang, Soon Haeng. 2007. *Sintassi dell'aggettivo italiano e coreano*. Doctoral dissertation, University of Venice.

Karanassios, Yorgos. 1992. *Syntaxe comparée du groupe nominal en grec moderne et dans d'autres langues*. Doctoral dissertation, Université de Paris VIII, Vincennes.

Katz, Jonah. 2008. Romance and Restriction. Ms., MIT.

Kayne, Richard S. 1975. *French Syntax*. Cambridge, MA: MIT Press.

Kayne, Richard S. 1994. *The Antisymmetry of Syntax*. Cambridge, MA: MIT Press.

Kayne, Richard S. 1998. Overt vs. covert movement. *Syntax* 1: 128–191.

Kayne, Richard S. 1999. Prepositional complementizers as attractors. *Probus* 11: 39–73.

Kayne, Richard S. 2000. A note on prepositions, complementizers, and word order universals. In R. S. Kayne, *Parameters and Universals*, 314–326. New York: Oxford University Press.

Kayne, Richard S. 2002. On some prepositions that look DP-internal: English *of* and French *de*. *Catalan Journal of Linguistics* 1: 71–115. (Reprinted in Richard S. Kayne, *Movement and Silence*. New York: Oxford University Press, 2005.)

Kayne, Richard S. 2004. Prepositions as probes. In A. Belletti, ed., *Structure and Beyond: The Cartography of Syntactic Structures*, vol. 3, 192–212. New York: Oxford University Press.

Kayne, Richard S. 2005a. *Movement and Silence*. New York: Oxford University Press.

Kayne, Richard S. 2005b. Some notes on comparative syntax, with special reference to English and French. In G. Cinque and R. S. Kayne, eds., *The Oxford Handbook of Comparative Syntax*, 3–69. New York: Oxford University Press. (Reprinted in Richard S. Kayne, *Movement and Silence*. New York: Oxford University Press, 2005.)

Kayne, Richard S. 2008a. Expletives, datives, and the tension between morphology and syntax. In T. Biberauer, ed., *The Limits of Syntactic Variation*, 175–217. Amsterdam: Benjamins. http://www.nyu.edu/gsas/dept/lingu/people/faculty/ kayne/papers/Kayne1006Expletives.pdf.

Kayne, Richard S. 2008b. Some preliminary comparative remarks on French and Italian definite articles. In R. Freidin, C. P. Otero, and M. L. Zubizarreta, eds.,

Foundational Issues in Linguistic Theory: Essays in Honor of Jean-Roger Vergnaud, 291–321. Cambridge, MA: MIT Press. http://www.nyu.edu/gsas/dept/lingu/people/faculty/kayne/papers/Kayne1004DefiniteArticles.pdf.

Keenan, Edward. 2002. Explaining the creation of reflexive pronouns in English. In D. Minkova and R. Stockwell, eds., *Studies in the History of English: A Millennial Perspective*, 325–355. Berlin: Mouton de Gruyter.

Kemmerer, David. 2000. Selective impairment of knowledge underlying prenominal adjective order: Evidence for the autonomy of grammatical semantics. *Journal of Neurolinguistics* 13: 57–82.

Kennedy, Christopher, and Louise McNally. 2005. Scale structure and the semantic typology of gradable predicates. *Language* 81: 345–381.

Kennedy, Christopher, and Jason Merchant. 2000. Attributive comparative deletion. *Natural Language and Linguistic Theory* 18: 89–146.

Kennedy, Christopher, and Jason Stanley. 2008. On *average*. Ms., University of Chicago and Rutgers University. http://semanticsarchive.net/Archive/TY2NzYxY/ks-average.pdf.

Kester, Ellen-Petra. 1996. *The Nature of Adjectival Inflection*. Doctoral dissertation, Utrecht University.

Kester, Ellen-Petra, and Petra Sleeman. 2002. N-ellipsis in Spanish. In H. Broekhuis and P. Fikkert, eds., *Linguistics in the Netherlands 2002*, 107–116. Amsterdam: Benjamins.

Kiefer, Ferenc. 2004. Sur l'ordre des adjectives. In C. Leclère, É. Laporte, M. Piot, and M. Silberzstein, eds., *Lexique, Syntaxe et Lexique-grammaire: Syntax, Lexis & Lexicon-Grammar. Papers in Honour of Maurice Gross*, 275–285. Amsterdam: Benjamins.

Kishimoto, Hideki. 2000. Indefinite pronouns and overt N-raising. *Linguistic Inquiry* 31: 557–566.

Kitahara, Hisatsugo. 1993. Numeral classifier phrases inside DP and the specificity effect. *Japanese/Korean Linguistics* 3: 171–186.

Knittel, Marie Laurence. 2005. Some remarks on adjective placement in the French NP. *Probus* 17: 185–226.

Koch, Karsten A. 2005. German prenominal modifiers. *Proceedings of the 2004 Annual Conference of the Canadian Linguistic Association*. http://http-server.carleton.ca/~mojunker/ACL-CLA/pdf/Koch-CLA-2004.pdf.

Kolliakou, Dimitra. 1995. *Definites and Possessives in Modern Greek: An HPSG Syntax for Noun Phrases*. Doctoral dissertation, University of Edinburgh.

Kolliakou, Dimitra. 1998. Linkhood and multiple definite marking. In G. Bouma, G.-J. M. Kruijff, and R. Oehrle, eds., *Proceedings [of] Joint Conference on Formal Grammar, Head-Driven Phrase Structure Grammar, and Categorial Grammar*, 14–24. http://folli.loria.fr/cds/1998/pdf/hpsg/gosse/proceedings.pdf.

Kolliakou, Dimitra. 1999. Non-monotone anaphora and the syntax of definiteness. In F. Corblin, C. Dobrovie-Sorin, and J.-M. Marandin, eds., *Empirical Issues in Formal Syntax and Semantics*, 121–143. The Hague: Phesus.

Kolliakou, Dimitra. 2003. *Nominal Constructions in Modern Greek: Implications for the Architecture of Grammar*. Stanford, CA: CSLI Publications.

Kolliakou, Dimitra. 2004. Monadic definites and polydefinites: Their form, meaning and use. *Journal of Linguistics* 40: 263–323.

König, Ekkehard. 1971. *Adjectival Constructions in English and German: A Contrastive Analysis*. Heidelberg: Julius Groos Verlag.

Koopman, Hilda. 1984. *The Syntax of Verbs*. Dordrecht: Foris.

Krapova, Iliyana, and Guglielmo Cinque. 2008. On the order of *wh*-phrases in Bulgarian multiple *wh*-fronting. In G. Zybatow, L. Szucsich, U. Junghanns, and R. Meyer, eds., *Formal Description of Slavic Languages*, 318–336. Frankfurt am Main: Lang.

Krause, Cornelia. 2001. *On Reduced Relatives with Genitive Subjects*. Doctoral dissertation, MIT.

Kremers, Joost. 2003. *The Arabic Noun Phrase: A Minimalist Approach*. Utrecht: LOT.

Laca, Brenda, and Liliane Tasmowski. 2001. Distributivité et interpretations dépendantes des expressions d'identité. In G. Kleiber, B. Laca, and L. Tasmowski, eds., *Typologie des groupes nominaux*, 143–166. Rennes: Presses Universitaires de Rennes.

Laca, Brenda, and Liliane Tasmowski. 2003. From non-identity to plurality: French *différent* as an adjective and as a determiner. In J. Quer, J. Schroten, M. Scorretti, P. Sleeman, and E. Verheugd, eds., *Romance Languages and Linguistic Theory 2001*, 155–176. Amsterdam: Benjamins.

Laca, Brenda, and Liliane Tasmowski. 2004. *Différents*. In F. Corblin and H. de Swart, eds., *Handbook of French Semantics*, 109–118. Stanford, CA: CSLI Publications.

Laczkó, Tibor. 2001. Another look at participles and adjectives in the English DP. In M. Butt and T. H. King, eds., *Proceedings of the LFG01 Conference*, University of Hong Kong. Stanford, CA: CSLI Publications. http://csli-publications.stanford.edu/LFG/6/lfg01/laczko.pdf.

Laenzlinger, Christopher. 2000. French adjective ordering: Perspectives on DP-internal movement types. *Generative Grammar in Geneva* 1: 55–104. http://www.unige.ch/lettres/linge/syntaxe/journal/pdf_volume_one/article3_laenzlinger.pdf.

Laenzlinger, Christopher. 2005a. French adjective ordering: Perspectives on DP-internal movement types. *Lingua* 115: 645–689.

Laenzlinger, Christopher. 2005b. Some notes on DP-internal movements. *Generative Grammar in Geneva* 4: 227–260. http://www.unige.ch/lettres/linge/syntaxe/journal/Volume4/LaenzlingerGG@G2004200522414735.pdf.

Laenzlinger, Christopher. Forthcoming. *Elements of Comparative Generative Syntax: A Cartographic Approach*. Padua: Unipress.

Lamarche, Jacques. 1991. Problems for N°-movement to NumP. *Probus* 3: 215–236.

Lance, Donald M. 1968. *Sequential Ordering in Prenominal Modifiers in English: A Critical Review*. Doctoral dissertation, University of Texas at Austin.

Langacker, Ronald, ed., 1977. *Studies in Uto-Aztecan Grammar, Volume 1: An Overview of Uto-Aztecan Grammar*. Arlington: University of Texas and Summer Institute of Linguistics.

Larson, Richard K. 1995. Olga is a beautiful dancer. Ms., SUNY Stony Brook (text of a paper delivered at the 1995 Winter Meeting of the LSA, New Orleans; available at: http://semlab5.sbs.sunysb.edu/~rlarson/lsa95.pdf).

Larson, Richard K. 1998. Events and modification in nominals. In D. Strolovitch and A. Lawson, eds., *Proceedings from Semantics and Linguistic Theory (SALT) VIII*, 145–168. Ithaca, NY: Cornell University Press. http://semlab5.sbs.sunysb.edu/~rlarson/salt8.pdf.

Larson, Richard K. 1999. *Semantics of Adjectival Modification*. Lectures presented at the Dutch National Graduate School (LOT), Amsterdam, The Netherlands. http://semlab5.sbs.sunysb.edu/~rlarson/LOT(99)/Contents.htmld/index.html.

Larson, Richard K. 2000a. ACD in AP? Paper presented at the 19th West Coast Conference on Formal Linguistics (WCCFL 19), Los Angeles. http://semlab5.sbs.sunysb.edu/~rlarson/wccfl19.pdf.

Larson, Richard K. 2000b. Temporal modification in nominals. Handout of paper presented at the International Round Table "The Syntax of Tense and Aspect," Paris, November 15–18, 2000. http://semlab5.sbs.sunysb.edu/~rlarson/ParisHandout.pdf.

Larson, Richard K., and Sungeun Cho. 1999. Temporal adjectives and the structure of possessive DPs. In S. Bird, A. Carnie, J. D. Haugen, and P. Norquest, eds., *Proceedings of the 18th West Coast Conference on Formal Linguistics*, 299–311. Somerville, MA: Cascadilla Press.

Larson, Richard K., and Sungeun Cho. 2003. Temporal adjectives and the structure of possessive DPs. *Natural Language Semantics* 11: 217–247. http://semlab5.sbs.sunysb.edu/~rlarson/Larson&Cho03.pdf.

Larson, Richard K., and Franc Marušič. 2004. On indefinite pronoun structures with APs: Reply to Kishimoto. *Linguistic Inquiry* 35: 268–287.

Larson, Richard K., and Naoko Takahashi. 2004. Order and interpretation in prenominal relative clauses. In M. Kelepir and B. Öztürk, eds., *Proceedings of the Workshop on Altaic Formal Linguistics II. MIT Working Papers in Linguistics* vol. 54: 101–120. Cambridge, MA: MITWPL. http://semlab5.sbs.sunysb.edu/~rlarson/larson-papers.html.

Laskova, Vesselina. 2006a. *The Structure of Adnominal Modification in Bulgarian*. Doctoral dissertation, University of Venice. http://dspace-unive.cilea.it/handle/10278/999.

Laskova, Vesselina. 2006b. Verbal participles and the prenominal position in English. Ms., University of Venice. http://lear.unive.it/handle/10278/207.

Ledgeway, Adam. 2007. La posizione dell'aggettivo nella storia del napoletano. In D. Bentley and A. Ledgeway, eds., *Sui dialetti italo romanzi: Saggi in onore di Nigel B. Vincent*, 104–125. The Italianist, No. 27, Special Supplement 1.

Lehmann, Christian. 1984. *Der Relativsatz*. Tübingen: Gunter Narr.

Lekakou, Marika, and Kriszta Szendrői. 2007. Eliding the noun in close apposition, or Greek polydefinites revisited. Paper presented at the Workshop on Greek Syntax and Semantics, MIT, May 20–22, 2007. http://the-source.dlp.mit.edu: 16080/greeksynsym/papers/Lekakou_Szendroi.pdf. (Also appeared in *UCL Working Papers in Linguistics* 19 (2007): 129–154. http://www.langsci.ucl.ac.uk/ linguistics/publications/WPL/07papers/uclwpl%2019%20Lekakou%20& %20Szendroi.pdf.)

Leko, Nedžad. 1988. X-bar theory and internal structure of NPs. *Lingua* 75: 135–169.

Leko, Nedžad. 1992. Restrictive and appositive forms of Serbo-Croatian descriptive adjectives. *Zeitschrift für Slawistik* 37: 621–629.

Leko, Nedžad. 1996. Definite and indefinite forms of descriptive adjectives in Bosnian. In R. Benacchio, F. Fici, and L. Gebert, eds., *Determinatezza e Indeterminatezza nelle Lingue Slave: Problemi di Morfosintassi delle Lingue Slave* 5: 147–162. Padua: Unipress.

Leko, Nedžad. 1999. Functional categories and the structure of the DP in Bosnian. In M. Dimitrova-Vulchanova and L. Hellan, eds., *Topics in South Slavic Syntax and Semantics*, 229–252. Benjamins: Amsterdam.

Leu, Thomas. 2004. Something invisible in English. *U. Penn Working Papers in Linguistics* 11: 143–154. http://ling.auf.net/lingBuzz/000010.

Leu, Thomas. 2007. These HERE Demonstratives. *U. Penn Working Papers in Linguistics* 13: 141–154. http://ling.auf.net/lingBuzz/000274.

Leu, Thomas. 2008. *The Internal Syntax of Determiners.* Doctoral dissertation, New York University. http://ling.auf.net/lingBuzz/000745 or http://gagl.eldoc.ub .rug.nl/FILES/root/2008-47/2008-47-01/2008-47-01.pdf.

Leu, Thomas. 2009. From Greek to Germanic: Poly-(*in)-definiteness and weak/ strong adjectival inflection. In J. M. Brucart, A. Gavarró, and J. Solà, eds., *Merging Features*. Oxford: Oxford University Press. http://ling.auf.net/lingBuzz/ 000392.

Levi, Judith. 1973. Where do all those other adjectives come from? In C. Corum, T. C. Smith-Stark, and A. Weiser, eds., *Papers from the Ninth Regional Meeting of the Chicago Linguistic Society*, 332–345. Chicago: Chicago Linguistic Society.

Levi, Judith. 1975. *The Syntax and Semantics of Non-predicating Adjectives in English.* Doctoral dissertation, University of Chicago.

Levi, Judith. 1978. *Syntax and Semantics of Complex Nominals.* New York: Academic Press.

Levin, Beth, and Malka Rappaport. 1986. The formation of adjectival passives. *Linguistic Inquiry* 17: 623–661.

Li, Xu-Ping. 2009. Semantics of pre-classifier adjectives. In S. Blaho, C. Constantinescu, and B. Le Bruyn, eds., *Proceedings of ConSOLE XVI, 2008*, 117–134. Leiden: University of Leiden. http://www.sole.leidenuniv.nl/.

Lindsey, Geoffrey, and Janine Scancarelli. 1985. Where have all the adjectives come from? In M. Niepokuj, M. VanClay, V. Nikiforidov, D. Feder, with C. Brugman, M. Macanlay, N. Beery and M. Emanatian, eds., *Proceedings of the*

Eleventh Annual Meeting of the Berkeley Linguistics Society, 207–215. Berkeley: Berkeley Linguistics Society.

Lombard, Alf. 1974. *La langue roumaine: Une présentation.* Paris: Klincksieck.

Longobardi, Giuseppe. 1994. Reference and proper names. *Linguistic Inquiry* 25: 609–665.

Longobardi, Giuseppe. 2001. How comparative is semantics? A unified parametric theory of bare nouns and proper names. *Natural Language Semantics* 9: 335–369.

Ludlow, Peter. 1989. Implicit comparison classes. *Linguistics and Philosophy* 12: 519–533.

Luján, Marta. 1973. Pre- and postnominal adjectives in Spanish. *Kritikon Litterarum* 2: 398–408.

Luján, Marta. 1980. *Sintaxis y semántica del adjetivo.* Madrid: Cátedra.

Lyons, John. 1968. *Introduction to Theoretical Linguistics.* Cambridge: Cambridge University Press.

Mackenzie, Ian. 2004. *Topics in Spanish Syntax.* Lecture notes. University of Newcastle upon Tyne. http://www.staff.ncl.ac.uk/i.e.mackenzie/syntax.htm.

MacLaughlin, Dawn. 1997. *The Structure of Determiner Phrases: Evidence from American Sign Language.* Doctoral dissertation, Boston University. ftp://louis-xiv.bu.edu/pub/asl/disserts/MacL97.pdf.

Madugu, Isaac S. George. 1976. Yoruba adjectives have merged with verbs: Or are they just emerging? *Journal of West African Languages* 11(1–2): 85–102.

Maho, Jouni. 1998. Notes on nouns and noun phrases in Iká. *Working Paper from the Gothenburgian Iká Sessions 1998.* Department of Oriental and African Languages, Göteborg University. http://www.african.gu.se/maho/downloads/mahoika.pdf.

Mahootian, Shahrzad. 1996. Code-switching and universal constraints: Evidence from Farsi/English. *World Englishes* 15: 377–384.

Maling, Joan. 1983. Transitive adjectives: A case of categorial reanalysis. In F. Heny and B. Richards, eds., *Linguistic Categories: Auxiliaries and Related Puzzles*, vol 1, 253–289. Dordrecht: Reidel.

Mallén, Enrique. 2001. Issues in the syntax of DP in Romance and Germanic. In J. Gutierréz-Rexach and L. Silva-Villar, eds., *Current Issues in Spanish Syntax and Semantics*, 39–63. Berlin: Mouton de Gruyter.

Mallén, Enrique. 2002. On the distribution of restrictive vs. nonrestrictive adjectives in Germanic and Romance. In I. Rauch and G. F. Carr, eds., *New Insights in Germanic Linguistics 3*, 177–210. Bern: Peter Lang.

Malouf, Robert. 2000. The order of prenominal adjectives in natural language generation. In *Proceedings of the 38th Annual Meeting of the Association for Computational Linguistics*, 85–92. Hong Kong: ACL.

Manolessou, Io. 2000. *Greek Noun Phrase Structure: A Study in Syntactic Evolution.* Doctoral dissertation, Cambridge University.

Marchis, Mihaela, and Artemis Alexiadou. 2008. On the properties of adjectival modification in Romanian: The *cel* construction. In E. Aboh, E. van der Linden, J. Quer, and P. Sleeman, eds., *Romance Languages and Linguistic Theory*. Amsterdam: Benjamins. http://ifla.uni-stuttgart.de/institut/mitarbeiter/artemis/handouts/celconstruction.pdf.

Marinis, Theodore, and E. Phoevos Panagiotidis. 2006. Determiner spreading as DP-predication. Ms., University of Reading and Cyprus College.

Markus, Manfred. 1997. "The men present" vs. "the present case": Word order rules concerning the position of the English adjective. *Anglia* 115: 487–506.

Martín, Juan. 1995. *On the Syntactic Structure of Spanish Noun Phrases*. Doctoral dissertation, University of Southern California.

Marušič, Franc, and Rok Žaucer. 2006. The "definite article" *TA* in colloquial Slovenian. In J. Lavine, S. Franks, M. Tasseva-Kurktchieva, and H. Filip, eds., *Annual Workshop on Formal Approaches to Slavic Linguistics: The Princeton Meeting 2005*, 189–204. Ann Arbor: Michigan Slavic Publications.

Marušič, Franc, and Rok Žaucer. 2007. On the adjectival definite article in Slovenian. To be published in *Forum Bosnae: Proceedings of Contemporary Linguistic Prospects*. http://ling.auf.net/lingbuzz/000479.

Marušič, Franc, and Rok Žaucer. 2009. Two strategies for combining adjectives with indefinite pronouns. In A. Schardl, M. Walkow, and M. Abdurrahman, eds., *Proceedings of the Thirty-Eighth Annual Meeting of the North East Linguistic Society*, 135–148. Amherst, MA: GLSA Publications.

Matushansky, Ora. 2002. *Movement of Degree/Degree of Movement*. Doctoral dissertation, MIT.

Matushansky, Ora. 2005a. Les adjectifs: Une introduction. In P. Cabredo Hofherr and O. Matushansky, eds., *L'adjectif* (*Recherches Linguistiques de Vincennes* 34: 9–54).

Matushansky, Ora. 2005b. Call me an ambulance. In L. Bateman and C. Ussery, eds., *Proceedings of the Thirty-Fifth Annual Meeting of the North East Linguistic Society*, 419–434. Amherst, MA: GLSA Publications.

Matushansky, Ora. 2006. How to be short: Some remarks on the syntax of Russian adjectives. Paper presented at the Séminaire de l'UMR 7023, Paris. (Long handout available at http://www.let.uu.nl/~Ora.Matushansky/personal/Downloads/rushort.pdf.)

Matushansky, Ora. 2008. On the attributive nature of superlatives. *Syntax* 11: 26–90.

McCawley, James D. 1970. Foreword to G. Lakoff, *Irregularity in Syntax*, v–viii. New York: Holt, Rinehart and Winston.

McKinney-Bock, Katy. 2009. *Effects of Focus on Adjective Ordering Restrictions*. Master's thesis, University of Southern California.

McLaughlin, John E. 2006. *Timbisha* (*Panamint*). Munich: Lincom Europa.

McNally, Louise. 2005. Lexical representation and modification within the noun phrase. *Recherches Linguistiques de Vincennes* 34: 191–206.

McNally, Louise, and Gemma Boleda. 2004. Relational adjectives as properties of kinds. In O. Bonami and P. Cabredo Hofherr, eds., *Empirical Issues in Formal Syntax and Semantics* 5, 179–196. http://www.cssp.cnrs.fr/eiss5.

Mehlhorn, Grit. 2001. Information structure of discontinuous constituents in Russian. In G. Zybatow, U. Junghanns, G. Mehlhorn, and L. Szucsich, eds., *Current Issues in Formal Slavic Linguistics*: 344–352. Frankfurt am Main: Lang.

Moltmann, Friederike. 1992. Reciprocals and same/different: Towards a semantic analysis. *Linguistics and Philosophy* 15: 411–462.

Moltmann, Friederike. 1997. *Parts and Wholes in Semantics*. New York: Oxford University Press.

Morzycki, Marcin. 2005. *Mediated Modification: Functional Structure and the Interpretation of Modifier Positions*. Doctoral dissertation, University of Massachusetts at Amherst.

Morzycki, Marcin. 2006. Size adjectives and adnominal degree modification. In E. Georgala and J. Howell, eds., *Proceedings from Semantics and Linguistic Theory (SALT)* XV. Ithaca, NY: CLC Publications, Cornell University. (A longer version of the article is available at https://www.msu.edu/~morzycki/papers/bigidiot_long.pdf.)

Morzycki, Marcin. 2008. Nonrestrictive modifiers in nonparenthetical positions. In L. McNally and C. Kennedy, eds., *Adjectives and Adverbs: Syntax, Semantics, and Discourse*, 101–122. Oxford: Oxford University Press.

Morzycki, Marcin. 2009. Degree modification of gradable nouns: Size adjectives and adnominal degree morphemes. *Natural Language Semantics* 17: 175–203.

Moshiri, Leila. 1988. *Colloquial Persian*. London: Routledge.

Motsch, Wolfgang. 1967. Können attributive Adjektive durch Transformationen erklärt werden? *Folia Linguistica* 1: 23–48.

Mouma, Evangelia. 1993. On some properties of DPs in Modern Greek. *UCL Working Papers in Linguistics* 5: 75–101.

Mui, Evelynne. 2002. Adjectival modification in Cantonese Chinese. In D. Hole, P. Law, and N. Zhang, eds., *Webfest for Horst-Dieter Gasde*. http://www.zas.gwz-berlin.de/mitarb/homepage/webfest/.

Müller, Stefan. 2009. A head-driven phrase structure grammar for Maltese. In B. Comrie, R. Fabri, E. Hume, M. Mifsud, T. Stolz, and M. Vanhove, eds., *Introducing Maltese Linguistics*, 83–112. Amsterdam: Benjamins. http://hpsg.fu-berlin.de/~stefan/Pub/maltese-sketch.html.

Muromatsu, Keiko. 2001. Adjective ordering as the reflection of a hierarchy in the noun system: A study from the perspective of numeral classifiers. *Linguistics Variation Yearbook* 1: 181–207.

Napoli, Donna Jo. 1993. *Syntax: Theory and Problems*. New York: Oxford University Press.

Noailly, Michèle. 1999. *L'adjectif en français*. Paris: Ophrys.

Noonan, Michael. 1992. *A Grammar of Lango*. Berlin: Mouton de Gruyter.

Nowak, Anita. 2000. On split PPs in Polish. Unpublished ms., University of Massachusetts.

Oersnes, Bjarne, and Stella Markantonatou. 2002. Group adjectives. *Journal of Greek Linguistics* 3: 139–178.

Osumi, Midori. 1995. *Tinrin Grammar*. Honolulu: University of Hawai'i Press.

Paniagotidis, Phoevos. 2007. Determiner spreading as DP-predication. http://ling.auf.net/lingBuzz/000159.

Partee, Barbara H. [1983] 1997. Uniformity vs. versatility: The genitive, a case study. Appendix to T. Janssen, "Compositionality." In J. van Bentham and A. ter Meulen, eds., *The Handbook of Logic and Language*, 464–470. New York: Elsevier.

Partee, Barbara H. 1995. Lexical semantics and compositionality. In L. Gleitman and M. Liberman, eds., *An Invitation to Cognitive Science, Volume 1: Language*, 311–360. 2nd ed. Cambridge, MA: MIT Press.

Partee, Barbara H. 2003a. Are there privative adjectives? Ms., University of Massachusetts. (Originally presented at the Conference on the Philosophy of Terry Parsons, Notre Dame, February 7–8, 2003. http://semanticsarchive.net/Archive/TFlNWIzO/AreTherePrivatives.pdf.)

Partee, Barbara H. 2003b. Privative adjectives: Subsective plus coercion. To appear in R. Bäuerle, U. Reyle, and T. E. Zimmermann, eds., *Presuppositions and Discourse*. Amsterdam: Elsevier. http://people.umass.edu/partee/docs/ParteeInPressKampFest.pdf.

Partee, Barbara H. 2007. Compositionality and coercion in semantics: The dynamics of adjective meaning. In G. Bouma et al., eds., *Cognitive Foundations of Interpretation*, 145–161. Amsterdam: Royal Netherlands Academy of Arts and Sciences. https://udrive.oit.umass.edu/partee/Partee2007CompositionalityCoercionAdjs.pdf.

Partee, Barbara H., and Vladimir Borchev. 2000. Genitives, relational nouns, and the argument-modifier distinction. In C. Fabricius-Hansen, E. Lang, and C. Maienborn, eds., *Approaching the Grammar of Adjuncts* (ZAS Working Papers in Linguistics 17), 177–201. Berlin: Zentrum für Allgemeine Sprachwissenschaft. http://www.zas.gwz-berlin.de/papers/zaspil/articles/zp17/160.pdf.

Pasqui, Rita. 2007. "Something interesting": Insights on the position of adjectival predicates in Romance. Paper presented at the 9th SUNY, CUNY, NYU Mini-Conference, December 1, 2007, New York University. http://www.nyu.edu/gsas/dept/lingu/events/miniconf9/abstracts/rita.pdf.

Paul, Waltraud. 2005. Adjectival modification in Mandarin Chinese and related issues. *Linguistics* 43: 757–793. (Prepublication version available at http://lodel.ehess.fr/crlao/docannexe.php?id=545.)

Paul, Waltraud. 2006. Zhu Dexi's two classes of adjectives revisited. In C. Anderl and H. Eifring, eds., *Studies in Chinese Language and Culture: Festschrift in Honour of Christoph Harbsmeier on the Occasion of His 60th Birthday*, 303–315. Oslo: Hermes Academic Publishing. http://crlao.ehess.fr/docannexe.php?id=486.

Paul, Waltraud. 2010. Adjectives in Mandarin Chinese: The rehabilitation of a much ostracized category. In P. Cabredo Hofherr and O. Matushansky, eds., *Adjectives: Formal analyses in syntax and semantics*, 115–152. Amsterdam: Benjamins.

Pawley, Andrew. 2006. Where have all the verbs gone? Remarks on the organization of languages with small, closed verb classes. Paper presented at the 11th Biennial Rice University Linguistics Symposium ("Intertheoretical Approaches to Complex Verb Constructions"), March 16–18, 2006. http://www.ruf.rice.edu/~lingsymp/Pawley_paper.pdf.

Pereltsvaig, Asya. 2000. Short and long adjectives in Russian: Against the Null-N° analysis. Ms., McGill University.

Pereltsvaig, Asya. 2001. Syntactic categories are not primitive: Evidence from short and long adjectives in Russian. In S. Franks, T. Holloway King, and M. Yadroff, eds., *Annual Workshop on Formal Approaches to Slavic Linguistics: The Bloomington Meeting 2000 (FASL 10)*, 209–227. Ann Arbor: Michigan Slavic Publications.

Pereltsvaig, Asya. 2006a. Head movement in Hebrew nominals: A reply to Shlonsky. *Lingua* 116(8): A1–A40.

Pereltsvaig, Asya. 2006b. Passing by cardinals: In support of head movement in nominals. In J. Lavine, S. Franks, M. Tasseva-Kurktchieva, and H. Filip, eds., *Annual Workshop on Formal Approaches to Slavic Linguistics: The Princeton Meeting 2005 (FASL 14)*, 277–292. Ann Arbor: Michigan Slavic Publications.

Pereltsvaig, Asya. 2007. The universality of DP: A view from Russian. *Studia Linguistica* 61: 59–94.

Picallo, M. Carme. 1994. A mark of specificity in indefinite nominals. *Catalan Working Papers in Linguistics* 4(1): 143–167. http://ddd.uab.cat/pub/cwpil/1132256Xv4n1p143.pdf.

Picallo, M. Carme. 2002. L'adjectiu i el sintagma adjectival. In J. Solà et al., eds., *Gramàtica del català contemporani*, vol. 2, 1641–1688. Barcelona: Empúries.

Plank, Frans, and Edith Moravcsik. 1996. The Maltese article: Language-particulars and universals. In A. J. Borg and F. Plank, eds., *The Maltese Noun Phrase Meets Typology* (*Rivista di linguistica* 8: 183–212).

Platzack, Christer. 1982. Transitive adjectives in Old and Modern Swedish. In A. Ahlqvist, ed., *Papers from the 5th International Conference on Historical Linguistics*, 273–282. Amsterdam: Benjamins.

Platzack, Christer. 1982–1983. Transitive adjectives in Swedish: A phenomenon with implications for the theory of abstract case. *Linguistic Review* 2: 39–56.

Posner, Roland. 1986. Iconicity in syntax: The natural order of adjectives. In T. A. Sebeok, P. Bouissac, and M. Herzfeld, eds., *Iconicity: Essays on the Nature of Culture*, 305–337. Tübingen: Stauffenburg Verlag.

Postal, Paul. 1972. The derivation of English pseudo-adjectives. Unpublished manuscript. Yorktown Heights, New York: IBM Thomas J. Watson Research Center.

Pullum, Geoffrey K., and Rodney Huddleston. 2002. Adjectives and adverbs. In R. Huddleston and G. K. Pullum, *The Cambridge Grammar of the English Language*, 525–595. Cambridge: Cambridge University Press.

Pustejovsky, James. 1995. *The Generative Lexicon*. Cambridge, MA: MIT Press.

Quirk, Randolph, Sidney Greenbaum, Geoffrey Leech, and Jan Svartvik. 1972. *A Grammar of Contemporary English*. London: Longman.

Radford, Andrew. 1989. The syntax of attributive adjectives in English and the problems of inheritance. Revised version of a paper titled "The syntax of attributive adjectives in English: Abnegating Abney" presented at the Colloquium on Noun Phrase Structure, University of Manchester, 1989. http://privatewww.essex.ac.uk/~radford/PapersPublications/adjectives.htm.

Ramaglia, Francesca. 2007. Monadic vs. polydefinite modification: The case of Greek. In A. Bisetto and F. E. Barbieri, eds., *Proceedings of the 33rd Incontro di Grammatica Generativa*, 162–177. Dipartimento di Lingue e Letterature Straniere Moderne, Università di Bologna. http://amsacta.cib.unibo.it/archive/00002397/01/PROCEEDINGS_IGG33.pdf.

Rasom, Sabrina. 2006. Il plurale femminile nel ladino dolomitico tra morfologia e sintassi. In N. Penello and D. Pescarini, eds., *Atti della XI Giornata di Dialettologia. Quaderni di lavoro dell'ASIS* 5: 20–35. http://www.maldura.unipd.it/ddlcs/.

Rasom, Sabrina. 2008. *Lazy Concord in the Central Ladin Feminine Plural DP: A Case Study on the Interaction between Morphosyntax and Semantics*. Doctoral dissertation, University of Padua. http://paduaresearch.cab.unipd.it/268/1/tesiSabrinaRasom.pdf.

Real Academia Española. 1973. *Esbozo de una nueva gramática de la lengua española*. Madrid: Espasa Calpe.

Reesink, Ger P. 1990. Adverbs in Papuan languages. Or: "Where have all the adverbs gone?" In H. Pinkster and I. Genee, eds., *Unity in Diversity: Papers Presented to Simon C. Dik on His 50th birthday*, 211–228. Dordrecht: Foris.

Rice, Keren. 1989. *A Grammar of Slave*. Berlin: Mouton de Gruyter.

Riemsdijk, Henk van. 1983. The case of German adjectives. In F. Heny and B. Richards, eds., *Linguistic Categories*, vol. 1, 223–252. Dordrecht: Reidel.

Riemsdijk, Henk van. 1998. Categorial feature magnetism: The endocentricity and distribution of projections. *Journal of Comparative Germanic Linguistics* 2: 1–48.

Riemsdijk, Henk van. 2001. A far from simple matter: Syntactic reflexes of syntax-pragmatics misalignments. In R. M. Harnish and I. Kenesei, eds., *Semantics, Pragmatics and Discourse: Perspectives and Connections. A Festschrift for Ferenc Kiefer*, 21–41. Amsterdam: Benjamins.

Rigau, Gemma. 1999. La estructura del sintagma nominal: Los modificatores del nombre. In I. Bosque and V. Demonte, eds., *Gramática Descriptiva de la Lengua Española*, 311–362. Madrid: Espasa Calpe.

Rijkhoff, Jan. 1998. Order in the noun phrase of the languages of Europe. In A. Siewierska, ed., *Constituent Order in the Languages of Europe*, 321–382. Berlin: Mouton de Gruyter.

Rijkhoff, Jan. 2002. *The Noun Phrase*. Oxford: Oxford University Press.

Risselada, Rodie. 1983. Coordination and juxtaposition of adjectives in the Latin NP. *Glotta* 62: 202–231.

Rizzi, Luigi. 1985. Two notes on the linguistic interpretation of Broca's aphasia. In M.-L. Kean, ed., *Agrammatism*, 153–164. New York: Academic Press.

Roca Urgell, Francesc. 1996. *La determinación y la modificatión nominal en español*. Doctoral dissertation, Universitat Autònoma de Barcelona. http://seneca.uab.es/ggt/Tesis/determinacion.pdf.

Roehrs, Dorian. 2006. *The Morpho-Syntax of the Germanic Noun Phrase: Determiners* Move *into the Determiner Phrase*. Doctoral dissertation, Indiana University. http://www.forl.unt.edu/~roehrs/entire%20diss.pdf.

Roehrs, Dorian. 2008. Something inner- and cross-linguistically different. *Journal of Comparative Germanic Linguistics* 11: 1–42.

Roehrs, Dorian. 2009. *Demonstratives and Definite Articles as Nominal Auxiliaries*. Amsterdam: Benjamins

Ronat, Mitsou. 1974. *Échelles de base et mutations en syntaxe française*. Doctoral dissertation, Paris VIII (Vincennes).

Ronat, Mitsou. 1977. Une contrainte sur l'effacement du nom. In M. Ronat, ed., *Langue*, 153–169. Paris: Hermann.

Ross, John Robert. 1964. *A Partial Grammar of English Superlatives*. Master's thesis, University of Pennsylvania.

Ross, John Robert. 1967. *Constraints on Variables in Syntax*. Doctoral dissertation, MIT.

Rowlett, Paul. 2007. *The Syntax of French*. Cambridge: Cambridge University Press.

Rubin, Edward J. 1994. *Modification: A Syntactic Analysis and Its Consequences*. Doctoral dissertation, Cornell University.

Rubin, Edward J. 1997. The transparent syntax and semantics of modifiers. In B. Agbayani and S.-W. Tang, eds., *Proceedings of the Fifteenth West Coast Conference on Formal Linguistics*, 429–439. Stanford, CA: Stanford Linguistics Association.

Rubin, Edward J. 2002. The structure of modifiers. Ms., University of Utah. http://www.linguistics.utah.edu/Faculty/rubin.htm.

Rutkowski, Paweł. 2007. The syntactic properties and diachronic development of postnominal adjectives in Polish. In R. Compton, M. Goledzinowska, and V. Savchenko, eds., *Annual Workshop on Formal Approaches to Slavic Linguistics (FASL 15): The Toronto Meeting*, 326–345. Ann Arbor: Michigan Slavic Publications.

Rutkowski, Paweł, and Ljiljana Progovac. 2005. Classification projection in Polish and Serbian: The position and shape of classifying adjectives. In M. Tasseva-Kurktchieva, S. Franks, and F. Gladney, eds., *Formal Approaches to Slavic Linguistics 13: The Columbia Meeting 2004*, 289–299. Ann Arbor: Michigan Slavic Publications.

Rutkowski, Paweł, and Ljiljana Progovac. 2006. Classifying adjectives and noun movement in Lithuanian. In *Proceedings of the 8th Seoul International Conference on Generative Grammar*. http://mercury.hau.ac.kr/kggc/Conferences/SICOGG10/SICOGG8_Program.htm.

Saba, Walid. 2008. Concerning Olga, the beautiful little street dancer (adjectives as higher-order polymorphic functions). Ms., American Institutes for Research. http://ling.auf.net/lingBuzz/000589.

Sadler, Louisa, and Douglas J. Arnold. 1994. Prenominal adjectives and the phrasal/lexical distinction. *Journal of Linguistics* 30: 187–226.

Saltarelli, Mario. 1999. An integrated theory of adjectives: The alternating adjectives of Romance. In P. Bouillon and E. Viegas, eds., *Description des adjectifs pour le traitment informatique: Proceedings of TALN*, 46–56. Cargess (Corsica).

Santorini, Beatrice, and Shahrzad Mahootian. 1995. Codeswitching and the syntactic status of adnominal adjectives. *Lingua* 96: 1–27.

Sauereisen, Britta. 2005. Against an underlying relative clause approach of attributive adjectives in German. Ms., University of Stuttgart. http://www.ims.uni-stuttgart.de/Graduiertenkolleg/Dokumente/Klausurtagung_2005/Sauereisen.pdf.

Saxon, Leslie. 2000. Head-internal relative clauses in Dogrib (Athapaskan). In A. Carnie, E. Jelinek, and M. A. Willie, eds., *Papers in Honor of Ken Hale: Working Papers in Endangered and Less Familiar Languages* 1. Cambridge, MA: MITWPL, Department of Linguistics and Philosophy, MIT.

Schachter, Paul. 1985. Parts-of-speech-systems. In T. Shopen, ed., *Language Typology and Syntactic Description*, 3–61. Cambridge: Cambridge University Press.

Schäfer, Martin. 2009. A N constructions in Mandarin and the compound versus phrase debate. *Word Structure* 2: 272–293.

Schäfer, Roland. 2007. On frequency adjectives. In E. Puig-Waldmüller, ed., *Proceedings of Sinn und Bedeutung* 11: 555–567. Barcelona: Universitat Pompeu Fabra. http://parles.upf.es/glif/pub/sub11/individual/schaefer.pdf.

Schiffman, Harold F. 1999. *A Reference Grammar of Spoken Tamil*. Cambridge: Cambridge University Press.

Schmitt, Cristina. 1996. *Aspect and the Syntax of Noun Phrases*. Doctoral dissertation, University of Maryland.

Schueler, David. 2005. Comparative superlatives in relative clauses. *Proceedings of the 29th Annual Penn Linguistics Colloquium*. http://www.linguistics.ucla.edu/people/grads/daschuel/SchuelerPLCProceedings2005.pdf.

Schwarz, Bernhard. 2006. Attributive *wrong*. In D. Baumer, D. Montero, and M. Scanlon, eds., *Proceedings of the 25th West Coast Conference on Formal Linguistics*, 362–370. Somerville, MA: Cascadilla Press. http://www.lingref.com/cpp/wccfl/25/paper1469.pdf.

Scott, Gary-John. 2002. Stacked adjectival modification and the structure of nominal phrases. In G. Cinque, ed., *Functional Structure in DP and IP: The Cartography of Syntactic Structures*, vol. 1, 91–120. New York: Oxford University Press.

Seiler, Hansjakob. 1978. Determination: A functional dimension for interlanguage comparison. In H. Seiler, ed., *Language Universals*, 301–328. Tübingen: Gunter Narr.

Sharvit, Yael, and Penka Stateva. 2002. Superlative expressions, context, and focus. *Linguistics and Philosophy* 25: 453–504.

Shlonsky, Ur. 2000. The form of Semitic noun phrases: An antisymmetric, non-N-movement account. Ms., University of Geneva.

Shlonsky, Ur. 2004. The form of Semitic noun phrases: An antisymmetric, non-N-movement account. *Lingua* 114: 1465–1526.

Shlonsky, Ur. 2006. Rejoinder to Pereltsvaig's head movement in Hebrew nominals: A reply to Shlonsky. *Lingua* 116: 1195–1197.

Shu, Chih-Hsiang. 2009. Sentential adverbs as focusing adverbs. Ms., Stony Brook University. http://www.linguistics.stonybrook.edu/files/u32/Glour_paper.pdf.

Sichel, Ivy. 2000a. Evidence for DP-internal Remnant Movement. In M. Hirotani, A. Coetzee, N. Hall, and J. Y. Kim, eds., *Proceedings of the Thirtieth North East Linguistic Society Meeting, Rutgers University*, vol. 2, 569–581. Amherst, MA: GLSA Publications.

Sichel, Ivy. 2000b. Remnant and phrasal movement in Hebrew adjectives and possessives. Ms., CUNY Graduate Center.

Sichel, Ivy. 2002. Phrasal movement in Hebrew adjectives and possessives. In A. Alexiadou, E. Anagnostopoulou, S. Barbiers, and H.-M. Gaertner, eds., *Dimensions of Movement: From Features to Remnants*, 297–339. Amsterdam: Benjamins.

Sichel, Ivy. 2003. Phrasal movement in Hebrew DPs. In J. Lecarme, ed., *Research in Afroasiatic Grammar*, vol. 2, 447–479. Amsterdam: Benjamins.

Siegel, Muffy E. A. 1976a. *Capturing the Adjective*. Doctoral dissertation, University of Massachusetts at Amherst.

Siegel, Muffy E. A. 1976b. Capturing the Russian adjective. In B. H. Partee, ed., *Montague Grammar*, 293–309. New York: Academic Press.

Siewierska, Anna, and Ludmila Uhlířová. 1998. An overview of word order in Slavic languages. In A. Siewierska, ed., *Constituent Order in the Languages of Europe*, 105–149. Berlin: Mouton de Gruyter.

Sigurðsson, Halldór Ármann. 1993. The structure of the Icelandic NP. *Studia Linguistica* 47: 177–197.

Sigurðsson, Halldór Ármann. 2005. The Icelandic noun phrase: Central traits. Ms., University of Lund. (Published in 2006 in *Arkiv för nordisk filologi* 121: 193–236.)

Siloni, Tal. 1995. On participial relatives and complementizer D°: A case study in Hebrew and French. *Natural Language and Linguistic Theory* 13: 445–487.

Siloni, Tal. 2001. Construct states at the PF interface. *Linguistic Variation Yearbook* 1: 229–266.

Silva-Villar, Luis, and Javier Gutiérrez-Rexach. 1997. Temporal adjectives and the feature structure of DP. In *MIT Working Papers in Linguistics 31: Papers from the Eighth Student Conference in Linguistics*, 449–466. Cambridge, MA: MITWPL, Department of Linguistics and Philosophy, MIT.

Simpson, Andrew. 2001. Definiteness agreement and the Chinese DP. *Language and Linguistics* 2: 125–156. http://www.ling.sinica.edu.tw/eip/FILES/journal/2007.3.9.59853761.7896917.pdf.

Simpson, Andrew. 2005. Classifiers and DP Structure in Southeast Asia. In G. Cinque and R. S. Kayne, eds., *The Oxford Handbook of Comparative Syntax*, 806–838. New York: Oxford University Press.

Sio, Joanna Ut-Seong. 2006. *Modification and Reference in the Chinese Nominal*. Doctoral dissertation, Universiteit Leiden. http://www.lotpublications.nl/index3.html.

Sleeman, Petra. 1993. Noun ellipsis in French. *Probus* 5: 271–295.

Sleeman, Petra. 1996. *Licensing Empty Nouns in French*. The Hague: Holland Academic Graphics.

Sleeman, Petra, and Els Verheugd. 1998a. How reduced are relative clauses? In R. Kager and R. van Bezooijen, eds., *Linguistics in the Netherlands*, vol. 15, 187–199. Amsterdam: Benjamins.

Sleeman, Petra, and Els Verheugd. 1998b. Licensing DP-internal predication. In A. Schwegler, B. Tranel, and M. Uribe-Etxebarria, eds., *Romance Linguistics: Theoretical Perspectives*, 271–282. Amsterdam: Benjamins.

Smith, Carlota. 1961. A class of complex modifiers in English. *Language* 37: 342–365.

Sproat, Richard, and Chinlin Shih. 1988. Prenominal adjectival ordering in English and Mandarin. In J. Blevins and J. Carter, eds., *Proceedings of NELS 18*, 465–489. Amherst: GSLA, University of Massachusetts.

Sproat, Richard, and Chinlin Shih. 1990. The cross-linguistic distribution of adjectival ordering restrictions. In C. Georgopoulos and R. Ishihara, eds., *Interdisciplinary Approaches to Language: Essays in Honor of S-Y. Kuroda*, 565–593. Dordrecht: Kluwer.

Stateva, Penka. 1999. In defense of the movement theory of superlatives. In R. Daly and A. Riehl, eds., *Proceedings of the Fiftieth Eastern States Conference on Linguistics (ESCOL) '99*, 215–226. Ithaca, NY: CLC Publications, Cornell University.

Stateva, Penka. 2000. Towards a superior theory of superlatives. In C. Czinglar, K. Köhler, E. Thrift, E. J. van der Torre, and M. Zimmermann, eds., *Proceedings of ConSole VIII*, 313–325. Leiden: SOLE.

Stavrou, Melita. 1995. Epexegesis vs. apposition. *Scientific Yearbook of the Classics Department*. Thessaloniki: Aristotle University of Thessaloniki.

Stavrou, Melita. 1996. Adjectives in Modern Greek: An instance of predication, or an old issue revisited. *Journal of Linguistics* 32: 79–112.

Stavrou, Melita. 1999. The position and serialization of APs in the DP: Evidence from Greek. In A. Alexiadou, G. Horrocks, and M. Stavrou, eds., *Studies in Greek Syntax*, 201–225. Dordrecht: Kluwer.

Stavrou, Melita. Forthcoming. Adnominal adjectives in Greek indefinite noun phrases. In L. Brugè, A. Cardinaletti, G. Giusti, N. Munaro, and C. Poletto, eds., *Functional Heads*. New York: Oxford University Press.

Stenson, Nancy. 1981. *Studies in Irish Syntax*. Tübingen: Gunter Narr.

Stenson, Nancy. 1990. Phrase structure congruence, government, and Irish-English code-switching. In R. Hendrick, ed., *The Syntax of the Modern Celtic Languages* (Syntax and Semantics 23), 167–197. San Diego: Academic Press.

Stowell, Tim. 1981. *Origins of Phrase Structure*. Doctoral dissertation, MIT.

Stowell, Tim. 1991. The alignment of arguments in adjective phrases. In S. Rothstein, ed., *Perspectives on Phrase Structure: Heads and Licensing*, 105–135 (Syntax and Semantics 25). New York: Academic Press.

Sulkala, Helena, and Merja Karjalainen. 1992. *Finnish*. London: Routledge.

Sumbatova, Nina R., and Rasul O. Mutalov. 2003. *A Grammar of Icari Dargwa*. Munich: Lincom Europa.

Sussex, Roland. 1971. *Aspects of the Syntax of Russian Adjectives*. Doctoral dissertation, University of London.

Sussex, Roland. 1974. The deep structure of adjectives in noun phrases. *Journal of Linguistics* 10: 111–131.

Sussex, Roland. 1975. *Attributive Adjectives in Polish*. Lisse: Peter De Ridder Press. (Originally published in *International Journal of Slavic Linguistics and Poetics* 20 (1975): 23–46.)

Sutcliffe, Edmund F. 1936. *A Grammar of the Maltese Language*. La Valletta: Progress Press.

Svenonius, Peter. 1992. The extended projection of N: Identifying the head of the noun phrase. *Working Papers in Scandinavian Syntax* 49: 95–121.

Svenonius, Peter. 1994. On the structural location of the attributive adjective. In E. Duncan, D. Farkas, and P. Spaelti, eds., *Proceedings of the Twelfth West Coast Conference on Formal Linguistics (WCCFL)*, 439–454. Stanford, CA: CSLI Publications.

Svenonius, Peter. 2008. The position of adjectives and other phrasal modifiers in the decomposition of DP. In L. McNally and C. Kennedy, eds., *Adjectives and Adverbs: Syntax, Semantics, and Discourse*, 16–42. Oxford: Oxford University Press. http://www.hum.uit.no/a/svenonius/paperspage.html.

Szabolcsi, Anna. 1986. Comparative superlatives. *MIT Working Papers in Linguistics* 8: 245–265.

Szendrői, Kriszta. 2008. A flexible approach to discourse-related word order variations in the DP. Ms., Department of Linguistics, University College, London. To appear in *Lingua*. http://www.phon.ucl.ac.uk/home/kriszta/flexifocusDPpaper_submit.pdf.

Tallerman, Maggie. 1998. *Understanding Syntax*. London: Arnold.

Tasseva-Kurktchieva, Mila. 2005. The possessor that came home. In J.-Y. Kim, Y. A. Lander, and B. H. Partee, eds., *Possessives and Beyond: Semantics and Syntax* (University of Massachusetts Occasional Papers in Linguistics 29), 279–293. Amherst, MA: GSLA Publications. http://www.mila.studiok-rfc.com/papers/TassevaPossWorkshop.pdf.

Taylor, John R. 1992. Old problems: Adjectives in cognitive grammar. *Cognitive Linguistics* 3: 1–35.

Teodorescu, Alexandra. 2006. Adjective ordering restrictions revisited. In D. Baumer, D. Montero, and M. Scanlon, eds., *Proceedings of the 25th West Coast Conference on Formal Linguistics*, 399–407. Somerville, MA: Cascadilla Press. http://www.lingref.com/cpp/wccfl/25/paper1473.pdf.

Thiella, Anna. 2008. Il sintagma nominale negli antichi volgari di area veneta e lombarda. *LabRomAn* (Laboratorio sulle Varietà Romanze Antiche, Università di Padova) Monografie LabRomAn 2/I, 1–163. http://www.maldura.unipd.it/ddlcs/laboratorio/home.html/.

Ticio, María Emma. 2003. *On the Structure of DPs*. Doctoral dissertation, University of Connecticut at Storrs.

Tonhauser, Judith. 2006. *The Temporal Semantics of Noun Phrases: Evidence from Guaraní*. Doctoral dissertation, Stanford University. http://www.ling.ohio-state.edu/~judith/tonhauser-dissertation.pdf.

Torrego, Esther. 1998. *The Dependencies of Objects*. Cambridge, MA: MIT Press.

Tovena, Lucia M., and Marleen Van Peteghem. 2003. Facets of "different" in French: *différent* and *autre*. In C. Beyssade, O. Bonami, P. Cabredo Hofherr, and F. Corblin, eds., *Empirical Issues in Syntax and Semantics* 4: 63–79. Paris: Presses de l'Université de Paris-Sorbonne.

Tredinnick, Victoria. 1992. Movement in the Modern Greek noun phrase. *Penn Review of Linguistics* 17: 194–207.

Trenkić, Danijela. 2004. Definiteness in Serbian/Croatian/Bosnian and some implications for the general structure of the nominal phrase. *Lingua* 114: 1401–1427.

Troseth, Erika. 2004. Negative inversion and degree inversion in the English DP. *Linguistics in the Big Apple: CUNY/NYU Working Papers in Linguistics*. http://web.gc.cuny.edu/linguistics/liba/papers/Troseth2004.pdf.

Troseth, Erika. 2009. Degree inversion and negative intensifier inversion in the English DP. *Linguistic Review* 26: 37–65.

Trugman, Helen. 2005. *Syntax of Russian DPs, and DP-Internal Agreement Phenomena*. Doctoral dissertation, Tel-Aviv University.

Trugman, Helen. 2007. Rudiments of Romance N-to-D movement in Russian. In P. Kosta and L. Schüreks, eds., *Linguistic Investigations into Formal Description of Slavic Languages*, 411–426. Frankfurt am Main: Lang.

Truswell, Robert. 2004a. *Attributive Adjectives and the Nominals They Modify*. Master's thesis, Oxford University. http://www.tufts.edu/~rtrusw01/mphil.pdf.

Truswell, Robert. 2004b. Non-restrictive adjective interpretation and association with focus. *Oxford Working Papers in Linguistics, Philology and Phonetics* 9: 133–154. http://www.ling-phil.ox.ac.uk/download/OWP2004.pdf.

Truswell, Robert. 2005. Adjectives and headedness. *Oxford Working Papers in Linguistics, Philology and Phonetics* 10: 1–19. http://www.ling-phil.ox.ac.uk/download/OWP2005.pdf.

Truswell, Robert. 2009. Attributive adjectives and nominal templates. *Linguistic Inquiry* 40: 525–533. http://www.tufts.edu/~rtrusw01/adjsquib.pdf.

Tuggy, David H. 1979. Tetelcingo Nahuatl. In R. Langacker, ed., *Uto-Aztecan Grammar, Volume 2: Modern Aztec Grammatical Sketches*, 1–140. Arlington: University of Texas and Summer Institute of Linguistics.

Turano, Giuseppina. 2002. On modifiers preceded by the article in Albanian DPs. *University of Venice Working Papers in Linguistics* 12: 169–215. http://dspace-unive.cilea.it/bitstream/10278/177/1/2002-6s-Turano.pdf.

Umbach, Carla. 2006. Non-restrictive modification and backgrounding. In B. Gyuris, L. Kálmán, C. Piñón, and K. Varasdi, eds., *Proceedings of the Ninth Symposium on Logic and Language*, 152–159. Budapest: Hungarian Academy of Sciences. http://www.linguistics.hu/lola9/proceedings.html.

Valassis, Ioannis. 2001. *Syntaxe positionnelle et épithètes: le cas des adjectifs relationnels*. Doctoral dissertation. Université de Paris X, Nanterre.

Valois, Daniel. 1991a. *The Internal Syntax of DP*. Doctoral dissertation, UCLA.

Valois, Daniel. 1991b. The Internal syntax of DP and adjectival placement in French and English. In T. Sheer, ed., *Proceedings of the Twenty-First North East Linguistic Society*, 367–382. Amherst, MA: GLSA Publications.

Valois, Daniel. 1996. On the structure of the French DP. *Canadian Journal of Linguistics* 41: 349–375.

Van Canegem-Ardijns, Ingrid. 2006. The extraposition of prepositional objects of adjectives in Dutch. *Linguistics* 44: 425–457.

Vandelanotte, Lieven. 2002. Prenominal adjectives in English: Structures and ordering. *Folia Linguistica* 36(3–4): 219–259.

Vander Klok, Jozina. 2009. Direct Adjectival Modification in Javanese. In Proceedings of AFLA 16. UC Santa Cruz http://frc.ucsd.edu/events/2fla.

Van de Velde, Danièle. 2006. Les adjectifs de groupe. *Travaux de Linguistique* 53: 135–154.

Vangsnes, Øystein Alexander. 2004. Rolling up the Scandinavian noun phrase. Paper presented at the 27th GLOW Colloquium. Athens, April 19–21, 2004. http://www.hum.uit.no/a/Vangsnes/papers/VangsnesGLOW2004.pd.

Van Peteghem, Marleen. 2002. Les différentes interprétations de *pareil* ou comment un adjectif relationnel devient un marqueur anaphorique. *Langue française* 136: 60–72.

Vendler, Zeno. 1968. *Adjectives and nominalizations*. The Hague: Mouton.

Vergnaud, Jean-Roger, and Maria Luisa Zubizarreta. 1992. The definite determiner and the inalienable constructions in French and in English. *Linguistic Inquiry* 23: 595–652.

Vincent, Nigel. 1986. La posizione dell'aggettivo in italiano. In S. Stammerjohann, ed., *Tema-Rema in italiano*, 181–195. Tübingen: Narr.

Wang, Lulu, and Haitao Liu. 2007. A description of Chinese NPs using head-driven phrase structure grammar. In S. Müller, ed., *Proceedings of the 14th International Conference on Head-Driven Phrase Structure Grammar*, 287–305. Stanford, CA: CSLI Publications.

Wang, Zhirong. 1995. Adjective-noun construction in Modern Chinese. In T.-F. Cheng, Y. Li, and H. Zhang, eds., *Proceedings of the 7th North American Conference on Chinese Linguistics/5th International Conference on Chinese Linguistics*, vol. 1, 303–316. Los Angeles: Department of Linguistics, University of Southern California, GSIL Publications.

Wasow, Thomas. 1997. Transformations and the Lexicon. In P. W. Culicover, T. Wasow, and A. Akmajian, eds., *Formal Syntax*, 327–360. New York: Academic Press.

Waugh, Linda. 1976. The semantics and paradigmatics of word order. *Language* 52: 82–107.

Waugh, Linda. 1977. *A Semantic Analysis of Word Order: Position of the Adjective in French*. Leiden: Brill.

Wegener, Claudia. 2008. *A Grammar of Savosavo: A Papuan Language of the Solomon Islands.* Doctoral dissertation, Radboud Universiteit, Nijmegen.

Wei, Ting-Chi. 2004. *Predication and Sluicing in Mandarin Chinese*. Doctoral dissertation, National Kaosiung Normal University. http://www.usc.edu/schools/college/ealc//chinling/WeiTingchi.htm.

Welmers, William E. 1973. *African Language Structures*. Berkeley: University of California Press.

Welmers, William E., and Beatrice Welmers. 1969. Noun modifiers in Igbo. *International Journal of American Linguistics* 35: 315–322.

Wetzer, Harrie. 1996. *The Typology of Adjectival Predication*. Berlin: Mouton de Gruyter.

Williams, Edwin. 1981. On the notions "lexically related" and "head of a word." *Linguistic Inquiry* 12: 245–274.

Williams, Edwin. 1982. Another argument that passive is transformational. *Linguistic Inquiry* 13: 160–163.

Williams, Edwin. 1994. *Thematic Structure in Syntax*. Cambridge, MA: MIT Press.

Williamson, Janis S. 1987. An indefinite restriction for relative clauses in Lakhota. In E. J. Reuland and A. G. B. ter Meulen, eds., *The Representation of (In)definiteness*, 168–190. Cambridge, MA: MIT Press.

Willim, Eva. 2000. Some aspects of the grammar and interpretation of adjectival modification. In P. Bánski and A. Przepiórkowski, eds., *Generative Linguistics in*

Poland. Proceedings of the GliP-1, 156–167. Warsaw: Instytut Podstaw Informatyki Polskiej Akademii Nauk.

Willim, Eva. 2001. On NP-internal agreement: A study of some adjectival and nominal modifiers in Polish. In G. Zybatow, U. Junghanns, G. Mehlhorn, and L. Szucsich, eds., *Current Issues in Formal Slavic Linguistics*, 80–95. Frankfurt am Main: Lang.

Winter, Werner. 1965. Transforms without kernels. *Language* 41: 484–489.

Wulff, Stefanie. 2003. A multifactorial corpus analysis of adjective order in English. *International Journal of Corpus Linguistics* 8: 245–282. http://www.linguistics.ucsb.edu/faculty/swulff/research/AdjectiveOrder@IJCL.pdf.

Yamakido, Hiroko. 2000. Japanese attributive adjectives are not (all) relative clauses. In R. Billerey and B. D. Lillehaugen, eds., *Proceedings of the Nineteenth West Coast Conference on Formal Linguistics*, 588–602. Somerville, MA: Cascadilla Press.

Yamakido, Hiroko. 2007. The nature of adjectival inflection in Japanese. *MIT Working Papers in Linguistics 54: Proceedings of the Workshop on Altaic Formal Linguistics II*, 365–377. Cambridge, MA: MITWPL, Department of Linguistics and Philosophy, MIT.

Yang, Henrietta Shu-Fen. 2005. *Plurality and Modification in Mandarin Nominal Phrases*. Doctoral dissertation, University of Texas at Austin.

Zamparelli, Roberto. 1993. Pre-nominal Modifiers, degree phrases and the structure of AP. *University of Venice Working Papers in Linguistics* 3(1): 138–163. http://dspace-unive.cilea.it/bitstream/10278/419/1/3.1.6.pdf.

Zlatić, Larisa. 1997. *The Structure of the Serbian Noun Phrase*. Doctoral dissertation, University of Texas at Austin. http://www.lztranslation.com/zlaticdissertation.html.

Zuber, Richard. 1996. Ordre des adjectifs et catégorisation multiple. *Studi Italiani di Linguistica Teorica e Applicata* 3: 534–545.

Zwart, Jan-Wouter. 1996. On the status and position of PPs inside APs in Dutch. Unpublished article, University of Groningen. http://www.let.rug.nl/~zwart/docs/ppinap.pdf.

Zwarts, Frans. 1974. On restricting base structure recursion in Dutch. Ms., University of Amsterdam.

Name Index

Abeillé, A., 6, 77, 116n7, 118n16
Abels, K., 126n20
Abney, S., 31, 44, 65, 128n16
Abusch, D., 14, 117n12
Adamson, S., 122n8
Ajíbóyè, O., 35–36, 125n15
Albro, D. M., 29
Alexiadou, A., 5, 50, 59, 104, 105, 106, 107, 114n1, 119n18, 121n1, 122n6,8, 126n18, 130n30, 135n2, 136n3, 146n25,27,29, 147n29, 148n30
Aljović, N., 6, 99, 100, 101, 102, 136n3, 137n9, 143n13, 144n13,14,15,16,17
Alrenga, P., 118n13
Androutsopoulou, A., 46, 104, 105, 106, 107, 108, 140n3, 147n29, 148n30
Aoun, J., 95, 96, 132n4, 141n4, 142n7, 143n9
Arnold, D., 6, 18, 59, 64, 114n2, 127n8
Authier, J.-P., 53
Azzopardi-Alexander, M., 99

Babby, L. H., 46, 109, 144n14, 148n32
Bach, E., 51
Backhouse, A. E., 127n4
Bailyn, J. F., 110, 144n14, 148n32,35
Baker, M., 31, 34, 35, 44, 124n14, 125n17, 129n20
Bakker, S. J., 122n8
Barbaud, P., 117n11
Barkaï, M., 70

Barrit, C. W., 122n8
Bartning, I., 135n2
Bartra, A., 137n9
Bartsch, R., 10
Bašić, M., 144n17
Beck, S., 15, 117n13
Benincà, P., 72
Bennis, H., 129n20
Bentley, D., 129n20
Berg, R. van den, 29
Berman, A., 44, 49, 50, 127n8, 130n29
Bernstein, J., 2, 5, 44, 47, 48, 51, 72, 76, 82, 83, 126n1, 128n17, 130n26, 136n5
Blackwell, A., 36
Blinkenberg, A., 52, 114n3, 136n4
Bloomfield, L., 131n3
Boleda, G., 137n9
Bolinger, D., 6, 7, 33, 50, 114n2,3, 121n1, 136n3
Borer, H., 134n16
Borg, A. J., 99
Borillo, A., 6
Borschev, V., 123n9
Borsley, R. D., 129n21
Bošković, Ž., 123n8
Bosque, I., 12, 14
Bouchard, D., 5, 6, 30, 33, 44, 49, 51, 77, 84, 85, 113n1,4, 114n5, 122n8, 136n3,5, 137n7,9
Boucher, P., 120n23
Bouillon, P., 119n16
Bouldin, J. M., 61
Boyd, V. L., 36

Brasoveanu, A., 118n13
Bresnan, J., 64
Brito, A. M., 136n4
Brucart, J. M., 129n23, 130n27
Brugè, L., 14, 82, 83, 139n18,21
Brugger, G., 14
Brunot, F., 6

Cabredo Hofherr, P., 129n22
Camacho, J., 88
Campos, H., 104, 105, 106, 132n4, 145n20, 146n26
Cardinaletti, A., 36–37, 65, 119n19
Carlson, G., 15, 147n29
Cetnarowska, B., 134n19
Champollion, L., 122n8
Cheung, C.-H. C., 96, 97, 132n4, 141n4
Chèvre, S., 139n18
Chierchia, G., 116n8
Cho, S., 118n16, 123n10, 124n13
Chomsky, N., 49, 52
Cinque, G., xiii, 2, 3, 6, 20, 34, 36, 38, 40, 41, 43, 45, 53, 54, 56, 72, 73, 74, 75, 76, 82, 113n1,2, 121n27,1, 122n3, 123n11, 124n13, 126n18,20,21,1,2, 129n20, 132n4,8, 133n12, 134n18, 135n2, 137n7,8, 138n14,15, 139n17
Citko, B., 119n20
Coene, M., 103
Cole, P., 39
Contreras, H., 6, 130n30
Corbett, G., 48, 148n32,35
Cornilescu, A., 6, 76, 103, 114n3, 135n1, 136n3, 145n20,24
Corver, N., 149n36
Coulter, J. M., 133n10
Crisma, P., 133n1

Dal Pozzo, L., 121n2, 122n2
Dayley, J. P., 44
DeGraff, M., 120n22, 128n17
Dehé, N., 126n18
Del Gobbo, F., 130n31, 133n14
Delomier, D., 6
Delsing, L.-O., 44, 46, 132n8, 140n1

Demeke, G., 132n4
Demonte, V., 6, 70, 88, 114n3, 115n4, 116n7, 123n11, 132n4, 136n3, 137n9, 138n16
den Dikken, M., 143n10
Dirven, R., 122n8
Di Sciullo, A.-M., 138n15
Dixon, R. M. W., 35, 43, 122n8, 126n2, 127n2,3,6
Dobrovie-Sorin, C., 102
Drăgan, R., 145n23
Duanmu, S., 96
Duffield, N., 99
Dumitrescu, D., 70
Dutta Baruah, 125n17

Emonds, J., 50, 65, 128n12
Escribano, J. L. G., 62, 64, 128n12
Español-Echevarría, M., 140n3
Ewert, M., 6

Fabb, N., 134n17
Fabian, E., 29
Fabian, G., 29
Fábregas, A., 135n2
Fabri, R., 98, 99, 143n12
Fanselow, G., 45, 55, 56, 130n33
Farkas, D., 117n9
Fassi Fehri, A., 122
Fedorowicz-Bacz, B., 130n30
Feist, J. M., 122n8
Felber, S., 48
Ferris, C., 6, 18, 61, 114n2, 119n19
Fiengo, R., 117n11
Fleisher, N., 127n8
Frank, P., 124n14
Frawley, W., 122n8
Fries, P. H., 122n8
Fudeman, K., 140n1
Fults, S., 129n20

Gengel, K., 115n5
Giannakidou, A., 107
Giegerich, H. J., 135n2
Giorgi, A., 45, 72, 114n3, 128n12, 135n1,2
Giurgea, I., 82, 138n15

Name Index

Giusti, G., 36–37, 48, 65, 72, 77, 82, 103, 126n18, 131n4, 145n20
Givón, T., 44, 51, 52
Godard, D., 6, 77, 116n7, 118n16
Gonzaga, M., 76, 136n3, 137n9
Gould, D., 44
Gouskova, M., 116n8
Gràcia, L., 129n23
Greenberg, J., 38
Groen, B. M., 148n32, 149n35
Grosu, A., 145n21
Grune, D., 44
Gutiérrez-Rexach, J., 14

Haegeman, L., 5, 50, 59, 114n1, 119n18, 122n8, 126n18, 130n30, 146n27
Haiman, J., 125n17
Hale, K., 126n2
Hamann, C., 49
Hansen, F., 6
Haroutyunian, S., 138n14
Haspelmath, M., 64
Hawkins, J., 121n2
Heim, I., 32, 124n13
Hendrick, R., 48
Hermon, G., 39
Hernanz, M. L., 137n9
Hetzron, R., 122n8
Higginbotham, J., 10, 117n11
Holmberg, A., 46, 127n8, 128n12
Horrocks, G., 146n25
Huang, S.-Z., 96, 142n5

Jackendoff, R., 33, 120n22
Jacobsson, B., 18, 132n10
James, D., 18
Jamrozik, E., 140n2
Jayaseelan, K. A., 138n14
Jespersen, O., 7
Jones, M. A., 6
Julien, M., 44, 48, 49, 128n11

Kamp, H., 116n8
Kang, S. H., 125n17, 130n30, 143n10
Karanassios, Y., 146n25
Karjalainen, M., 121n2

Kayne, R. S., 20, 26, 32, 39, 47, 48, 52, 53, 67, 79, 80, 82, 84, 85, 121n1, 123n11, 124n13, 126n20,1,2, 128n15, 130n31,32, 133n15, 138n12, 139n16,20
Keenan, E., 133n10
Kemmerer, D., 127n7
Kennedy, C., 48, 117n9, 134n16, 147n29
Kester, E.-P., 127n8, 129n22, 132n8, 149n36
Keyser, S. J., 126n2
Kiefer, F., 122n8
Kishimoto, H., 65
Kiss, E. K., 117n9
Knittel, M. L., 30, 49, 126n18, 137n7, 140n1
Koch, K., 130n32
Kolliakou, D., 104, 105, 106
König, E., 132n8
Koopman, H., 125n17
Kornfilt, J., 138n14
Krapova, I., 46, 47, 53, 82, 134n19
Krause, C., 149n36
Kremers, J., 30

Laca, B., 118n13
Laenzlinger, C., 2, 49, 126n18, 129n19, 137n7,9, 138n14
Lam, C. F., 141n5
Lamarche, J., 44, 45, 49, 139n17
Lance, D. M., 122n8
Langacker, R., 44
Larson, R. K., xi, 6, 7, 8, 9, 18, 19, 26, 33, 60, 63, 65, 66, 110, 114n2,3, 115n5,6, 118n16, 119n20,23, 123n10, 124n13, 131n1, 132n10, 133n14, 134n19
Laskova, V., 134n17, 147n30
Lehmann, C., 121n2
Lekakou, M., 105, 107
Leko, N., 99, 100, 101, 143n13, 144n14,16, 145n19
Leu, T., 48, 65, 82, 84, 106, 108, 130n30, 133n10, 139n19,20, 148n31
Levi, J., 50, 130n29
Levin, B., 64

Li, A., 95, 96, 132n4, 141n4, 142n7, 143n9
Lindsey, G., 127n5
Liu, H., 143n9
Loether, C., 44
Lombard, A., 145n21
Longobardi, G., 114n3, 126n18, 128n12, 135n2
Ludlow, P., 116n8
Luján, M., 136n3
Lyons, J., 126n2

Mackenzie, I., 114n3
Madugu, I. S. G., 125n16
Mahajan, A., 138n14
Maho, J., 125n16
Mahootian, S., 129n18
Mallén, E., 126n18
Malouf, R., 30
Mandelbaum, D., 120n22, 128n17
Manolessou, I., 105
Marinis, T., 105, 107, 146n27
Markantonatou, S., 135n2
Martín, J., 114n3
Martinez Atienza, M., 116n7
Marušič, F., 7, 18, 19, 60, 63, 65, 66, 114n2,3, 132n10, 134n19, 147n30
Matushansky, O., 31, 32, 48, 49, 53, 122n8, 127n8, 148n22, 149n35
McConnell-Ginet, S., 116n8
McLaughlin, J. E., 44
McNally, L., 33, 134n16, 137n9
Mehlhorn, G., 116n8
Merchant, J., 48
Moltmann, F., 15, 117n13
Moravcsik, E., 98, 99, 143n11
Morzycki, M., 114n3, 115n4, 116n7
Moshiri, L., 124n13
Motsch, W., 50
Mouma, E., 105
Mui, E., 141n2
Murumatsu, K., 122n8
Mutalov, R. O., 121n2

Napoli, D. J., 132n9
Neeleman, A., 126n20
Noailly, M., 88, 89

Noonan, M., 35
Nowak, A., 108, 116n8

Oersnes, B., 135n2
Osumi, M., 125n17

Panagiotidis, P., 105, 107, 146n27
Partee, B. H., 78, 116n8, 123n10
Pasqui, R., 5
Paul, W., 96, 115n6, 128n14, 141n3,4, 142n5, 143n7
Pawley, A., 127n2
Pereltsvaig, A., 108, 122n7, 136n6, 144n14, 148n32,34, 149n35
Picallo, C., 12, 136n3
Plank, F., 98, 99, 143n11
Platzack, C., 45
Posner, R., 122n8, 123n9
Postal, P., 135n2
Prévost, P., 140n3
Progovac, L., 101, 134n19
Pustejovski, J., 33
Pysz, A., 134n19

Quirk, R., 122n8

Radford, A., 127n8
Rae, M., 64, 65, 124n11,13
Ramaglia, F., 146n27
Rappaport, M., 64
Rasom, S., 140n1
Reesink, G. P., 126n2
Rice, K., 35, 124n14
Riemsdijk, H. van, 108, 111, 127n8, 132n8
Rigau, G., 6
Rijkhoff, J., 46, 121n2, 127n8, 130n32
Risselada, R., 122n8
Rizzi, L., 44, 135
Roehrs, D., 48, 66, 141n1
Ronat, M., 51
Rooth, M., 14, 117n12
Ross, J. R., 39, 117n9
Rowlett, P., 48
Rubin, E. J., 122n3
Rutkowski, P., 101, 134n19

Saba, W., 115n6
Sadler, L., 6, 18, 59, 64, 114n2, 127n8
Saltarelli, M., 70, 73
Samek-Lodovici, V., 126n18
Santorini, B., 129n18
Sauereisen, B., 120n22, 123n9
Saxon, L., 124n14
Scancarelli, J., 127n5
Schachter, P., 125n17, 126n2
Schäfer, R., 142n5
Schiffman, H. F., 125n17
Schmitt, C., 131n1
Schueler, D., 117n9
Schwarz, B., 115n5, 131n1
Schweikert, W., 54, 70
Scott, J.-G., 59, 120n22, 122n7,8, 131n2
Seiler, H., 122n8
Sharvit, Y., 32, 117n9
Shih, C., 22, 25, 28, 31, 33, 44, 45, 54, 95, 96, 97, 105, 120n25, 121n1, 122n8, 131n3, 140n1, 141n4, 142n7
Shlonsky, U., 126n18, 136n6
Sichel, I., 126n18
Siegel, M. E. A., 109, 110, 119n18, 121n1, 125n17, 144n14, 148n32,35, 149n35
Siewierska, A., 127n9
Sigurðsson, H. A., 45
Siloni, T., 131n34, 136n6
Silva-Villar, L., 14
Simpson, A., 96, 143n9
Singhapreecha, P., 143n10
Sio, J.-U., 96, 97, 141n2,4, 142n7, 143n8,10
Sleeman, P., 84, 129n22,23
Smith, C., 49
Sproat, R., 22, 25, 28, 31, 33, 44, 45, 54, 95, 96, 97, 105, 120n25, 121n1, 122n8, 131n3, 140n1, 141n4, 142n7
Stateva, P., 32, 117n9
Stavrou, M., 104, 105, 106, 107, 114n1, 119n18, 122n8, 126n18, 130n30, 146n25,26,27, 147n29, 148n31
Stenson, N., 129n18
Stowell, T., 64, 87, 129n20

Sulkala, H., 121n2
Sumbatova, N. R., 121n2
Sussex, R., 49, 134n19, 148n32
Sutcliffe, E. F., 98
Svenonius, P., 6, 48, 49, 59, 127n8
Szabolcsi, A., 117n9, 119n17
Szendři, K., 30, 105, 107

Takahashi, N., 133n14
Tallerman, M., 47
Tasmowski, L., 118n13
Tasseva-Kurktchieva, M., 46
Taylor, J. R., 119n16, 138n11
Teodorescu, A., 122n8, 124n12
Ticio, E., 12, 114n3, 137n9
Tjung, Y. N., 39
Tomić, O. M., 101
Tonhauser, J., 124n10
Tovena, L., 118n13
Trenkić, D., 101, 144n13
Troseth, E., 48, 128n16
Trugman, H., 134n19
Truswell, R., 30, 44, 59
Tuggy, D. H., 44
Turano, G., 148n30

Uhlířová, L., 127n9
Umbach, C., 33

Valassis, I., 135n2
Valois, D., 3, 44, 45, 48, 49
Van Canegem-Ardijns, I., 62
Vandelanotte, L., 122n8
Vander Klok, J., 140n1
Van de Velde, D., 135n2
Vangsnes, Ø., 139n20
Van Peteghem, M., 118n13
Vendler, Z., 58, 122n8, 130n28
Venneman, T., 10
Vergnaud, J.-R., 114n3
Verheugd, E., 65, 84

Wang, Z., 96, 141n5, 143n7,9
Wasow, T., 64
Waters, B., 29
Waugh, L., 5
Wegener, C., 125n16

Wei, T.-C., 96
Welmers, B., 125n17
Welmers, W., 125n17
Wetzer, H., 125n17
Wilder, C., 104, 105, 106, 107, 121n1, 135n2, 146n25,27,29
Williams, E., 128n12, 132n6, 133n10
Williamson, J. S., 134n18
Willim, E., 134n19
Wiltschko, M., 130n32
Winter, W., 50
Wu, T., 143n9
Wulff, S., 122n8

Xu, L., 143n9

Yamakido, H., 130n30, 143n10
Yang, H.S.-F., 96, 97, 132n4, 140n2, 141n3, 142n7, 143n9

Zamparelli, R., 128n17, 135n3
Žaucer, R., 147n30
Zlatić, L., 101
Zuber, R., 122n8
Zubizarreta, M.-L., 114n3
Zwart, J.-W., 62
Zwarts, F., 128n12

Subject Index

adjacent, 61
Adjective
  A-bar moved, 48
  absolute reading, 10–11, 16, 17, 117n9, 122n4
  absolute reading in the superlative form, 11–12, 119n17
  acquisition, 36–37
  adnominal, 25–41, 43, 44, 48, 49, 52, 63, 64, 95, 96, 97, 99, 100, 101, 102, 103, 105, 107, 108, 109, 110, 122n3, 124n14, 140, 142n5, 143n10, 149n35
  adnominal-only, 36, 125n17
  adverbial, 9, 27, 29, 100, 116n8, 117n8
  agreement, 111, 143n9
  articleless, 28, 29, 99, 104, 105, 146n27
  articulated, 28, 98, 99, 105, 106, 107, 108, 129n20, 145n21, 146n25,27, 147n29,30, 148n30
  associative, 135n2
  attributive, 49, 64, 115n5, 124n14, 125n16, 129n20, 130n30, 132n5,8, 144n14, 147n29, 149n35
  bare, 61–63, 65, 81, 85, 97, 98, 102, 132n8, 133n13, 134n19,20, 138n15, 142n5, 143n7,8, 144n16
  -*ble*, 61, 63
  Bosnian/Croatian/Serbian, 28, 99–102, 108, 140
  Chinese, 28, 95–97, 120n25, 140–143

Classificatory, 29, 41, 71, 72, 93, 98, 101, 130n29, 134n19, 136n5, 140, 147n29
closed class, 36, 43, 126n2
color, 32, 38–41, 58
comparative, 9, 124n13, 127n8
comparative reading in the superlative form, 11–12, 16, 17, 23, 24, 27, 33, 119n17, 122n4
complex (or nonbare) vs. bare, 62, 65, 133n13, 144n16
"complex" [Chinese], 142n5
coordinated, 31, 48, 88–90, 138n10,15, 145n19
de-less, 27, 28, 95–97, 120n25
dimension (size), 125n15
direct modification (*see* Modification)
discourse anaphoric reading (of 'different'), 15–16
epistemic reading (of 'unknown'), 14–17, 20, 27, 33
ergative, 129n20
ethnic, 135n2
evaluative reading (of 'unknown'), 14–17, 20, 27, 33
evidential, 123n11
extraction, 108 (*see also* NP/PP Splitting)
focalized, 77, 126n21
focusing, 123n11
followed by a complement, 60, 62, 81, 85, 138n15

Adjective (*cont.*)
  French, 3, 6, 12, 44, 49, 51, 53, 67, 70, 76, 77, 81, 84–85, 88–89, 102, 113n4, 114n3, 115n5, 116n7, 118n13,16, 119n16, 120n23,134n20, 136n3,4,5, 137n7,9, 139n15,18, 140n1
  functional, 36, 43–44, 126n1,2, 127n7
  German, 45, 54, 66, 90, 111, 115n6, 117n13, 120n22, 123n9, 130n32, 132n8
  gradable, 129n20
  Greek, 28, 104–108
  idiomatic reading (*see* Idiomatic readings of adjectives)
  implicit relative clause reading, 8–9, 115n5
  indirect modification (*see* Modification)
  individual-level, 6–7, 28, 36–37, 44, 63, 77, 96, 110, 114n2, 120n23, 133n14, 135n3, 149n35
  intersective, 9–10, 16, 17, 19, 21, 23, 24, 26, 27, 33, 60, 62, 77, 78, 88, 93, 105, 109, 110, 115n6, 116n8, 119n18,19, 120n22, 122n3, 123n9, 124n13, 125n14, 136n3, 142n7
  Italian, 5–22, 26, 27–30, 32, 36, 45, 46, 47, 48, 50, 53, 54, 69–84, 87–90, 92, 93, 113n3, 114n1,3, 115n6, 116n7, 117n8,11, 118n16, 120n22,24, 122n4, 128n14,17, 130n31, 133n13, 134n20, 135n1, 136n3,4, 140n2, 141n5, 142n7
  Japanese, 43, 124n14, 130n30, 143n10
  Korean, 125n17, 130n30, 143n10
  Long-form, 27, 99–102, 108, 109, 110, 140, 144n14,16, 145n19, 146n28, 147n30, 148n35, 149n35
  Maltese, 98–99
  Manner, 75, 76, 113n1
  Modal, 8–9, 16, 17, 18, 19, 21, 22, 23, 24, 27, 33, 113n1, 116n8
  modified by *hen*, 141n5, 142n5
  movement, 32, 48, 77, 126n21, 132n5, 148n31
  nationality, 38–41, 58, 71, 72, 134n19, 136n5, 140n2
  nonbare, (*see* complex)
  nonintersective, 9–10, 16, 17, 19, 21, 22, 23, 24, 26, 32, 33, 60, 62, 77, 78, 88, 93, 96, 97, 98, 100, 101, 105, 106, 107, 109, 110, 115n6, 116n7, 119n18, 120n22, 123n9, 132n7, 135n3, 142n7
  nonpredicative, 2, 3, 4, 6, 47, 48, 51, 58, 60, 65, 77, 89, 96, 97, 103, 114n1, 122n6, 124n14, 128n13,14,16, 130n28,29, 132n4, 136n6, 141n4, 142n7, 143n8, 147n29
  nonrestrictive, 44, 52, 130n31
  nonspecific, 117n10, 119n17, 122n5, 144n13
  nonspecificity-inducing, 12–14, 16, 17, 22, 28, 120n26
  NP dependent reading (of 'different'), 15–16
  order
    nonrigid, 28–31, 50, 58, 95–96, 105
    rigid, 28–31, 52, 58, 74, 95–96, 100, 101, 105, 122n7, 125n15,16, 137n7, 142n6
  possessive, 30, 51, 144n15
  postnominal, xiv, 1–4, 5–24, 44, 50, 57, 59, 60, 61, 69, 73, 87, 88, 89, 91, 93
  predicate, 35, 43, 49
  predicate-only, 127n6
  predicative, 18, 28, 29, 30, 31, 33, 34, 35, 36, 49, 52, 61, 77, 87, 103, 105, 109, 113n3, 115n5, 122n3,6, 132n8, 139n18, 142n7
  prefixed, 44
  prenominal, xiv, 1–4, 5–24, 44, 45, 47, 49, 50, 57–59, 61, 69, 74, 75, 76, 87, 88, 91, 93, 101, 102, 110, 111, 114n2,3, 115n3, 116n7, 117n10,11, 118n16, 119n17,19, 120n23,24, 121n2, 122n3,4, 124n13, 127n7,9, 128n13, 128n17, 129n18,19,20, 132n8,10, 133n14, 134n16,17,19, 135n1,3, 136n3,5,

137n9, 138n10, 140, 141n5, 142n7, 144n18, 145n25, 146n27, 147n29, 148n31
privative, 78, 116n8
provenance (*see* nationality)
pseudo, 135n2
quality, 125n15
rearticulated, (*see* articulated)
reduplicated, 142n5
relational, 135n2
relative (to a comparison class) reading, 10–11
restrictive, 7–8, 44, 105
Romanian, 102–104, 114n3, 136n3, 138n15
Russian, 45–46, 108–111, 122n7, 127n9, 134n19, 144n14, 147n30, 148n32, 149n35
shape, 32, 58, 71, 136n3, 143n9
short-form, 27, 99–102, 108, 109, 144n15,16, 145n19, 146n28, 148n32,35, 149n35
"simple" [Chinese], 142n5
size, 32, 38–41, 58, 71, 116n7, 131n3
specific, 117n10,11, 119n17, 122n5, 144n13
specificity-inducing, 12–14, 27, 28, 33, 120n26, 144n18
stage-level, 6–7, 28, 36–37, 44, 63, 110, 114n2, 120n23, 133n14, 136n3, 149n35
subject-oriented, 76
subsective, 116n7,8
superlative, 11–12, 16, 17, 23, 24, 27, 31–32, 59, 117n9, 119n17, 124n12,13, 128n14, 135n1, 141n5, 145n21
thematic, 135n2
unaccusative, 129n20
utsukushi, 124n14
value, 58, 71
with complements or adjuncts, 59–61
with *de*, 27
with prefix *a*-, 61, 63, 133n10
Yoruba, 29, 35–36, 38, 125n15,17
Adverb, 44, 51, 57, 74, 76, 77, 123n11, 126n2, 135n1, 141n5

Adverbial adjective, 9, 27, 29, 100, 116n7,8, 117n8, 123n8
afraid, 61
Afrikaans, 139n19
Agrammatic speech, 44
Agreement, 148n34,35
Akimbo, 119n19
Albanian, 131n4, 148n30
Alethic modal, 113
alive, 18–19, 61
allegat (cf. *alleged, ipotithemenos, navodni*), 143n11
alleged (cf. *allegat, ipotithemenos, navodni*), 30, 51, 52, 58, 59, 60, 116n8, 123n11, 124n11
allora, 77
alone, 61
alt (cf. *lao, lou, old, vecchio, vieux*), 120n22
American Sign Language, 140n1
Antecedent Contained Deletion, 8, 18, 115n5, 131n1
Antisymmetry, 38, 48, 61, 122, 133n11
aplenty, 119n19
Approximate use, 77
AP reduced relative clauses. *See* Reduced relative clause
Arabic, 28, 122n7
  Maltese, 28, 98–99, 140
Aromanian, 145n20
Article. *See also* Determiner
  definite, 26, 50, 53, 98, 104, 105, 107, 143n11
  indefinite, 143n11, 146n25, 148n31
  ta, 29
Arvantovlaxika, 145n20
asleep, 61
autre, 134n20
available, 64
average, 147n29

Babungo, 125n17
bad, 52
Balanta, 140n1
Balkan
  feature, 148n30
  languages, 102

beautiful (cf. *krasivyi, meraviglioso, orea*), 9–10, 19, 57, 62, 65, 110, 115n6, 119n18
beden/bednyj (cf. *biet, ftohos, kaimenos, poor, povero*), 149n35
biet (cf. *beden/bednyj, ftohos, kaimenos, poor, povero*), 103
big, 10, 48, 116n7, 128n13, 143n9
bivši (cf. *byvshij, ex, former, proighoumenos, proin, qian, yiqian*), 147n30
blu, 135n3
bon, 77
Bosnian/Croatian/Serbian, 27, 28, 99–102, 108, 122n7, 143–145, 146n28, 147n30
Broca's aphasia, 44
brutale, 75–76
Bulgarian, 45–47, 102, 107, 127n9, 133n19, 134n19, 147n30
buono, 10, 21, 77, 115n6, 128n14
byvshij (cf. *bivši, ex, former, proighoumenos, proin, qian, yiqian*), 148n35

Cantonese. *See* Chinese
Catalan, 12, 72, 136n3, 137n9
Category
  functional, 126n2
  lexical, 126n2
cel, 102–104, 145n20,21,22,24, 146n24, 148n30
celui, 81, 84–85, 139n15
Central Italian dialects. *See* Italian
certain, 5
Cherokee, 43
chief, 52
Chinese
  Cantonese, 96, 141n2, 142n7, 143n7,8
  Mandarin, 27, 38, 44, 78, 95–97, 120n25, 128n14, 130n31, 132n4, 133n14, 140–143, 146n28
Classifier, 97, 143n9
Closed Class, 35–36, 43, 124n14, 125n17, 127n6
Code-switching, 48–49
completo, 138n10
Compound, 45, 96, 97, 120n25, 139n17, 140, 141n3

Coordination of adjectives. *See* Adjective, coordinated
Czech, 127n9

Danish, 128n11
dannato, 53
Dargwa, 121n2
de
  Chinese, 95–97, 120n25
  French, 67
  Spanish, 84
Degree Inversion, 48
Deictic, 26
Demonstrative (Dem), 38, 83, 97, 125n15, 129n22, 130n32, 132n4, 133n12, 138n14, 139n18,19,21, 144n14,15
  reinforcers, 82–84, 139n19,21
destro, 119n19
Determiner, 55, 84. *See also* Article
  adjectival, 98, 145n22
  indefinite, 146n25
  Spreading, 105, 145n22, 146n25,26,27, 147n29, 148n30,31
different, 15, 20, 117n13
différent, 118n13
differente, 16, 22, 118n14
Direct modification. *See* Modification
Discourse anaphoric reading (of 'different'), 15–17
Dogrib, 124n14
dP, 34, 89
Dravidian (languages), 125n17
Dutch, 62, 66, 130n32, 132n8, 149n36
Dyrbal, 43

early, 52
easy-to-please, 127n8
ehemalig, 54
einer nach dem anderen, 55–56
Elliptical DP/N, 107, 140, 147n30
English, xv, 2, 5–24, 27, 28, 29, 30, 32, 36, 38, 39, 43, 44, 45, 47, 48, 50, 57–67, 70, 73, 74, 76, 78, 81, 84, 87, 90, 99, 101, 110, 117n8, 118n15,16, 119n16, 120n22,23,24, 122n2,4,7, 125n15,16,17, 127n8,

128n12,13, 129n18,25, 130n32,
  132n5,7,8, 133n13,14,
  134n17,19,20, 135n1, 136n6,
  137n7, 138n11, 139n15,20, 142n7,
  144n16, 146n27, 147n30
 New Zealand, 64–65
 nonstandard, 139n20
enough, 47, 128n15
epithet, 87, 140n1
estremamente (cf. *feichang*), 141n5
evaluative reading (of 'unknown'), 14, 17
ex (cf. *bivši, byvshij, former, proighoumenos, proin, qian, yiqian*), 74
Extraction
 from DP, 117n11
 of *di* phrases, 117n11
 LF, 117n11
Extraposition, 133n11
 PP, 139n16
 reduced relative clause, 62
 relative clause, 62, 133n13, 139n16
 with adjectives, 62

fake, 60, 62, 116n8, 142n7
falso, 77–78, 138n13, 142n7
famoso, 13–14
famous, 30
faux, 77
feichang (cf. *estremamente*), 141n5
Fijian, 44
Final-Over-Final Constraint, 128n12
Finnish, 121n2, 122n2,7
finto, 142n7
Focus
 movement, 59, 132n5
former (cf. *bivši, byvshij, ex, proighoumenos, proin, qian, yiqian*), 30, 50, 51, 57, 59, 116n8, 123n11, 124n14, 130n32
French, 3, 6, 12, 44, 49, 51, 53, 65, 67, 70, 72, 76, 77, 81, 84–85, 88–89, 102, 113n4, 114n5,3, 115n5, 116n7, 118n13, 118n16, 119n16, 120n23, 131n34, 134n20, 136n3,4,5, 137n7,9, 138n10,15, 139n15,17,18, 140n1
frequent, 124n11, 131n4, 132n6

Frisian, 130n32
ftohos (cf. *beden/bednyj, biet, kaimenos, poor, povero*), 106, 107, 147n29
Functional adjective. *See* Adjective, functional
Function composition, 122n3
future (cf. *futuro, janglai*), 124n14, 138n10
futuro (cf. *future, janglai*), 72, 74

galore, 119n19
Gbadi, 125n17
Generic, 26
genug, 66
German, 45, 46, 54, 55–56, 66, 70, 90, 108, 110, 111, 115n6, 117n13, 120n22, 122n2, 123n9, 130n32, 132n8, 148n31
 Swiss, 65
Germanic (languages), xiii, xiv, 2, 3, 4, 5, 6, 22–24, 37, 41, 43, 45, 52, 57, 58, 59, 60, 61, 66, 70, 73, 87, 91, 123n9, 127n8, 132n8, 134n20, 135n1, 139n20
giovane, 4, 92, 114n3, 115n3
glad, 129n21
good, 120n22
grande, 116n7, 118n16, 140n2
Greek (Modern), 28, 45, 46, 47, 102, 104–108, 122n7, 140, 145n21,22, 146n25,27, 147n29, 148n30,31
gros, 118n16
groß, 115n6, 123n9
Guaraní, 123n10
guilty, 61

habile, 5
handy, 61
hard, 59
Head movement. *See* Movement
heavy, 30, 57, 59, 65, 123n9, 132n7
Hebrew, 136n6
here, 139n19
Hixkaryana, 35, 127n6
Hmar, 125n17
Hopi, 44
Hua, 125n17

Ibibio, 122n7
Icelandic, 140–141
Idiomatic readings of adjectives, 26, 27, 44, 87–88, 97, 100, 101
Idiom chunk, 56
Igbo, 125n17
Ika, 124n14
Iká, 125n16
ill, 129n21
Indefinite DP, 12–14
Indefiniteness restriction, 134n18
Indirect modification. *See* Modification
Individual-level adjective. *See* Adjective
industrioso, 79–80
invisibile, 7
invisible
 English, 119n20
 French, 120n23
ipotithemenos (cf. *allegat, alleged, navodni*), 106
Irish, 38, 129n18
Irrealis context, 13, 117n10
Island, 131n34
Italian, xiii, xv, 1, 2, 3, 5, 6, 7, 8, 9, 10, 11, 12, 13, 14, 15, 16, 17, 20, 22, 23, 26, 27, 28, 29, 30, 32, 36, 45, 47, 48, 50, 53, 54, 69–84, 87–90, 113n3, 114n1,3, 115n6, 116n7, 117n8,10,11, 118n16, 120n22,24, 122n4, 128n14,17, 130n31, 131n34, 133n13,14, 134n20, 135n1, 136n3,4,6, 137n7, 138n10, 139n18,21, 140n2, 141n5, 142n7, 144n14, 145n23, 146n27
 Central dialects, 73
 Literary, 45, 46
 Old, 72

janglai (cf. *future, futuro*), 143n7
Japanese, 43, 124n14, 130n30, 133n14, 143n10
Javanese, 140n1
jeune, 114n3

kaimenos (*beden/bednyj, biet, ftohos, poor, povero*), 107, 147n29

Kassena, 125n17
Korean, 125n17, 130n30, 133n14, 143n10
krasivyi (cf. *beautiful, meraviglioso, orea*), 110

Ladin, 140
Lango, 35
lao (cf. *alt, lou, old, vecchio, vieux*), 142n7
lì, 83–84
Liaison, 49
Light verb. *See* Verb
Linear Correspondence Axiom, 39, 126n20
Literal (reading), 100
live, 18–19
lou (cf. *alt, lao, old, vecchio, vieux*), 143n7
lucky, 52

Macedonian, 127n9
main, 47, 52, 57, 60, 113n3
Malayalam, 138n14
Maltese. *See* Arabic
Mandarin. *See* Chinese
Mbodómó (Gbaya), 36, 43, 125n17
medio, 83, 147n29
meraviglioso (cf. *beautiful, krasivyi, orea*), 115n6, 119n18
mero, 72, 128n17, 130n26, 138n10
Modal context, 13, 117n10
Modification
 direct, 22, 23, 24, 25, 26, 27, 28, 29, 30, 31, 32, 33, 43–54, 57, 58, 59, 62, 63, 64, 69, 71, 73, 74, 75, 76, 77, 78, 79, 80, 81, 82, 83, 84, 85, 88, 89, 90, 91, 92, 93, 95, 96, 97, 98, 99, 101, 102, 107, 108, 110, 111, 117n8, 119n18,19, 120n25, 121n2, 122n3, 123n11, 124n13,14, 127n7,10, 128n14, 129n20, 130n26, 131n4, 132n5, 133n15, 135n3, 136n5,6, 137n7, 139n17, 140, 142n7, 143n7, 146n27
 indirect, 25, 27, 28, 33, 35, 36, 44, 47, 54, 57, 58, 64, 69, 75, 77, 78, 79,

80, 81, 82, 84, 85, 89, 90, 91, 92, 93, 95, 98, 99, 100, 101, 105, 108, 121n2, 127n10, 130n32, 131n1, 133n15, 136n5, 137n7, 139n17, 140
parallel, 31
molto, 141n5
Movement
 of adjectives with *enough*, 128n15
 head, xiii, 1–4, 22–24, 37–41
 phrasal, 37–41
 remnant, 61, 62, 77, 79, 133n11, 134n20, 139n21
much, 64–65, 127n8, 134n16
Muna, 29

Nabak, 29
navigable, 28, 114n2
navodni (cf. *allegat, alleged, ipotithemenos*), 100
Nawdm, 29
nearby, 12, 28, 61, 63, 133n15
Negative Degree Inversion, 48
Negative polarity, 32
Neurolinguistic evidence, 44, 127n7
Ngamambo, 125n17
N-modifying, 118n16
noioso, 8, 119n18
Nonintersective. *See* Adjective
Nonpronunciation, 140n3
Nonrestrictive. *See* Adjective; Relative clause
no one, 65
Norwegian, 139n20
nothing, 65
NP
 extraction from, 117n11
 movement to Spec,DP, 126n18
NP dependent reading (of 'different'), 117n13
NP/PP Splitting, 116n8
N-raising, xiii, 1–4, 22–24
N-to-D movement (cf. NP movement to Spec,DP), 126n18
Numeral, 34, 54, 97, 124n13, 125n15, 130n32, 131n1, 133n12, 143n9, 146n25
numeroso, 75

occasional, 124n11
old (cf. *alt, lao, lou, vecchio, vieux*), 47, 48, 119n16, 120n22, 128n16, 138n11
only, 52
Open class, 43, 126n2
orea (cf. *beautiful, krasivyi, meraviglioso*), 105

Papuan (languages), 125n17
Participle
 past, 135n1
 prenominal, 64–65, 128n12, 130n32, 145n23
 present, 135n1
 present in -*ing*, 134n16
particular, 52
perfetto, 76, 138n10
Pied-piping, 39–41
più (cf. *zui*), 141n5
Polish, 108, 116n8, 127n9, 130n30, 134n19
Polydefinite construction, 105
poor (*beden/bednyj, biet, ftohos, kaimenos, povero*), 47, 51, 52, 65, 116n8, 128n16
Portuguese, 72, 77, 136n3,4, 137n9
Possessive. *See* Adjective
possibile, xiii, 1, 3, 9, 21, 74, 76, 92, 113n1
possible, 8, 18, 64
POSS-modifying, 118n16
Postnominal. *See* Adjective
povero (*beden/bednyj, biet, ftohos, kaimenos, poor*), 13, 29, 53, 72, 92
PP complement, 79–82
Predicate inversion, 128n16, 143n10
Predicate noun, 148n35
Predicative. *See also* Adjective
 noun phrase, 125n17
Prenominal. *See* Adjective
Preposition
 accusative, 14
present, 18, 61, 63, 64, 129n21
présent, 51, 81
presente, 50, 81, 129n25, 130n25
présumé, 3

presunto, 74
primo (= *principale*) (cf. *main, zhuyao*), 2, 113n3
principale (*main, primo, zhuyao*), 6, 51, 114n1, 139n17
PRO, 55–56, 129n20, 131n34
probabile, 2, 6, 51, 113n3
probable, 47
proighoumenos (cf. *bivši, byvshij, ex, former, proin, qian, yiqian*), 107
proin (cf. *bivši, byvshij, ex, former, proighoumenos, qian, yiqian*), 106
puro, 77, 138n10
puro e semplice, 48, 130n26

qian, 141n4
qui, 83–84

ready, 50, 61, 63, 64
Realis context, 12
Recursion restriction. *See* Right recursion restriction
Reduced relative clause, 2, 3, 18, 19, 20, 25, 26, 28, 29, 34, 37, 43, 47, 49, 52, 54, 55, 56, 57, 58, 59, 60, 61, 62, 64, 65, 66, 69, 70, 71, 74, 80, 81, 85, 91, 92, 95, 97, 98, 100, 102, 103, 105, 107, 109, 110, 111, 115n5, 117n8, 120n25, 121n2, 122n2,3, 125n14, 128n12, 130n32, 131n34,1, 133n12,13,14, 135n1, 136n1,5, 144n16, 145n20,22,24, 146n27, 147n30, 148n30,33
 bare AP, 62–63, 133n13, 134n19,20
 complex AP, 62, 133n13
 extraposition, 91
Reference, 33
Referent, 33
Relative clause (RC), 2, 3, 17, 18, 19, 22, 28, 29, 31, 34, 35, 49–54, 58, 66, 71, 74, 80, 95, 96, 97, 98, 100, 102, 104, 118n15, 119n19, 121n2, 124n13,14, 130n28,29,30, 131n1, 133n13, 136n6, 141n4, 146n7
 Chinese, 133n14, 142n6, 143n7

extraposition, 62, 139n16
full finite, 60, 62, 63, 69, 81, 85, 133n12,13,14
Head, 34, 55
Head-internal, 124n14, 134n18
implicit, 8–9, 16, 17, 19, 21, 27, 33, 115n5
individual-level, 133n14
Japanese/Korean, 133n14, 143n10
matching derivation of, 56, 134n18
nonrestrictive, 52–54, 130n31, 133n12,13
participial, 54, 62, 63, 130n32, 132n8, 133n13
postnominal, 49
prenominal, 45, 54, 69, 121n2
prenominal origin of, 122n3, 133n14
raising derivation of, 56, 134n18
reduced (*see* Reduced relative clause)
restrictive, 18, 32, 124n13, 133n12,13
source, 3, 26–31, 44, 47, 64, 89, 102, 110, 136n6, 140, 142n6, 144n16, 146n27,28
stage-level, 133n14
subjunctive, 117n10
Remnant (movement). *See* Movement
Restrictive Elliptic Appositive construction, 111
right, 129n21
Righthand Head Rule. *See* Right recursion restriction
Right recursion restriction, 59, 62, 128n12, 132n5, 133n10
Romance (languages), xiii, xiv, 5–24, 37, 41, 43, 52, 53, 54, 61, 69–85, 87–90, 91–92, 102, 113n4, 115n5, 116n7, 118n16, 119n17, 128n17, 129n23, 130n27, 133n13, 134n20, 135n1, 136n5, 137n7, 138n10, 139n20, 144n18, 147n29, 149n35
Romanian, 6, 70, 72, 76, 77, 102–104, 107, 114n3, 135n1, 136n3, 138n15, 140, 145n20, 147n30, 148n30
rosa, 135n3
rotten, 59–60

Russian, 45, 46, 108–110, 122n7, 127n9, 134n19, 144n14, 147n30, 148n32,35, 149n35

Sardinian, 72
Sbagliato (cf. *wrong*), 120n24
Scandinavian, 44, 132n8
sconosciuto, 15
Scope, 2–4, 30, 44, 48, 58, 59, 60, 92, 117n11, 123n11, 124n13, 137n7
sedicente, 74
semplice, 77, 138n10
Serbo-Croatian. *See* Bosnian/Croatian/Serbian
seule, 5
shocked, 52
Shoshoni, 44
sicuro, 4, 92
sinistro, 119n19
skillful, 116n8
Slave, 35
Slavic (languages), 43, 116n8, 127n9, 134n19
Slovak, 127n9
Slovenian, 66, 127n9, 133n19, 147n30
solo, xiii, 1, 130n26
someone, 65
something, 65
Sorbian, 127n9
Spanish, 6, 12, 14, 45, 70, 72, 76, 77, 84, 88, 114n3, 115n4, 116n7, 129n22, 130n30, 132n4, 136n3, 137n9, 138n16, 139n18,21
Spanish *a*, 14
specialmente (cf. *tebie*), 141n5
Specific, 13, 14, 18, 101, 117n11, 119n17, 122n5, 144n13
Specificity Condition, 117n11
Specificity-inducing, 12–14, 16, 17, 22, 27, 33, 144n18
Stacking
  adjectives, 31, 50, 96
  relative clauses, 52
Stage-level. *See* Adjective
sterk, 48

stretto, 147n29
Subjunctive. *See* Relative clause
Subsective, 116n7,8
Superiority, 82
Superlative, 11–12
  adjective (*see* Adjective)
  position of, 32, 124n13
Swedish, 45, 46, 70, 132n8

Tamil, 125n17
tebie (cf. *specialmente*), 141n5
Tetelcingo Nahuatl, 44
Thematic. *See* Adjective
there, 139n19
Thursday, 26
Tinrin, 125n17
Tiriyó, 35, 127n6
Turkish, 138n14

Ukrainian, 127n9
undisclosed, 117n12
unexpected, 117n12
unico, 74, 83, 123n11, 147n29
unknown, 14–15, 16, 17, 20, 27, 33
unspecified, 117n12
unsuitable, 7–8
Ute, 44
Utsukushi. See Adjective
utter, 47, 48

Vata, 125n17
vecchio (cf. *alt, lao, lou, old, vieux*), 13, 47, 72, 92, 114n3, 115n3, 118n16, 119n16, 128n14,17, 140n2, 142n7
Verb
  lexical, 126n2
  light, 126n2
vero, 77
vero e proprio, 6
very, 52, 64–65
vieux (cf. *alt, lao, lou, old, vecchio*), 114n3, 119n16
visible
  English, 6–7, 19, 49, 57, 119n20
  French, 120n23
vrais, 77

Walloon, 136n5
Western Jutlandic, 140–141
wh-feature, 39
wh-in-situ, 39
wrong (cf. *sbagliato*), 115n5, 120n21,24, 131n1

Yagaria, 125n17
yiqian (cf. *former, bivši, byvshij, ex, proighoumenos, proin, qian*), 141n4, 142n7, 143n7
Yoruba, 29, 35–36, 38, 43, 58, 125n15,16,17

zhuyao (cf. *main, primo, principale*), 141n4
zui (cf. *più*), 141n5

Linguistic Inquiry Monographs
Samuel Jay Keyser, general editor

1. *Word Formation in Generative Grammar*, Mark Aronoff
2. *X̄ Syntax: A Study of Phrase Structure*, Ray Jackendoff
3. *Recent Transformational Studies in European Languages*, S. Jay Keyser, editor
4. *Studies in Abstract Phonology*, Edmund Gussmann
5. *An Encyclopedia of AUX: A Study of Cross-Linguistic Equivalence*, Susan Steele
6. *Some Concepts and Consequences of the Theory of Government and Binding*, Noam Chomsky
7. *The Syntax of Words*, Elisabeth O. Selkirk
8. *Syllable Structure and Stress in Spanish: A Nonlinear Analysis*, James W. Harris
9. *CV Phonology: A Generative Theory of the Syllable*, George N. Clements and Samuel Jay Keyser
10. *On the Nature of Grammatical Relations*, Alec P. Marantz
11. *A Grammar of Anaphora*, Joseph Aoun
12. *Logical Form: Its Structure and Derivation*, Robert May
13. *Barriers*, Noam Chomsky
14. *On the Definition of Word*, Anna-Maria Di Sciullo and Edwin Williams
15. *Japanese Tone Structure*, Janet Pierrehumbert and Mary E. Beckman
16. *Relativized Minimality*, Luigi Rizzi
17. *Types of Ā-Dependencies*, Guglielmo Cinque
18. *Argument Structure*, Jane Grimshaw
19. *Locality: A Theory and Some of Its Empirical Consequences*, Maria Rita Manzini
20. *Indefinites*, Molly Diesing
21. *Syntax of Scope*, Joseph Aoun and Yen-hui Audrey Li
22. *Morphology by Itself: Stems and Inflectional Classes*, Mark Aronoff
23. *Thematic Structure in Syntax*, Edwin Williams
24. *Indices and Identity*, Robert Fiengo and Robert May
25. *The Antisymmetry of Syntax*, Richard S. Kayne
26. *Unaccusativity: At the Syntax–Lexical Semantics Interface*, Beth Levin and Malka Rappaport Hovav
27. *Lexico-Logical Form: A Radically Minimalist Theory*, Michael Brody
28. *The Architecture of the Language Faculty*, Ray Jackendoff
29. *Local Economy*, Chris Collins

30. *Surface Structure and Interpretation*, Mark Steedman

31. *Elementary Operations and Optimal Derivations*, Hisatsugu Kitahara

32. *The Syntax of Nonfinite Complementation: An Economy Approach*, Željko Bošković

33. *Prosody, Focus, and Word Order*, Maria Luisa Zubizarreta

34. *The Dependencies of Objects*, Esther Torrego

35. *Economy and Semantic Interpretation*, Danny Fox

36. *What Counts: Focus and Quantification*, Elena Herburger

37. *Phrasal Movement and Its Kin*, David Pesetsky

38. *Dynamic Antisymmetry*, Andrea Moro

39. *Prolegomenon to a Theory of Argument Structure*, Ken Hale and Samuel Jay Keyser

40. *Essays on the Representational and Derivational Nature of Grammar: The Diversity of* Wh-*Constructions*, Joseph Aoun and Yen-hui Audrey Li

41. *Japanese Morphophonemics: Markedness and Word Structure*, Junko Ito and Armin Mester

42. *Restriction and Saturation*, Sandra Chung and William A. Ladusaw

43. *Linearization of Chains and Sideward Movement*, Jairo Nunes

44. *The Syntax of (In)dependence*, Ken Safir

45. *Interface Strategies: Optimal and Costly Computations*, Tanya Reinhart

46. *Asymmetry in Morphology*, Anna Maria Di Sciullo

47. *Relators and Linkers: The Syntax of Predication, Predicate Inversion, and Copulas*, Marcel den Dikken

48. *On the Syntactic Composition of Manner and Motion*, Maria Luisa Zubizarreta and Eunjeong Oh

49. *Introducing Arguments*, Liina Pylkkänen

50. *Where Does Binding Theory Apply?*, David Lebeaux

51. *Locality in Minimalist Syntax*, Thomas S. Stroik

52. *Distributed Reduplication*, John Frampton

53. *The Locative Syntax of Experiencers*, Idan Landau

54. *Why Agree? Why Move?: Unifying Agreement-Based and Discourse-Configurational Languages*, Shigeru Miyagawa

55. *Locality in Vowel Harmony*, Andrew Nevins

56. *Uttering Trees*, Norvin Richards

57. *The Syntax of Adjectives: A Comparative Study*, Guglielmo Cinque

www.ingramcontent.com/pod-product-compliance
Lightning Source LLC
Chambersburg PA
CBHW021827300426
44114CB00009BA/351